Exploring Diary Methods in High Education Research

This methodologically oriented collection brings together higher education diary research studies from international contexts to showcase the versatility of the method and its adaptability to higher education research.

While keeping a diary is a familiar personal practice, diary method is a neglected form of research in higher education studies as well as the social sciences more broadly. This book showcases the range of options within diary method, as well as the benefits and challenges that this fascinating but mysterious method may bring to students and academic researchers alike. The benefits and the risks and challenges of diary research are discussed across the empirical studies included in the volume. Using a variety of solicited diary techniques, including audio, written and photo diaries, and focusing on different aspects of higher education including undergraduate and postgraduate students and academics, these studies include salient topics such as:

- LGBTQ identities,
- faith,
- caring responsibilities,
- international students,
- socioeconomically disadvantaged students and
- employability.

This important contribution to methodological innovation in the higher education research field promotes diary method as a viable option in social sciences and beyond. Whether new to the method or a seasoned diary researcher, this book is ideal reading for anyone who would like to learn the fundamentals of diary research and explore its feasibility in empirical contexts.

Xuemeng Cao is an Early Career Fellow in the Institute of Advanced Study and the Department of Education Studies, at the University of Warwick, UK.

Emily F. Henderson is Associate Professor in the Department of Education Studies, at the University of Warwick, UK.

Research into Higher Education

Series Editors:
Jennifer M. Case, Virginia Tech, USA
Jeroen Huisman, Ghent University, Belgium

This exciting new series aims to publish cutting edge research and discourse that reflects the rapidly changing world of higher education, examined in a global context. Encompassing topics of wide international relevance, the series includes every aspect of the international higher education research agenda, from strategic policy formulation and impact to pragmatic advice on best practice in the field.

Titles in the series:

For more information about this series, please visit: https://www.routledge.com/Research-into-Higher-Education/book-series/SRHE

Exploring Diary Methods in Higher Education Research

Opportunities, Choices and Challenges

Edited by
Xuemeng Cao and Emily F. Henderson

Routledge
Taylor & Francis Group

LONDON AND NEW YORK

First published 2021
by Routledge
2 Park Square, Milton Park, Abingdon, Oxon OX14 4RN

and by Routledge
52 Vanderbilt Avenue, New York, NY 10017

Routledge is an imprint of the Taylor & Francis Group, an informa business

British Library Cataloguing-in-Publication Data
A catalogue record for this book is available from the British Library

Library of Congress Cataloging-in-Publication Data
Names: Cao, Xuemeng, 1991- editor. | Henderson, Emily F., editor.
Title: Exploring diary methods in higher education research : opportunities, choices and challenges / edited by Xuemeng Cao and Emily F. Henderson.
Identifiers: LCCN 2020044830 (print) | LCCN 2020044831 (ebook) |
ISBN 9780367345204 (hardback) | ISBN 9780367345211 (paperback) |
ISBN 9780429326318 (ebook)
Subjects: LCSH: Education, Higher--Research--Methodology. |
College students--Diaries. | Narrative inquiry (Research method)
Classification: LCC LB2326.3 .E96 2021 (print) | LCC LB2326.3 (ebook) |
DDC 378.0072--dc23
LC record available at https://lccn.loc.gov/2020044830
LC ebook record available at https://lccn.loc.gov/2020044831

ISBN: 978-0-367-34520-4 (hbk)
ISBN: 978-0-367-34521-1 (pbk)
ISBN: 978-0-429-32631-8 (ebk)

Typeset in Galliard
by Taylor & Francis Books

Contents

Illustrations

Figures

Tables

Contributors

Xuemeng Cao is an early career fellow in the Institute of Advanced Study and the Department of Education Studies, University of Warwick. She achieved her doctoral degree from the Department of Education Studies, University of Warwick, funded by China Scholarship Council (CSC). Xuemeng is also a co-convenor and the blog editor for Academic Mobilities and Immobilities Network (AMIN) at Warwick. Her research interests include higher education, graduate employability, academic (im)mobilities, internationalisation/cross-cultural studies in education.

Emily F. Henderson is an associate professor in the Department of Education Studies, University of Warwick. She is author of *Gender Pedagogy: Teaching, Learning and Tracing Gender in Higher Education* (Palgrave, 2015) and *Gender, Definitional Politics and 'Live' Knowledge Production: Contesting Concepts at Conferences* (Routledge, 2019), and co-editor of *Starting with Gender in International Higher Education Research* (Routledge, 2019). She is co-editor of the academic blog Conference Inference: Blogging the World of Conferences and has co-edited a special issue of the journal *Gender and Education* on gender and conferences, 'Thoughtful Gatherings' (2020) and a special issue of the journal *Higher Education* on academic mobility (forthcoming). Emily's research lies in the areas of gender and higher education, particularly the production of knowledge about gender; the academic profession, academic mobility and conferences; and poststructuralist and feminist theory and research methodology, including diary method.

Zoe Baker is currently a visiting fellow in the Centre for Development and Research in Education (CDARE) at Sheffield Hallam University. Her research interests include widening participation, the sociology of education, educational inequalities, social justice and transitions.

Anil C. Bankar is an assistant professor in the Department of Political Science at Vasantrao Naik Government Institute of Arts and Social Sciences Nagpur. Anil Bankar has published many research papers and chapters in journals and edited books. He was a member in the Maharashtra State team for the CPRHE research project on diversity and inclusion in higher educational institutions of India that was conducted across six states of India. He is working as a PhD supervisor in the Faculty of Humanities at Rashtrasant Tukdoji Maharaj Nagpur University Nagpur and four research scholars are pursuing PhD under his guidance.

James Burford is a lecturer in researcher education and development at La Trobe University, Australia. He coordinates a researcher development programme for graduate researchers and contributes to institutional initiatives focused on academic writing and research communication. James's work is broadly situated within critical university studies. His research interests include doctoral education, the academic profession and international higher education. His recent collaborative projects have explored academic migration to Thailand, academic conferences, and the spatial practices of doctoral education. James co-edits the blog Conference Inference and tweets as @jiaburford.

Dangeni is currently completing her doctorate in the School of Education at the University of Glasgow. Her current research project investigates Chinese students' experience of learning engagement and conceptual change in UK Master's programmes, employing a combination of creative research tools such as audio diaries and drawing-featured interviews. Dangeni's research interests include international students, student engagement, language teacher education and creative research methods.

Dely Lazarte Elliot is a senior lecturer in the School of Education at the University of Glasgow. She convenes educational psychology, which is part of the MSc in psychological studies programme. With an MSc in counselling psychology and a PhD in the psychology of education in the higher education context, Dely actively researches on the cross-cultural facets of sojourners' experience (e.g. international doctoral researchers) and their impact on sojourners' acculturation, academic performance and psychological well-being. Dely favours the use of creative research methods, particularly the use of images, metaphors and artefacts in research. As part of a team, Dely's recent publications include the book 'The Hidden Curriculum in Doctoral Education'. Dely is an associate editor for *Higher Education Research & Development.*

Olivia Groves is an early career researcher from the University of Wollongong. Olivia's research interests lie understanding the conditions under which learning takes place in order to maximise the potential for learning and success of all students. Her current research activity examines how student equity can be achieved in the higher education sector and beyond – including research into best practice career education in schools, supporting student success in higher education, and investigating equity in graduate outcomes.

Lauri L. Hyers is a social psychologist in the Psychology Department of West Chester University of Pennsylvania, USA (in the Philadelphia area). Her teaching expertise and published scholarship focus on diversity and social justice. She conducts primarily qualitative narrative research, about which she has recently published a book, *Diary Methods: Understanding Qualitative Research* (Oxford University Press, 2018).

Divya Jindal-Snape is Professor of Education, Inclusion and Life Transitions in the School of Education and Social Work, University of Dundee, Scotland. She is director of the Transformative Change: Educational and Life Transitions (TCELT) Research Centre. She has over 200 publications and, to make her research accessible to different audiences, she has used a variety of media, for example, books, papers, comics and multi-media outputs.

Roma Smart Joseph is an associate professor in the Department of Teacher Education in Isabella Thoburn College, Lucknow, UP, India. She is the recipient of Bharat Gaurav Ratna, Shikshak Gaurav, Chancellor's Gold Medal (Lucknow University) and is honoured by CSIR-IITR, and Vigyan Bharti for her outstanding contribution in the field of education. She is also involved in national and international projects and has presented in many national and international conferences, seminars and workshops. She is working in the field of blended learning and has published number of e contents in the form of ebooks, presentations (on SlideShare, author stream and thinkling), podcast, blogs, glogs, videos and webinars etc. She has developed technology integrated Smart lesson plan. She has been the part of team from Uttar Pradesh for CPRHE project on diversity and inclusion in higher educational institutes of India, a study that was conducted across states of India.

Michael Keenan is a senior lecturer in sociology at Nottingham Trent University. Michael's research interests are primarily focused on exploring sexual and religious identity. He is particularly interested in the ways in which identities are lived in everyday experiences and interactions. Michael's ESRC-funded doctoral study explored the lived experiences of gay men in the Anglican clergy with a focus on the ways in which sexual, religious and 'clergy' identities interacted and were managed in everyday experiences. Michael has been co-investigator on the ESRC/AHRC funded study 'Religion, Youth and Sexuality: A Multi-faith Exploration' (AH/G014051/1). More recently Michael's research has been focused on the university experiences of LGBTQ identifying students. Michael has been principal investigator on two Society for Research into Higher Education funded studies in this area (2012 Prize for Newer Researchers, 2016 Annual Award).

Sarah Lawther is a postgraduate researcher at Nottingham Trent University. Her PhD explores the student experience of religion and belief at university, starting from the students' individual experience rather than affiliation, to capture all forms of meaning-making as described by the students themselves and takes a research approach that does not privilege any forms of meaning-making over others. The project explores the use of research methodologies to capture the complexity of everyday beliefs and practices, including a postcard method and a diary-like photo-elicitation method. This builds on her previous research in higher education such as: the first year experience, student retention and success, student transition and learning analytics. Her research interests also include: lived religion, religious literacy, religion and the media, and mixed methods research.

Jennifer Leigh is a senior lecturer in higher education and academic practice in the Centre for the Study of Higher Education, University of Kent. She is a founder member and Vice Chair of WISC (an international network for Women In Supramolecular Chemistry) and the only social scientist in the team. Her research weaves together threads of embodiment, reflective practice, identity, inclusivity, and creative research methods in higher education. She has three projects underway with WISC that bring embodied research approaches (and glitter) into the world of chemistry. She edited Conversations on Embodiment in Higher Education: Teaching, practice and research (Routledge), and is co-editor on Ableism in academia: Theorising experiences of disabilities and chronic illnesses in higher education (UCL Press). Her next books, Embodied Inquiry: Research Methods and The boundaries of qualitative research: with art, education, therapy and science will be published by Bloomsbury and Bristol University Press respectively.

Carole MacDiarmid is English for academic purposes (EAP) manager for teacher development, within the School of Modern Languages and Cultures at the University of Glasgow. She co-runs two masters in TESOL in conjunction with the School of Education and lectures on a number of courses, including teaching English for academic purposes (TEAP). Carole is a BALEAP Accreditation Scheme Assessor of EAP programmes across the UK and was a core member of the BALEAP TEAP Working Party which developed the BALEAP TEAP Fellowship Scheme award. Her research interests include spoken academic discourse, teacher development and EAP. Carole's most recent research includes a UK–Brazil British Council supported collaborative project investigating EAP teacher needs.

Carmen Martinez-Vargas is currently based at the SARCHI Chair's Higher Education and Human Development Research Programme at the University of the Free State, South Africa, as a post-doctoral fellow. She has several years' experience working with participatory approaches (participatory methods, methodologies and research processes) within the Global North and Global South having collaborated in more than six national and international participatory projects. Since 2018, she has been the coordinator of the participatory methods thematic group at the Human Development and Capabilities Association (HDCA). Her research interest problematises the intersection of decoloniality and social justice in the context of human development using participatory research. She has facilitated training workshops about different participatory practices in South Africa, and has published in international journals about these studies. Her forthcoming monograph is titled *Democratising Participatory Research: Pathways to Social Justice from the Global South.*

Mikateko Mathebula is senior researcher on the Miratho Project and at the SARCHI Chair's Higher Education and Human Development Research Programme at the University of the Free State, South Africa. Her research interests lie in the relationship between processes of higher education, 'development', and human flourishing. She is also interested in the role of storytelling in advancing inclusive knowledge-making and knowledge-sharing processes developed in the Global South, and she is passionate about research and pedagogic approaches that are underpinned by decolonial thought. Recent publications include the articles 'Recognising Poor Black Youth from Rural Communities in South Africa as Epistemic Contributors' and 'Low-income Rural Youth Migrating to Urban Universities in South Africa: Opportunities and Inequalities', as well as the monograph *Engineering Education for Sustainable Development: A Capabilities Approach.*

Jenna Mittelmeier is lecturer in international education at the University of Manchester. Her mixed methods research focuses on the transition experiences of international students and broader aspects of curriculum internationalisation. In her teaching practice, she has expertise in educational research methods and curriculum design in the context of internationalisation.

Bart Rienties is professor of learning analytics and head of academic professional development at the Institute of Educational Technology at the Open University UK. As associate director, he leads a group of academics who provide university-wide academic professional development. As educational psychologist, he conducts multi-disciplinary research on work-based and collaborative learning environments and focuses on the role of social interaction in learning.

Nidhi S. Sabharwal is associate professor at the Centre for Policy Research in Higher Education, National Institute of Educational Planning and Administration, New Delhi. Dr Sabharwal has previously served as the Director at the Indian Institute of Dalit Studies, New Delhi. She has recently completed multistate studies on 'Student Diversity and Inclusion in Higher Education Institutions in India' across six states and 'Higher Education Success and Social Mobility: A Study on Coaching Schemes for SC/ST/OBC and Minorities in Universities and Colleges' across ten states. Her recent publications include *Caste, Discrimination, and Exclusion in Modern India* (co-authored with Vani K. Borooah et al.; Sage, 2015), *Bridging the Social Gap: Perspectives on Dalit Empowerment* (co-edited with Sukhadeo Thorat; Sage, 2014) and *India Higher Education Report 2016: Equity in Higher Education* (co-authored with N. V. Varghese and C. M. Malish; Sage, 2018). Her current research focuses on college readiness, student diversity, inclusive excellence and equity in higher education.

Avinash V. Talmale is an assistant professor in the Department of Geography at Vasantrao Naik Government Institute of Arts and Social Sciences Nagpur. Talmale has published many research papers and chapters in journals and edited books. He was a member in the Maharashtra State team for the CPRHE research project on diversity and inclusion in higher educational institutions of India that was conducted across six states of India. He currently works as a PhD supervisor in the Faculty of Humanities at Rashtrasant Tukdoji Maharaj Nagpur University Nagpur and two research scholars are pursuing PhD under his guidance. He is an advisory body member of Board of Studies of Rashtrasant Tukdoji Maharaj Nagpur University.

Jenna Walmer is a graduate student in Holocaust and genocide studies and general psychology at West Chester University of Pennsylvania. The guiding theme of Jenna's research is the overlap of social/peace psychology and mass atrocities. She is specifically interested in taking an interdisciplinary and transnational approach to studying violence by addressing themes of religion, political science, history and psychology to better understand genocides.

Ben Watson is the accessible information adviser at the University of Kent. He also leads the OPERA project (Opportunity, Productivity, Engagement, Reducing barriers, Achievement), which seeks to implement a range of accessibility initiatives to raise awareness of the potential for inclusive design and assistive technologies to improve access to learning for all.

Kate Yue Zhang is associate professor of international business administration at the American University of Paris. Her research interests focus on human resource management and international students.

Introduction

The (re)naissance of diary method research in and beyond higher education studies

Xuemeng Cao and Emily F. Henderson

Diary research is a somewhat mysterious form of empirical research, in part because it has remained under-used in the social sciences, and yet it pops up in many different forms, often associated with creative and/or emancipatory projects. The diary itself is a commonly understood artefact, taking multiple forms across the world and across time, with purposes ranging from detailed private personal journaling to keeping basic records of appointments and activities. However the use of diaries in research is not so commonly understood, and arguably it is the over-familiarity of the form and the under-familiarity of the research method that have resulted in a relative dearth of critically engaged methodological literature in this field, in comparison with the wealth of literature on, for example, interviews, observations and questionnaires. This volume, with its focus on methodological processes, undertakes to provide a new reference point for diary method research, and it is to our knowledge the first edited collection focusing on this method.

As we were finalising the chapters of this book and preparing to write this introduction, the COVID-19 pandemic hit and suddenly diary research experienced something of a (re)naissance as a method that enables research to be conducted remotely, from the home if necessary. This is an intriguing development for this neglected method, and it will be important to track how this trend develops, and the legacy of the pandemic for empirical social sciences research in general. There are however concerns that the sudden orientation of research projects towards the use of diaries may also result in slapdash approaches to diary research. It is hoped that this book can provide an orientation for those who reach for diaries due to the challenges of conducting in-person fieldwork (during the pandemic and its aftermath as well as for other reasons affecting researchers and participants alike, such as dis/ability and chronic illness, border controls, natural disasters and conflict), as well as a source of critically engaged methodological discussion for those who are already experienced with this method.

As diary researchers, we have constructed this book to meet three specific challenges that we have encountered in relation to using diary method in our own higher education research projects (see Chapters 2 and 5 in this volume). Each of these challenges results from the fact that diary method is both under-used and misunderstood in higher education research, as well as education research and social sciences more broadly. Firstly, diary researchers encounter gate-keeping regarding their methodological choices, which can appear in the form of the assessment of student work, doctoral examination, peer reviewing of publications and question time at conferences, and which is owing to the widespread lack of understanding of both the method and the possibilities within the method. This book aims to provide a marker for future diary researchers to use to legitimise their choices. Secondly, we have encountered unwillingness on the part of colleagues and students to engage with the method, even when it is highly appropriate for the study in question. We conjecture that this may be due to the absence of diary method in research training courses and its minimal coverage in textbooks, as well as the paucity of specific methodological literature on diary research; this book encourages researchers of all levels to try this intriguing and exciting method. Thirdly, when diary method is adopted, it can be adopted in inappropriate or unimaginative ways, again because of the lack of expert knowledge, guidance and training on this method. We hope that this book will lead to the development of rich, creative, nuanced diary research projects.

While this book is aimed at researchers – and teachers of research methods and research project supervisors – across education studies and the social sciences more broadly, we proposed the project to the Society for Research into Higher Education (SRHE) series because we also wanted to make a specific methodological intervention into higher education research. Higher education research is subject to critique regarding what has been perceived as its limited set of research methods. Given the burgeoning nature of the international higher education research field, higher education is more than ever in need of methodological innovation. Moreover the increased focus on equality, diversity and inclusion in higher education research begs for methodological creativity, which diary method can provide (see Chapters 9 and 10, this volume). Our ongoing literature survey of diary methods in higher education research has shown us that a small but not insignificant number of researchers are already using diary methods across a variety of country contexts, yet the lack of a discipline-specific reference guide for the method has resulted in a disjointed, dissipated use of the method. Indeed when we advertised for contributors to this volume, several researchers across different contexts expressed the need for a volume of this kind, particularly as a number of researchers wrote to us that they had struggled to yield high quality diary data in their studies. There is insufficient methodological guidance or reference on how to design and conduct a diary research study in a higher education context. Therefore, this book will contribute to filling this gap, injecting vitality into the methodological repertoire for international higher education research. The book includes contributions based on studies in Australia, India, New Zealand, South Africa, the UK and the US, and this range of contributors itself speaks to the international relevance of this volume.

In this introduction, we set out some of the foundations, key considerations and indeed challenges of diary research, in order to allow chapter authors to circumvent this necessity and to permit them to enter into the specific detail pertaining to their chapters. However it is impossible to do justice to the method in this small space, so we urge readers to turn to the three existing diary research methodological guidebooks for more information (Alaszewski, 2006; Bartlett & Milligan, 2015; Hyers, 2018). We would like to recognise the achievements of these initial books, which have given the foundation for us to offer an edited collection that goes into more of the nuance of the method through the presentation of a range of rich and diverse studies. In this introduction, in addition to introducing the method, we also give a comprehensive description of the organisation of the book.

Diary methods: nature, implementation and effectiveness

The diaries that this book focuses on are *solicited diaries*, which are different from personal diaries (also known as archival or *unsolicited diaries*) that people choose to keep voluntarily without this being requested by researchers. Unsolicited diaries can also be used for research, usually as a type of secondary source, when researchers explore a historical phenomenon from individuals' subjective accounts of experiences in which they were involved (Gottschalk, Kluckhohn & Angell, 1945). Unsolicited diaries are usually adopted as a stand-alone method particularly for qualitative historical analysis. Solicited diaries are diaries that are intentionally created for the purpose of research, which means that participants are required to write diary entries regularly over a period of time, reporting their own experiences and interpretations of events related to a particular research topic (Braun & Clarke, 2013; Cucu-Oancea, 2013). Solicited diaries therefore serve as a flexible research method which can be designed and adapted to fit different research questions and target participants in a wide range of research areas (Kaur, Saukko & Lumsden, 2018). The remainder of this section introduces the solicited diary method, in relation to structure, duration, frequency of entries, compatibility with other methods and forms diaries may take for the research design, together with the effectiveness, and indeed challenges, of adopting diary method for research purposes.

Diaries range from highly structured to unstructured, and therefore can be aligned with the full gamut of epistemological and theoretical positionings and produce data for both quantitative and qualitative analysis. As such, diary data can resemble that arising from a structured observation or questionnaire (Mullan, 2019) or a biographical narrative interview (Taylor & Gannon, 2018), with semi-structured diaries always seeking for a balance between enabling participants' flexibility in data provision and preventing their reports straying too far from the topic. Diary research can follow both short and intense timescales, even a matter of hours or days (Henderson, 2020), and periods of months or more (Chapters 3 and 5, this volume). The time span of diary keeping does not have a universal standard; a sufficient duration is considered to be neither too short to obtain sufficient data, nor too long to diminish participant fatigue and/or reactive effects. The design of diary studies also requires decisions to be taken concerning the frequency of required diary recording. Diary recording occurs in the form of event-based sampling, which requests diary entries to be provided when the researched phenomenon occurs (Chapter 7, this volume); and interval-based sampling, which collects diary data regularly at pre-determined intervals (Cohen et al., 2003). Solicited diaries may serve as stand-alone data, but they are often incorporated into a multi-faceted methodology (Chapter 1, this volume). Most commonly, diaries are combined with interviews in what is known as the diary-interview method (Zimmerman & Wieder, 1977). In this method, the diaries constitute the basis for successive or retrospective interviews.

As a cultural artefact with a long history, the traditional paper-and-pencil diary is still an acceptable form when it acts as a research method (Chapter 9, this volume). However, written diaries are increasingly assisted with the use of software (e.g. diaries using word-processing software), internet (e.g. email diaries) and social media (e.g. blog-based diaries), which make diary keeping more convenient and traceable. In addition, more innovative forms of diaries have emerged, including audio (Chapter 3, this volume; Monrouxe, 2009), video (Kaur, Saukko & Lumsden, 2018; Scott, Green & Cashmore, 2012), photo (Chapters 4, 6, 8 and 10, this volume) or collage diaries (Bartlett, 2012), which can provide a more vivid and multi-dimensional dataset for research projects. Indeed, researchers might be uncertain whether their research even counts as diary research, particularly as their diary-like or diary-inspired data collection may have been facilitated by digital tools and constituted an already-identified method (e.g. photo-elicitation). It is indeed difficult to define what counts as a diary and what does not, considering the very diverse types and forms of diaries as we have showcased above and in this volume. We understand solicited diaries as: *records of researched phenomena, produced under researchers' guidance, based on events or recorded at regular intervals, which records in essence contain participants' perceptions and reflections on their experiences.* There are many ways this definition can be pushed, as shown in the chapters in this volume. Concepts such as 'regularity' require further exploration. Moreover, the perception of diary research as obtaining personal reflections may be misplaced when some highly structured studies are consulted, where for example a diary entry involves recording details of asthma symptoms (Smith et al., 2000; Dietrich, Kracke & Nurmi, 2011).

Diary method facilitates researchers' effectiveness and convenience in research practices which other methods cannot easily achieve. It enables researchers to enter into the everyday lives of participants in a range of contexts that researchers are unable to enter, or that are too geographically distant to access. Diaries document life as it is lived, rather than recounting a past event or feeling as retrospective questionnaires or interviews do, which in theory improves the accuracy of the data. Diary research, longitudinal studies in particular, can examine daily rhythms of life or within-person changes over a period of time, which challenges the snapshot view of social practice that other research methods often offer. Furthermore, aided by digital tools, diaries taking the forms of audio and video can provide unique insights about the body and creative practices, which allow researchers to conduct multi-level data analyses.

At the same time, diary methods also pose challenges for researchers, which we summarise here. Diaries are explicitly constructed as 'interventions' in some research areas such as psychology (Levine & Calvanio, 2007) and healthcare (Furness &

Garrud, 2010), where diaries are intentionally used as a research instrument that also may have positive effects, for example on health and wellbeing. In higher education research, there is more reticence to deliberately engage in a research practice that has a demonstrable effect on participants' lives – rather the tendency is to minimise reactive effects. While all empirical research on human subjects arguably has an effect on participants' lives, diary method may pose a particular challenge to researchers working in this mindset, as keeping diaries of behaviours and practices is likely to have an impact on these behaviours and practices. Diary method, in its common form, obliges researchers to relinquish control of part of the research process to their participants. Researchers are usually absent from the diary data provision, which leads to the fact that they cannot spontaneously put the participants back on track as they can do in interviews and focus groups. There is thus considerable uncertainty surrounding the quantity and quality of diary data, and researchers are at risk of receiving partially completed diaries. Giving feedback to participants during longitudinal diary research is, arguably, an effective remedy for this issue (Chapter 5, this volume); and researchers also cope with this by complementing or triangulating diary data with data from other methods (Chapter 11, this volume). Diaries can easily trigger ethical concerns considering their confessional nature and the likelihood that they contain personal and private data, with ethical issues ranging from foreseeable issues such as participant protection and confidentiality (Chapter 8, this volume) to unforeseen issues such as participants' emotion changes (Chapter 7, this volume). Diaries may produce holistic accounts of participants' lives, which is clearly an advantage, but this can also give rise to ethical concerns about the possibility of anonymising accounts that contain so much detailed information. Last but not least, the comprehensive dataset can also impose huge pressure on researchers' workloads for data organisation and analysis.

Moving from the perspective of researcher to participant, diary method arguably can be considered a participant-friendly mode of research, depending on the requirements. Solicited diaries can appear less obtrusive or daunting than other research instruments, considering participants' initial familiarity with diary keeping as a practice – though this familiarity can also pose a challenge if participants confuse the research diary process with keeping a private diary. Diaries allow participants to represent and interpret their world from their own standpoint, in their own time, before they bring this to the researcher (Bartlett & Milligan, 2015; Hyers, 2018), which can diminish the potential interference from the researcher's agenda in the data-gathering and may lead to surprising data. Furthermore, because of the possibility of recording data away from the gaze of the researcher, participants may confront less pressure in providing data through diaries compared to face-to-face observations and interviews; this makes diaries a particularly feasible method for researching marginalised groups (Eidse & Turner, 2014; Chapters 4 and 9, this volume) and sensitive topics (Harvey, 2011; Chapter 8, this volume). Diary keeping, as an activity requiring some intellectual effort (depending on the study in question), encourages participants' in-depth engagement with the data production process; the act of recording the data is already akin to an initial layer of analysis. This can and often does lead to an information source with profound reflections on the researched phenomena.

There are also a number of common challenges and issues associated with the participants of diary research:

i   Though participant-friendly in some respects, diary methods also demand higher investment in terms of time and effort than many other methods, which may prevent people from signing up to and staying in diary studies.

ii   There is also the challenge for participants to retain a commitment to recording relevant, informative data at the required interval or in temporal proximity to the occurrence of the researched phenomenon.

iii   Diary keeping also requires a series of skills, including but not necessarily limited to: information selection, reflection, critical thinking and summarising, with different types of diaries requesting different specific skills (e.g. literacy in written diaries; IT skills in online diaries; digital skills in photo, audio and video diaries).

iv   Moreover, diary research, especially longer-duration studies, may cause respondent fatigue and reactive effects on participants' lives (which may be positive or negative, intended or accidental); the changes in participants' diary-keeping behaviour can be interwoven with their broader life experiences during the research period (Cao & Henderson, 2020).

All of these challenges need to be carefully considered by researchers in order to achieve a high quality of data from this innovative research method.

Overall, solicited diaries are a flexible research method which can take various types and forms to facilitate a wide range of research purposes. Diary method enables researchers to capture the minutiae of personal events, motives, feelings and reflections across time and across contexts. Diary research has high potential to be used more widely in higher education research and more broadly across the social sciences. However, researchers may hesitate to adopt diary method considering the challenges outlined above, including recruitment issues, attrition of participants, variation in quality and quantity of entries, a lack of control from the perspective of the researcher over the nature of the data, the modification of behaviour that results from diary-keeping, and ethical issues relating to personal and private content. Rather than dismiss these challenges, we explicitly set out to expose and explore these issues, so that more researchers feel confident to work with a diary research design. In this volume, we and the contributing authors showcase how methodological issues of diary research may be encountered and negotiated in empirical studies on aspects of higher education.

Organisation of this book

As stated above, the core aim of this book is to make a significant contribution to the diary methods literature within and beyond higher education studies. The chapters therefore focus less on the empirical findings of the studies that are showcased in the book, and rather place methodological discussions centre stage. Each chapter is based on one empirical study in the field of higher education research; the study and the area of higher education are introduced, and then a specific aspect of diary research is discussed with reference to diary method literature and to the empirical study in question. As such the book provides real examples of diary research – including the challenges and quirks, as well as the benefits, and a multitude of diary method sources in and beyond higher education research which, now that they are collated in one volume, provide a treasure trove of references to look up for future diary researchers. The chapters are organised into three sections, covering the design and evaluation of diary studies; the nuances of the research process; the use of diaries to explore hidden phenomena.

Following this Introduction, Part I, 'Critically designing and evaluating diary studies', includes four chapters. In Chapter 1, Mittelmeier, Rienties, Zhang and Jindal-Snape elaborate the advantages and challenges of accommodating diaries with other techniques to form a mixed method research design. Against the empirical context of doctoral students' social transitions, the authors demonstrate how diary data were triangulated with data from social network analysis surveys and interviews, and how these two methods in turn may help overcome the drawbacks of diary data. Moreover, they also outline the challenges associated with participation fatigue, self-selection bias, and ethical issues in developing mixed methods diary design.

Chapter 2, by Henderson, exemplifies the way she used diary method for a research project on the conference participation of academics with caring responsibilities; the academics in the study were predominantly based in the UK but also Australia, North America and Europe. Employing diaries in exploring short-term, time-bound phenomena, the methodological issue focused on in this chapter is diary duration. Exploring the underlying assumptions of value attached to duration for longitudinal diary studies, this chapter reverses the debate by asking 'how short is too short' for a diary study, considering that it is necessary to balance the feasibility of diary keeping with the richness of the data.

Chapter 3, by Dangeni, Elliot and MacDiarmid, showcases the audio diary form of diary research, which they used to investigate the learning engagement experience and subsequent conceptual changes of Scotland-educated Chinese students on TESOL (teaching English to speakers of other languages) courses. The authors articulate why this novel type of diary study design was chosen and how the study was implemented. They reflect on the positionality of the researcher and the role of the researcher in relation to the data collection and data management as challenges for audio diary research. Overall, the authors highlight the method's capacity to capture participants' complex psychological, emotional and cognitive changes and to gain higher rates of data provision.

The final chapter in Part I is Chapter 4, by Mathebula and Martinez-Vargas, drawing on data from a project that applied photovoice to explore the experiences of inclusion and exclusion within universities, for low-income rural and township youth in South Africa. This chapter focuses on an important but neglected aspect of diary study design: that of study evaluation. While many diary studies have emancipatory aims, trying to capture the voices of participants, few studies incorporate an evaluation element of these aims. Adopting capabilities approach as the theoretical underpinning, this chapter assesses the impact of photovoice on enhancing research participants' opportunities for epistemic contribution, well-being achievement and collective agency. This chapter highlights the role of photo diaries, a participatory visual research method, in promoting decoloniality in Global South contexts.

Part II of this book, 'Exploring the nuances of the diary research process', moves from diary study design to the intricacies of conducting diary research. The first of four chapters in this section, by Cao (Chapter 5), places issues associated with participant recruitment and retention in longitudinal diary studies under the spotlight. She discusses the strategies which supported her success in recruiting a suitable number of participants within an intensive time frame and realising almost full participant retention in her one-year diary-interview study on the employability management of UK-educated Chinese students, setting out processes which may be effective in facilitating desirable results of participant recruitment and retention in longitudinal diary studies.

Keenan's contribution (Chapter 6) directs our attention to LGBTQ students in the UK, bisexual- and trans-identifying undergraduate students in particular, where he reflects on how photo diary offers insight and access to deep, diverse and unexpected narratives of these students' everyday lives in higher education contexts. The chapter explores participants' intentions in taking photos to express their experiences, and the way they make sense of these images. This chapter provides an important argument on the unique combination of distance and intimacy between participant and experience due to the dual role that participants in photo diary studies play as creators and interpreters of the visual images with which they record their lives.

Chapter 7, by Baker, concentrates on ethical issues of diary methods. Baker provides a chapter based on her research on how UK students in further education make decisions about higher education. She explains how an event-based diary (see the previous section for an explanation of this term) results in the study having some impacts – positive and negative alike – on participants' decision-making; the diary also captured emotions throughout the decision-making process, and then potentially led to self-protection responses to participants' unfulfilled plans. The chapter accordingly addresses the ethical concerns that need to be treated with caution in diary studies regarding the impact on participants' psychosocial wellbeing of recording past events, thoughts, and plans via diaries.

Concluding Part II, in Chapter 8 Lawther focuses on the ethical issues which arose from the photo diary method she used for her research project on students' experience of religion and belief in higher education in the UK. While demonstrating the strengths of diary-like photo-elicitation method in permitting participants a degree of flexibility in providing data from their own starting point, she emphasises the ethical tension between giving the students voice and protecting their confidentiality in religious identity and practices, which is caused by the visual nature of the method.

Part III of this book, 'The importance of diaries for researching hidden issues', captures one of the key strengths of diary method: the possibility of using diaries to research phenomena which are otherwise hidden or difficult to capture. The first chapter in this part, by Sabharwal, Joseph, Bankar and Talmale (Chapter 9), is based on a mixed-method study with a diary element on higher education experiences of students from socially excluded groups in India. The chapter outlines the reasons for using diary method, its design, its use alongside questionnaires and focus group discussions, and the challenges in implementation. This chapter argues that diaries can offer a safe space to socially excluded students to record their otherwise unspoken reflections on their everyday encounters in higher education, which helps researchers in developing a comprehensive understanding of the life-world of these students.

Chapter 10, by Watson and Leigh, is based on a research project which engages with the issues associated with print disability in higher education in the UK. This study adopted the 'diary-photograph: diary-interview' method to explore the information-related experiences of students both with and without a print disability. Focusing on the potential inclusivity of diary research and its capacity to capture 'hidden' issues in higher education, the chapter addresses the challenges of implementing this method. Challenges include the variation in quality of diaries, the lack of researcher control, the selectivity of responses, and possible inequities of the format; however, the authors highlight the value of photo diary method in broadening their understanding of the barriers students experienced in accessing information.

In Chapter 11, Burford draws on a study on doctoral writing, based in Aotearoa/New Zealand. The study incorporated diaries in combination with interviews and a writing retreat, and aimed to capture the emotions related to doctoral writing in the neoliberal academy. The chapter focuses on using diaries to capture affective phenomena. Emotions are notoriously difficult to capture, and this study explores how diaries can be designed to capture fleeting, ephemeral feelings which may be omitted from data gained through other methods.

The final chapter in this section, by Groves (Chapter 12), is based on a study involving Australia-based international students, adopting interval-based, semi-structured learner diaries to explore participants' situated English language learning experiences. Diary method is presented as powerful in the creation of data on everyday, routine and forgettable activities of the students, which are extremely important when considering student experience, but which may not be captured by retrospective methods. This chapter includes discussions of respondent fatigue and the fullness and quality of data as the main challenges faced in diary studies.

The book concludes with an Afterword penned by Hyers, diary expert and author of *Diary Methods* (Hyers, 2018), with co-author Walmer. The Afterword includes reflections on the volume as a whole, including thoughts on the motivations of participants for engaging with diary research studies on higher education phenomena, as well as the strengths of diary method for higher education research. The Afterword includes a valuable discussion of pedagogical strategies for educating others about diary research, and an exhortation to diary researchers to communicate their processes in order to shore up the future of diary method.

Overall, this book provides a wide range of discussions of different types of diary study, in different higher education contexts, and as a volume exceeds our hopes and aims for the project. However, there are still omissions which should be recognised as eventualities of the academic publishing process and the inequalities of global knowledge production. Some studies which we had at different stages of the planning process hoped to include did not unfortunately come to fruition as chapters. Other studies never came to our attention as our wide-ranging search process inevitably reached some corners of academia and not others. There are also many questions that remain unanswered and even unasked by this volume. This is inevitable for a research approach which has been comparatively neglected in the methodological literature – the nuanced discussions of interviews, observations, questionnaires, of ethnography, case study and survey methodologies, are in a different league due to the sustained critical and theoretical engagement with these methods and their widespread treatment in methods courses and textbooks. Nonetheless, as the first of its kind as an edited collection on the processes of conducting diary research, this volume broaches new ground for diary method and for higher education research alike. It is our sincere hope that this volume will inspire readers to seriously consider diary method for your research studies, and that the production of further critical, nuanced literature on diary research will also be prompted by the rich discussions presented by authors in this volume.

References

Alaszewski, A. (2006) *Using diaries for social research*. London: Sage.

Bartlett, R. (2012) Modifying the diary interview method to research the lives of people with dementia. *Qualitative Health Research*, 22, 12: 1717–1726.

Bartlett, R. & Milligan, C. (2015) *What is diary method?* London: Bloomsbury.

Braun, V. & Clarke, V. (2013) *Successful qualitative research: A practical guide for beginners*. London: Sage.

Cao, X. & Henderson, E. F. (2020) The interweaving of diaries and lives: diary-keeping behaviour in a diary-interview study of international students' employability management. *Qualitative Research*. DOI: 10.1177/1468794120920260

Cohen, J., Cohen, P., West, S. G. & Aiken, L. S. (2003) *Applied multiple regression/correlation analysis for the behavioral sciences*. Mahwah, NJ: Lawrence Erlbaum Associates.

Cucu-Oancea, O. (2013) Using diaries – A real challenge for the social scientist. *Procedia – Social and Behavioral Sciences*, 92, October: 231–238.

Dietrich, J., Kracke, B. & Nurmi, J. E. (2011) Parents' role in adolescents' decision on a college major: A weekly diary study. *Journal of Vocational Behavior*, 79, 1: 134–144.

Eidse, N. & Turner, S. (2014) Doing resistance their own way: Counter-narratives of street vending in Hanoi, Vietnam through solicited journaling. *Area*, 46, 3: 242–248.

Furness, P.J. & Garrud, P. (2010) Adaptation after facial surgery: Using the diary as a research tool. *Qualitative Health Research*, 20, 2: 262–272.

Gottschalk, L., Kluckhohn, C. & Angell, R. (1945) *The use of personal documents in history, anthropology and sociology*. New York: Social Science Research Council.

Harvey, L. (2011) Intimate reflections: private diaries in qualitative research. *Qualitative Research*, 11, 6: 664–682.

Hyers, L. L. (2018) *Diary methods*. New York: Oxford University Press.

Kaur, H., Saukko, P. & Lumsden, K. (2018) Rhythms of moving in and between digital media: a study on video diaries of young people with physical disabilities. *Mobilities*, 13, 3: 397–410.

Levine, M. & Calvanio, R. (2007) The recording of personal information as an intervention and an electronic health report. In L. L'Abate, (ed.), *Low-cost approaches to promote physical and mental health*. New York: Springer, pp. 227–250.

Monrouxe, L. V. (2009) Solicited audio diaries in longitudinal narrative research: a view from inside. *Qualitative research*, 9, 1: 81–103.

Mullan, K. (2019) A child's day: trends in time use in the UK from 1975 to 2015. *The British Journal of Sociology*, 70, 3: 997–1024.

Scott, J., Green, P. & Cashmore, A. (2012) Bioscience students' first year perspectives through video diaries: Home, family and student transitions. *Bioscience Education*, 20, 1: 53–67.

Smith, B. J., Nitschke, M., Pilotto, L. S., Ruffin, R. E., Pisaniello, D. L. & Willson, K. J. (2000) Health effects of daily indoor nitrogen dioxide exposure in people with asthma. *European Respiratory Journal*, 16, 5: 879–885.

Taylor, C. A. & Gannon, S. (2018) Doing time and motion diffractively: Academic life everywhere and all the time. *International Journal of Qualitative Studies in Education*, 31, 6: 465–486.

Zimmerman, D. & Wieder, D. (1977) The diary-interview method. *Urban Life*, 5, 4: 479–497.

Part I

Critically designing and evaluating diary studies

Chapter 1

Using diaries in mixed methods designs

Lessons from a cross-institutional research project on doctoral students' social transition experiences

Jenna Mittelmeier, Bart Rienties, Kate Yue Zhang and Divya Jindal-Snape

Introduction

In higher education research, as well as across the wider social sciences, there is increased awareness that combining multiple research methods enables researchers to better understand the complex and often non-linear phenomena that occur in today's societies (Creswell & Creswell, 2018; Creswell & Plano Clark, 2017; Greene, Caracelli & Graham, 1989; Johnson & Onwuegbuzie, 2004). In this chapter, we consider solicited diaries as one possible method to incorporate within a mixed methods higher education research design. We start by defining mixed methods research broadly and outlining various approaches, purposes and key considerations for its use. The second half of this chapter highlights the benefits and challenges of mixed methods diary designs through reflection on our own research examining doctoral students' social community building experiences. The chapter closes with six key considerations for higher education researchers for developing rigorous mixed methods diary studies.

Approaches and considerations for mixed methods research

While there is debate about how to label and define mixed methods research, we define it in this chapter in line with Bazeley (2017, p. 7): 'Any research that involves multiple sources and types of data and/or multiple approaches of those data, in which *integration* of data and analyses occurs before drawing final conclusions about the final topic of the investigation.' Some mixed methods researchers argue that mixed methods must involve both *quantitative* and *qualitative* elements (see, for example: Johnson, Onwuegbuzie & Turner, 2007), but there is increasing recognition that this strict dichotomy between research paradigms is perhaps superficial (Bazeley, 2017).

Mixed methods diary research offers many benefits for approaching complex research topics, including those present in many higher education studies. One consideration is that researchers can draw upon the strengths and counterbalance the weaknesses of chosen methods, as well as more broadly balance quantitative versus qualitative research paradigms (Symonds & Gorard, 2010). One additional strength of mixed methods approaches is that they allow for data triangulation by combining multiple insights into a phenomenon from different perspectives. As described by Cohen, Manion and Morrison (2018, p. 195), 'triangular techniques in the social sciences attempt to map out, or explain more fully, the richness and complexity of human behaviour by studying it from more than one standpoint.'

Mixed methods designs are inherently flexible and allow researchers to think pragmatically about research approaches, paradigms and methods that best answer their research questions (Johnson & Onwuegbuzie, 2004). In higher education research, the underlying pragmatism of mixed methods research is well suited, given that research topics often combine more subjective perspectives (such as students' experiences or preferences) with more positivistic approaches (such as measuring students' learning behaviours or progression routes) (Scoles, Huxham & McArthur, 2014).

Despite this flexibility, there are many considerations researchers must make in designing mixed methods diary research, including managing the sample across multiple methods, developing complementary research instruments, deciding on approaches to analysis, and outlining procedures for drawing together findings from multiple sources (Teddlie & Tashakkori, 2009). Plano Clark and Ivankova (2016) also note that considerations must be made related to timing (when and in what order to collect data), priority (the relative importance of the various research strands in light of the research questions), and integration (the strategies used to combine multiple sets of data throughout the research design). Taken together, this means there is no single, 'right' way to design a mixed methods diary study, as approaches are often complex and unique to the aims of the individual study. Indeed, Creswell and Plano Clark (2017) highlight six overall approaches for developing a mixed methods research design, all of which could be incorporated into a solicited diary study:

1 **Convergent parallel design**: data from multiple methods are collected separately, but at the same time, and then drawn together in the analysis.
2 **Explanatory sequential design**: an initial quantitative data collection phase is followed by qualitative data collection, explaining the initial results of the quantitative analysis.
3 **Exploratory sequential design:** an initial qualitative data collection phase is followed by quantitative data collection, allowing for an initial exploration phase before bringing the study to scale.
4 **Embedded design:** data from multiple methods are collected together at the same time in one single research phase.
5 **Transformative design:** a transformative theoretical framework is used to inform all decisions within the mixed methods design.
6 **Multiphase design:** convergent and sequential designs are combined over a larger programme of study.

An additional consideration in mixed methods research is the careful design of when, where and how multiple methods are integrated throughout the research process (Bazeley, 2017). Woolley (2009, p. 7) describes integration in mixed methods research as:

> the extent that these components [multiple research methods] are explicitly related to each other within a single study and in such a way as to be mutually illuminating, thereby producing findings that are greater than the sum of the parts.

Decisions related to integration are important to mixed methods diary designs, particularly as there are multiple approaches to integrating data in mixed methods research (see Creswell and Plano Clark 2017).

Mixed methods diary research

Mixed methods diary research offers great potential, particularly as many diary research features are well-suited for mixed methods designs. The most striking is the flexibility of diary approaches, which can be easily moulded across the broad range of mixed methods research design options outlined by Creswell and Plano Clark (2017). Diary instruments can be developed in many ways: as highly structured and questionnaire-like (Mullan, 2019), unstructured and more open-ended (Martinez-Vargas, Walker & Mkwananzi, 2020), or a hybrid (Swim, Hyers, Cohen, Fitzgerald & Bylsma, 2003). This means diaries' role and function can vary greatly between different studies. For example, some mixed methods studies in higher education have used diaries at the study's start to provide a baseline understanding of participants' experiences in an initial exploratory phase (Chen, Yarnal, Hustad & Sims, 2016), while others have used diaries towards the study's end to explain or complement initial quantitative findings (Swim et al., 2003).

Triangulating findings from diary research with other methods provides many benefits to researchers. For example, one common approach is the diary-interview method (Harvey, 2011), whereby preliminary findings from a diary study are used to develop interview questions. This allows researchers to expand upon preliminary diary findings with the interviewee, shedding greater light on findings that seem unclear or providing more depth into the sentiments expressed. Other research designs have collected diary data after a questionnaire (for example: Swim et al., 2003), which can help explain preliminary quantitative findings or provide deeper understandings about why certain patterns were exhibited. In higher education research, triangulating diaries with other methods has previously provided researchers access into more in-depth and well-rounded understandings of highly sensitive or personal research topics, such as students' experiences with racism (Swim et al., 2003) and sexism (Swim, Hyers, Cohen & Ferguson, 2001) or international students' experience (Heng, 2017; Chapters 3 and 12, this volume).

Incorporating other methods alongside diaries can additionally help overcome perceived drawbacks or challenges of the method. For example, one consideration is self-reflection bias, as participants select themselves what to include in their diaries, which may not fully represent their experiences or may demonstrate only extreme examples (Cohen et al., 2018). Responses might also be influenced by social desirability bias; in recognition that their writing will be read by another person for research purposes, participants may wish to portray their lives and experiences in a more positive light (Cohen et al., 2018). However, using mixed methods diary approaches allows for triangulation and member checking, meaning researchers can confirm or contradict the findings from multiple sources to create a more complete picture. An additional consideration is that some participants may not provide much depth in their diary writing or there might be a waning response depth over time, particularly in more unstructured diaries. Mixed methods diary approaches can help overcome such problems by allowing researchers to follow up on interesting ideas that were perhaps initially only explored superficially in the diaries.

Altogether, mixed methods diary approaches have the potential to offer unique insights into participants' worlds in higher education research through flexible engagement with multiple facets of their experiences. In the next sections, we critically reflect on the benefits and challenges associated with mixed methods diary research in the higher education field through an in-depth exploration of our own research.

Research methodology adopted

The remainder of this chapter reflects on our experiences conducting a longitudinal mixed methods diary study entitled Social Transition Research into International Doctoral Experiences (STRIDE). This project, situated within doctoral education research, focused on the social transitions and peer community development experiences of 53 doctoral students studying in three higher education departments in institutions based in England, Scotland and China. The study's underlying goal was to understand how doctoral students develop social support from peers within their departments and the roles doctoral communities play in supporting students' well-being. In recognition that social relationships and social transitions in higher education are complex experiences, we opted for a mixed methods approach using an explanatory sequential design (Creswell & Plano Clark, 2017). Altogether three research methods were used in this study:

- *Social network analysis surveys*: Social network analysis is a research method that measures and maps existing social structures and networks (Wasserman & Faust, 1994). In this study, we used a closed network questionnaire, whereby we provided doctoral students with a list of peers in their higher education departments and asked them to mark those from whom they had received social support. These data were then used to visualise the existing network structure and identify quantitative patterns of social support between doctoral students.

- *Reflective diaries:* The second research method was a semi-structured reflective diary study that lasted for six weeks. Participants were asked to reflect in their diaries about the social community in their higher education departments, including how they had interacted socially within their doctoral communities, what social opportunities occurred, and what factors they felt affected the social support they received. The diary data provided an understanding of the types of social behaviours participants exhibited, as well as a reflective account of why they did or did not feel socially supported in their academic departments.
- *Semi-structured interviews:* The final research method used was semi-structured interviews with doctoral students. In the interviews, participants were given the social network analysis visualisation as a mediating artefact and asked to reflect on the social network structure and their own role in the doctoral community. Data from the diaries were also used as prompts to explore participants' behaviours or reflections in greater depth. Altogether, the interviews provided an opportunity to member check (i.e. check understandings of the findings with the population being studied) and develop a greater understanding of initial findings.

The mixed methods research design investigated doctoral students' social support networks on multiple levels by considering what were students' existing social networks in their higher education departments (using social network analysis), what behaviours or factors impacted students' positions within their doctoral social community (using diaries), and why these patterns were exhibited (using interviews). In the following sections, we reflect on the benefits and challenges of incorporating diary research into a large-scale and complex mixed methods design in a higher education setting. For more information about the study, including its preliminary findings, readers may refer to Mittelmeier, Jindal-Snape and Rienties (2018).

Reflections on using a mixed methods diary approach

Added value to research

Perhaps the greatest benefit of adopting a mixed methods diary approach in this piece of higher education research was the opportunity to triangulate findings and examine the complex phenomena of doctoral students' social transitions. At the start, we recognised that social relationships between students in higher education were not necessarily rational or linear and that students' reflections on their social support networks may change over time (or even day-to-day). We also felt there was value in exploring social support networks from both a macro, group-level perspective and a micro, individual-level perspective, as this would add depth to our understanding of experiences within individual university departments. Therefore, the opportunity to explore convergence and divergence in the findings across multiple methods helped us develop a more complete answer to our research questions in a higher education setting.

The first step of our research was a quantitative, social network analysis approach whereby we mapped existing social relationships in each department and analysed various individual-level measures related to students' position within their social network. From this analysis, we concluded there were different engagement patterns: some doctoral students received substantial social support and were central to their social networks, while others received demonstrably less social support and appeared to be more isolated. While these findings were valuable, one weakness of social network analysis is that it does not necessarily explain why or how networks have formed in a particular way (Froehlich, Rehm & Rienties, 2020). Indeed, our initial quantitative findings brought up many questions: Why were some doctoral students more engaged in their social community? Why did other doctoral students not receive as much social support from their peers? What factors influenced doctoral students' social experiences in their departments?

As seen in other higher education studies (Swim et al., 2001; Swim et al., 2003), we followed up our initial findings by asking doctoral students to keep a diary, where they recorded their social behaviours in the department and reflected on what may have influenced doctoral social communities. By using the initial quantitative findings as a lens for comparing participants' diary responses, we identified several patterns of behaviour that linked to or explained the varying social support levels doctoral students received. For example, the diaries illuminated several factors that influenced students' social connections with peers and staff, such as their physical presence or attendance on campus, physical working spaces allocated in the department, or whether they had recently relocated for doctoral study. However, we found that, at times, the diary submissions lacked depth in some areas of participants' reflections. We also felt our findings thus far did not establish whether these behaviours and reflections were a cause or an effect of participants' role within their social network. For instance, lower attendance could mean that doctoral students have fewer opportunities to establish social support, but equally an existing lack of support might lead to less motivation to be present in the department.

Our third research method, semi-structured interviews with doctoral students, provided an opportunity to bring these initial findings back to the participants and develop more in-depth understandings of their experiences. In our interviews, we used a mediating artefact, which was a social network analysis visualisation depicting relationships between doctoral students as nodes and lines (see Mittelmeier et al., 2018). Participants were asked to reflect on the visualisation and why certain patterns might be exhibited in the doctoral students' social networks. We also brought in preliminary findings from the diary data and asked more direct questions to expand upon students' experiences. For example, we noted that several participants had taken the initiative to plan social activities for their peers and we were able to ask participants to comment upon why and what motivated these behaviours. Similarly, we asked participants who were less involved in the community what influenced their decision not to attend certain social events or why they more frequently worked from home rather than in the department.

Altogether, bringing together these three research strands helped explain initial findings, provided more depth in responses, and allowed us to triangulate findings from multiple perspectives. The diary approach's flexibility also meant that we could strategically embed it within our research in ways that best supported answering our research questions (Creswell & Plano Clark, 2017). In our design, this was as the second of three data collection phases, which allowed us to use the diaries to provide more depth for the initial quantitative findings and simultaneously act as a foundation for follow-up interviews. Nonetheless, incorporating diaries into a mixed methods design brought up distinct challenges, which we turn our attention to next.

Challenges of adopting a diary method

As our research project was longitudinal and sequential, participants were asked to contribute to several data collection phases (an initial survey, a 6-week diary collection, and an interview). As is common in longitudinal and mixed methods designs (Lavrakas, 2008), some participants in our project shared informally with the researchers that they experienced participation fatigue during the research process, leading to a decline in motivation and attention. For example, there were frequent comments in the follow-up interview data that reflected on participants' experiences using diaries, such as:

> I probably should have said this in my diary, but I was a little bit lazy ...
>
> (Interview Participant 2)

> I ran out of time so didn't write much about this ...
>
> (Interview Participant 11)

The consequences for diary collection included data quality deterioration over time, shorter diaries and repetition in the entries. Various factors that contributed to this were informally shared by participants, such as enthusiasm fading when writing the diary became a routine, when there was a lack of new experiences or events to reflect on, or when participants had to balance participation with a busy agenda (such as towards the semester end). As a result, we observed diary quality discrepancies between the earlier and later phases of data collection. Hence, one significant challenge for researchers using a mixed methods diary approach is how to design mechanisms for motivating participants to ensure consistency in the diary data's quality and volume. This has particular implications for higher education research, as researchers will need to ensure that diary collection timing does not coincide with busy or stressful periods (such as during exams) or when attention is likely elsewhere (such as during university breaks).

Second, we recognised that there were likely self-selection or self-reflection biases that might have occurred in our data collection in terms of the experiences that participants chose to share in their diaries. Unlike private diary writers, participants in diary research are aware that their diaries are being read by researchers (Wechtler, 2018). In our own study, one consideration was the implications of perceived power dynamics between the doctoral students and the research team, who were university staff members. Participants might share experiences and emotions that they assume would meet the researchers' expectations, perhaps leading to an unwillingness to be critical of the institution or its staff. Participants might additionally select certain parts of their lives to create a particular image, such as highlighting behaviours to portray themselves as 'good' students. In our study, for example, we found there were instances when a participant portrayed themselves as active within their doctoral social community in a face-to-face interview, but this was unsubstantiated by evidence in the social network analysis survey or diaries. Therefore, a distinct challenge for mixed methods diary research is disentangling such self-reflection biases in the findings by triangulating multiple pieces of evidence.

As noted previously, integration is at the heart of mixed methods research (Bazeley, 2017; Woolley, 2009). However, many mixed methods theorists argue that integration often remains superficial and focused on research conclusions, rather than substantially embedded across the research design (Bazeley, 2017; Woolley, 2009). However, getting integration 'right' can be exceptionally challenging, particularly as it requires careful planning and consideration (Bazeley, 2017; Plano Clark & Ivankova, 2016). In our study, we found that careful considerations were needed at the project's start to map and plan to ensure that integration was purposeful. This included considering the order of the methods used related to our research questions (first outlining *what* with the social network analysis survey, then unpacking *why* and *how* with the diaries and interviews). We also needed to consider the research instrument development and plan for how preliminary analysis and findings would shape subsequent data collection. For example, preliminary findings from the diary study informed the questions developed for our semi-structured interviews. Finally, we needed to carefully consider from the start of the project our approach to analysing the data and how to integrate findings to develop a more complete picture of the student communities we were investigating. Altogether, in line with Bazeley (2017), we found that data integration was a dynamic (and time-intensive) process which required integrating multiple forms of data at different research stages. At times, this meant unexpected challenges that required collaborative reflection by the research team, such as how to handle missing data or contradictions in findings between different methods. As we conducted the project in different steps with information unfolding over time, it was important to balance both careful planning at the start of the project and flexibility to adjust approaches as findings were developed. Nonetheless, we found that incorporating a mixed methods approach encouraged collaboration and methodological reflection to a degree that might not have been as valuable using one method alone.

Ethical considerations

Several ethical issues must be considered when conducting diary research (Filep, Turner, Eidse, Thompson-Fawcett & Fitzsimons, 2017). In particular to a mixed methods design, important considerations in our study were issues related to privacy and anonymisation of participants' responses. As we were taking an in-depth look at doctoral students' experiences within single departments, the participants were well known to one another and to other non-participants in the department (including their supervisors or other staff), which increased risks that participants may be identifiable in the dissemination of our findings. This was exacerbated in a mixed methods design, as triangulating multiple pieces of sensitive information about individuals could make it easier to 'guess' who the individual might be. For instance, we explored demographic and lifestyle variables related to students' experiences, and there were instances when there was only one individual who matched a certain profile in the department. In these cases, we needed to take consistent and careful consideration in writing up and disseminating our findings to ensure that the way we discussed participants' experiences respected their privacy. In some cases, this meant choosing not to share certain results or excluding certain examples in our writing, as the explanation would compromise a particular participant's confidentiality.

As our participants discussed their daily lives in the diaries and provided location-specific details throughout our study, our data collection included many identifying markers, such as discussions about other doctoral students, supervisors, staff members, and university or departmental signifiers. For example, there were instances in which participants spoke about negative impacts their doctoral supervisor had on their social support provisions, where that supervisor was named or described. We recognised that this had implications on several levels, should careful steps not be taken to ensure anonymisation. Further, we needed to consider the privacy and dignity of non-participants, who might find themselves identifiable or recognisable in the dissemination of our findings. We also felt there were potential issues related to power dynamics and social harmony should a supervisor or staff member recognise negative sentiments expressed by their student, particularly considering we were researching within our own departments (Malone, 2003). Therefore, the project required a strict anonymisation protocol that was developed at the start of the study and was revisited throughout the data collection and analysis processes. This included removing names and place markers and deleting any statements that may have made the participant identifiable. We also made sure that all transcripts were anonymised by members of the research team who were not in a position of power over the participant (such as being their supervisor). At the same time, the mixed methods design required the researchers to have a signifying marker (for us, a unique identifying number) to link the data from multiple collection points. An additional step was taken by sending participants a copy of their anonymised data and allowing them to make any additional anonymisations if they felt uncomfortable or unsure whether they could be identified, of which several participants suggested further changes.

Our research focused on a highly personal and sensitive topic and we recognised that social transitions can have an influential impact on higher education students' mental health and well-being. Given that we collected such in-depth data about challenging subjects such as social isolation or social anxiety, we also recognised the potential that our participants may disclose information that might lead the research team to be concerned for their well-being or safety (for example, suicidal thoughts or severe anxiety). This is a particular concern for diary studies, given they often facilitate in-depth and personal reflection on sensitive topics (Harvey, 2011). As such, the research team developed a protocol at the start of the study for addressing any issues that might arise, including outlining what circumstances might warrant intervention, dedicating who would be designated with addressing any concerns and establishing easily accessible resources and referrals for students in crisis. However, it is worth noting that, unlike interviews, diary data are often submitted at particular intervals and may not be immediately available to the researcher, leaving no recourse for immediate action to safeguard participants.

Altogether, it is important to be aware that the nature of mixed methods diary research means more complex, personal and identifiable information is often collected about an individual, giving way to an increased potential for ethical issues. Developing clear protocol at the start of a mixed methods diary study for issues such as privacy, anonymisation, opportunities to withdraw data and circumstances that warrant breaking participants' confidentiality is essential for supporting ethical research and easing the concerns of both participants and researchers alike.

Considerations for developing a rigorous mixed methods diary study

Based on these reflections, we offer several suggestions to researchers considering adopting a mixed methods diary approach in higher education settings:

- *Reflect on the role diaries play in a mixed methods study.* As outlined at the start of our chapter, mixed methods designs can vary greatly, depending on the research questions and study aims (Cohen et al., 2018; Creswell & Creswell, 2018; Creswell & Plano Clark, 2017; Greene et al., 1989). When developing a mixed methods study, it is important to critically reflect at the start of the design process about the overarching goals of the study and carefully consider how different research methods might best address the complex experiences of students in higher education (Creswell & Creswell, 2018). The role, purpose and priority of diary research for answering research questions has strong implications for when diary data is collected and how diary instruments are designed to capture the reflections of students or other stakeholders (Filep et al., 2017).
- *Consider methods of integration throughout a study.* A frequent critique in mixed methods research is that researchers often only consider the integration of the findings at the conclusion of the study (Bazeley, 2017; Woolley, 2009). However, a stronger form of integration should be developed throughout the

research design, data collection, analysis and dissemination of findings. For example, considerations might be made about how the preliminary findings from diary data can inform the instrument design or purposeful sampling of follow-up data collection about experiences in higher education (or vice versa).

- *Consider the strengths and weaknesses of each research method.* One important added value of a mixed methods approach in our own study was balancing the strengths and weaknesses of the different methods used to form a more complete picture of doctoral students' social transitions. By carefully considering those strengths and weaknesses at the start of our study design, we could order and design our data collection in a way that was more logical for addressing the research questions. Therefore, it is recommended to reflect on what is gained by including a diary method into a higher education research design and what gaps or weaknesses remain at the end of each data collection phase so that these can be compensated for in the next method employed in a study (Creswell & Creswell, 2018; Creswell & Plano Clark, 2017; Greene et al., 1989). In particular to diary research in higher education settings, challenges such as self-reflection bias, participation fatigue, or lack of depth in responses should be considered, especially in consideration for distracting periods during the academic year (such as exam times).

- *Consider mechanisms for motivating continued participation.* One challenge for mixed methods research is that participation often occurs over a longer period or over multiple phases, which may lead to participation fatigue or participant dropout. This is of particular concern for diary studies in higher education settings, where there is often a longitudinal element that requires sustained effort and contribution (Harvey, 2011), in addition to participants' competing priorities and deadlines as university students or staff. Although there is debate about the merits of financial incentives or gifts for participants (Head, 2009), it is worth noting that mixed methods diary designs often do need some form of incentive or motivation for continued participation. The appropriateness of these choices for participants in higher education are likely circumstantial and it is suggested to reflect upon this at the start of a study design process.

- *Develop a plan for anonymisation and merging of the data.* As experienced in our own study, one challenge for mixed methods diary research is that the triangulation of multiple methods might make it easier to identify participants in the analysis and dissemination of findings. This can be exacerbated for higher education researchers working in their own departments, where participants may be known to the researchers or other staff members (Malone, 2003). It can also be difficult to merge data from multiple methods without a designated identifier for individual participants. To avoid ethical or organisational problems, it is suggested to create a strict anonymisation protocol at the start of a study for all data collection methods. When working in a team, assigning one researcher to be in charge of anonymisation and data merging can also be beneficial, particularly if they have limited power over participants' progression, completion or promotion. Finally, we found it was good practice in our own research to allow student participants the opportunity to review their own anonymised data and suggest changes to make them less identifiable to each other and departmental staff. This approach is especially well-suited for higher education research, where participants are likely to be highly literate and potentially aware (in the case of our doctoral participants) of research processes and ethical protocols.

- *Create strong ethical protocols to guide the research.* As identified previously, the nature of mixed methods diary research design means that large volumes of personal and identifiable information are often collected about participants. For this reason, the research team needs to reflect carefully about potential issues that might arise in the study, including in the data collection, analysis and dissemination (Filep et al., 2017). Researchers in higher education who are developing such studies should consider issues such as power dynamics between researchers (likely university staff) and participants (students or colleagues), the privacy of non-participants, identification of participants in the dissemination, anonymisation of people or university place markers discussed in the data, and the increased risk of identification due to triangulation of multiple pieces of information about participants.

Conclusion

We identified in our research on doctoral students' social transitions that solicited diaries can offer several advantages in a mixed methods research design by allowing participants to reflect on their experiences and providing researchers with more in-depth and 'in the moment' data. However, as with any research method, the use of diaries must be considered carefully, particularly in light of potential issues, such as participation fatigue and issues of anonymity. In higher education settings, many considerations impact the overall research design approach, such as timing in the academic year, existing power dynamics between researcher staff and participants (often students), and competing academic priorities over participation. In this way, considering a mixed methods diary approach brings up several questions for researchers: Why is a mixed methods diary design appropriate to the research questions in higher education settings? When and how can other methods be incorporated alongside diaries? In what order should data be collected? How will multiple methods be integrated throughout the study? How will participants' identities be protected? Yet, with careful planning, mixed methods diary designs promote breadth and depth of the findings about complex issues facing higher education, alongside an ability to look at phenomena from multiple angles and balance the inherent strengths and weaknesses that exist between research paradigms.

Acknowledgements

This study was funded by the UK Council for International Student Affairs (UKCISA) through the 2017–2018 Grant Scheme and the Ministry of Education in China, grant number 15YJC880140.

References

Bazeley, P. (2017) *Integrating analyses in mixed methods research*. London: Sage.

Chen, H.-Y., Yarnal, C., Hustad, J. T. P. & Sims, D. (2016). Take a selfie of life: A qualitative exploration of college students' self-reflections on free time use and personal values. *Journal of College and Character*, 17, 2: 101–115.

Cohen, L., Manion, L. & Morrison, K. (2018) *Research methods in education*. London: Routledge.

Creswell, J. W. & Creswell, J. D. (2018) *Research design: Qualitative, quantitative, and mixed methods approaches* (5th ed.). London: Sage.

Creswell, J. W. & Plano Clark, V. L. (2017) *Designing and conducting mixed methods research* (3rd ed.). London: Sage.

Filep, C. V., Turner, S., Eidse, N., Thompson-Fawcett, M. & Fitzsimons, S. (2017) Advancing rigour in solicited diary research. *Qualitative Research*, 18, 4: 451–470.

Froehlich, D., Rehm, M. & Rienties, B. (2020) *Mixed method approaches to social network analysis*. London: Routledge.

Greene, J. C., Caracelli, V. J. & Graham, W. F. (1989) Toward a conceptual framework for mixed-method evaluation designs. *Educational Evaluation and Policy Analysis*, 11, 3: 255–274.

Harvey, L. (2011) Intimate reflections: Private diaries in qualitative research. *Qualitative Research*, 11, 6: 664–682.

Head, E. (2009) The ethics and implications of paying participants in qualitative research. *International Journal of Social Research Methodology*, 12, 4: 335–344.

Heng, T. T. (2017) Voices of Chinese international students in USA colleges: 'I want to tell them that …'. *Studies in Higher Education*, 42, 5: 833–850.

Johnson, R. B. & Onwuegbuzie, A. J. (2004) Mixed methods research: A research paradigm whose time has come. *Educational Researcher*, 33, 7: 14–26.

Johnson, R. B., Onwuegbuzie, A. J. & Turner, L. A. (2007) Toward a definition of mixed methods research. *Journal of Mixed Methods Research*, 1, 2: 112–133.

Lavrakas, P. (2008) *Encyclopedia of survey research methods*. London: Sage.

Malone, S. (2003) Ethics at home: informed consent in your own backyard. *International Journal of Qualitative Studies in Education*, 16, 6: 797–815.

Martinez-Vargas, C., Walker, M. & Mkwananzi, F. (2020). Access to higher education in South Africa: Expanding capabilities in and through an undergraduate photovoice project. *Educational Action Research*, 28, 3, 427–442.

Mittelmeier, J., Jindal-Snape, D. & Rienties, B. (2018) *STRIDE: Social transition research into international doctoral experiences*. London: UK Council for International Student Affairs (UKCISA).

Mullan, K. (2019) A child's day: Trends in time use in the UK from 1975 to 2015. *The British Journal of Sociology*, 70, 3: 997–1024.

Plano Clark, V. L. & Ivankova, N. V. (2016) *Mixed methods research: A guide to the field*. London: Sage.

Scoles, J., Huxham, M. & McArthur, J. (2014) *Mixed-methods research in education: Exploring students' response to a focused feedback initiative*. London: Sage. Retrieved from https://methods.sagepub.com/case/mixed-methods-education-students-response-focused-feedback-initiative.

Swim, J. K., Hyers, L. L., Cohen, L. L. & Ferguson, M. J. (2001) Everyday sexism: Evidence for its incidence, nature, and psychological impact from three daily diary studies. *Journal of Social Issues*, 57, 1: 31–53.

Swim, J. K., Hyers, L. L., Cohen, L. L., Fitzgerald, D. C. & Bylsma, W. H. (2003) African American college students' experiences with everyday racism: Characteristics of and responses to these incidents. *Journal of Black Psychology*, 29, 1: 38–67.

Symonds, J. E. & Gorard, S. (2010) Death of mixed methods? Or the rebirth of research as a craft. *Evaluation & Research in Education*, 23, 2: 121–136.

Teddlie, C. & Tashakkori, A. (2009) *Foundations of mixed methods research: Integrating quantitative and qualitative approaches in the social and behavioral sciences*. London: Sage.

Wasserman, S. & Faust, K. (1994) *Social network analysis: Methods and applications*. Cambridge: Cambridge University Press.

Wechtler, H. (2018) 'Life if elsewhere': A diary study of female self-initiated expatriates' motivation to work abroad. *Career Development International*, 23, 3: 291–311.

Woolley, C. M. (2009) Meeting the mixed methods challenge of integration in a sociological study of structure and agency. *Journal of Mixed Methods Research*, 3, 1: 7–25.

Chapter 2

How short is too short?

Exploring diary study duration from the perspective of researching conferences and other short-term phenomena in higher education and beyond

Emily F. Henderson

Introduction – how long is too long ... or how short is too short?

In diary method studies, often a key question in designing the study is, 'how long is too long?' This question stems from the fact that diary method is known to be an effort-intensive form of data collection for participants, as, unlike with for example questionnaires or one-off interviews, they have to produce the data themselves over a period of time (Reynolds et al., 2016). As such, when researchers justify their diary design, they often include a statement relating to how they made the diary design less onerous for participants, in order to increase the chances of participant recruitment and retention. We can see examples of this in the studies represented in other chapters of this book, such as where Cao (Chapter 5) asked participants to complete a diary for one week per month, or where Dangeni et al. (Chapter 3) justified audio diaries based on the convenience for participants. The question of 'how long is too long?' pertains to diary studies which focus on capturing ongoing experiences, such as how people with chronic health conditions manage their health (Jacelon & Imperio, 2005), or in higher education how students choose where to study (Beckers, van der Voordt & Dewulf, 2016). Secondly, it pertains to diary projects aiming to study time-bound phenomena, but which are of longer durations, such as a sports season (Day & Thatcher, 2009) or, in higher education, students' experiences of their first year of a course (Scott, Green & Cashmore, 2012). Neglected in diary method literature is the question, 'how short is too short?'

Researching short-term, intense phenomena means researching *people when they are at their busiest*. This may seem to be a disadvantageous set of circumstances for using diary method – a method which specialises in gathering nuanced reflections (Alaszewski, 2006) – but there may be particular reasons why we wish to capture the micro-level detail of short-term, intense phenomena, which would be easily forgotten or glossed over in retrospective methods. This applies to anything where importance is placed on understanding *process* – the decisions that are taken, the feelings and actions which play out at a mundane level, but which encompass experience at a more general level. Hyers (2018, p. 28) expresses this as 'studying the ephemera of everyday life'. In relation to higher education, this could apply to various phenomena – meetings and away days, engaging in assessment and feedback, planning teaching, conducting empirical fieldwork. The short-term phenomenon addressed in this chapter is conferences, in particular conference participation for academics who have caring responsibilities.

Conferences remain an under-researched phenomenon within the higher education research field (Henderson, 2015, 2020a; Nicolson, 2017), and issues of inequality and conferences are no exception. There have been a number of studies relating to access to conferences, which have used survey and/or secondary data analysis methods to examine gender inequality (e.g. Eden, 2016) and 'international' representation (e.g. Derudder & Liu, 2016) at conferences. However, the experiences of academics while they are at conferences remain clouded in mystery. This chapter is based on a project entitled 'In Two Places at Once' (Henderson, Cao & Mansuy, 2018; Henderson, 2019a, 2020b; Henderson & Moreau, 2020), which set out to understand more about how academics with caring responsibilities manage attending and participating in conferences, following a previous study that uncovered some of these issues (Henderson, 2020a). The study employed an adapted form of diary-interview method (Zimmerman & Wieder, 1977), using the diary to capture the minutiae of academic-carers' experiences of attending conferences, and the interview to compare the 'case' conference to other conference experiences, thus widening the purview of the study. The diary, which was a simple form with a grid for completion during the conference (explained further below), produced fascinating, detailed information on how care and conferences intertwine.

The chapter engages specifically with two principal issues. The first is that of time in relation to diaries: how short is too short to keep a diary? And what counts as 'short'? The second issue is the notion of sampling, which has a specific meaning in diary research – in addition to the usual meaning of participant selection, sampling in diary research refers to the selection of timings for participants to record diary entries (Bartlett & Milligan, 2015). While the chapter focuses on the use of diary method to research caring practices at conferences, the issues covered are applicable to any short-term diary study, in higher education or beyond. Overall the chapter argues that diary method yields a great degree of flexibility in terms of its adaptability to phenomena of different durations, but that there are particular considerations for short-term diary studies relating to the duration of the diary versus duration of the phenomenon, and to the functioning of the sampling strategy within a short, intense experience.

Exploring diary duration in and beyond higher education research

In their guide to diary method research, Bartlett and Milligan (2015, p. 38) emphasise that 'there is no "right" or "wrong" period of time for keeping a diary'. However, the examples they provide to exemplify a range of diary study durations range from 40 days to 18 months (ibid.). Indeed, as noted in the introduction, guidance on diary method often rests on a normative assumption of the longevity of a study. One of the common ways of defining diary method is to note that it involves collecting data 'over time' (see e.g. Bartlett & Milligan, 2015, p. 30; Hyers, 2018, p. vii), with the longitudinal aspect of this method held up as a defining feature. In view of this assumption of longevity, guidance on diary design is likely to discuss for how long it is possible to maintain a diary study while avoiding participant attrition or a dip in diary quality (e.g. Alaszewski, 2006). Given that diary method obtains its methodological kudos from its longitudinal nature, there is another question underlying 'how long is too long?', which is 'how short is too short?': does a diary study gain methodological legitimacy from being *long enough*? In which case, is it possible for a diary to be *not long enough*? This section of the chapter engages with the notion of diary duration, situating short-term diary studies in the wider landscape of this discussion.

Diary studies tend to fall into one of two categories in relation to temporality. First, there are diary studies which attempt to capture ongoing phenomena, where the researcher determines the time-scale of the study. These studies try to capture the reality of everyday life relating to a particular phenomenon, such as chronic health issues (Jacelon & Imperio, 2005), non-normative sexuality (Kenten, 2010) or practices of street vending (Eidse & Turner, 2014), or, in relation to higher education, students' choices relating to where they study (Beckers, van der Voordt & Dewulf, 2016) or how they use their time (Chen, Yarnal, Hustad & Sims, 2016; Nonis, Philhours & Hudson, 2006), or the prevalence of sexism on campus (Swim, Hyers, Cohen & Ferguson, 2001). Second, diary studies may also be designed around time-bound phenomena, where the phenomenon in question imposes the time-scale of the study. These studies seem to be less common than the former type, but may include the specific time period after a birth (Williamson, Leeming, Lyttle & Johnson, 2012) or operation (Furness & Garrud, 2010), a sports season (Day & Thatcher, 2009), or, in higher education, an academic year (Scott, Green & Cashmore, 2012). Time-bound studies encompass a wide range of durations, from a few days to a year.[1] Short-term diary studies may be used to research both ongoing and time-bound phenomena.

The focus of this chapter is short-term diary studies, but there is no formal definition of what counts as 'short'. In reviewing literature for this chapter, I explored diary studies where the diary-keeping period was one month or less, as a working definition of 'short'. The most common durations were two weeks or one week, with the shortest period I found being three days for a study on the experiences of compulsions for those with a diagnosis of obsessive compulsive disorder (Bucarelli & Purdon, 2015). There is also a grey area where time-use studies, which are a specific type of study aiming to survey how populations use time, overlap with diary studies, and where the typical length of the time-use log is one day, or at times two units of one day each (Sullivan & Gershuny, 2018, Kitterød & Pettersen, 2006). However, the majority of these studies, time-use studies included, focus on capturing ongoing phenomena, with few examples of time-bound phenomena. Moreover there is very little discussion in these papers of the choice of short-term diary duration, and interestingly, where justifications of duration are included, they still err towards the 'as long as possible' argument, where the duration of the diary study is curbed by the nature of the study or the availability or potential tenacity of participants (rather than by the duration of the phenomenon). This chapter therefore specifically focuses on the somewhat neglected discussion of 'how short is too short?' in relation to short-term, time-bound phenomena (i.e. are there phenomena which are too short to be researched using diary method?).

The question of 'how short is too short' is intimately linked with the chosen sampling strategy of a diary study, which in turn is closely related to the phenomenon in question. As noted in the introduction, in diary research there are specific sampling procedures related to the timing of diary entries. In this form of sampling, as discussed by Hyers (2018, p. 96), 'diary entries represent a sampling of the hours, days, weeks and months of an individual's ongoing experiences'. There are two broad types of sampling in diary research: *interval-based*, which is based on recording information at specific, regular intervals (which may be triggered by a reminder from the researcher, in which case it is *signal-based*), and *event-based* (or *event-contingent*), which is based on recording information when the phenomenon of interest occurs (Bartlett & Milligan, 2015). Both forms of sampling are related to the duration of the study, as in both cases the researcher has to design the study to ensure that the phenomenon of study is captured in sufficient detail.

If the study lasts a week and uses an *interval-based* sampling strategy to capture a frequent *ongoing phenomenon*, participants may be requested to complete a diary once a day (e.g. in Swim et al., 2001, researching sexism on campus), while a more infrequent phenomenon may involve keeping a diary once per week (e.g. Hyers, Syphan, Cochran & Brown, 2012, studying professional development interactions of faculty members). If a study lasts a week and uses an *event-based* strategy to capture an *ongoing phenomenon*, the choice of a one-week study implies that the phenomenon of study will occur several times during that week. For example, in the aforementioned study of where students study (Beckers, van der Voordt & Dewulf, 2016), the duration was one week, presumably based on the assumption that the participants would engage in study activities several times during that week. In the case of an event-based diary study used to research an ongoing phenomenon, the question of 'how short is too short' is linked to the requirement that the phenomenon of study occur several times during the chosen time period.

However, a different question arises for a study which is based on a short-term *time-bound phenomenon*. In this research context, *interval-based* entries may be much more frequent, as in the time-use surveys which may ask participants to record what they are doing every ten minutes for one or two days (Kitterød & Pettersen, 2006). An *event-based* sampling strategy would need to assume that the phenomenon of interest would occur frequently during the phenomenon of study (Hyers, 2018); for example a study of breastfeeding in the post-birth month

(Williamson et al., 2012). The choice of duration and the choice of sampling are based on researching an activity, feeling or process that occurs frequently during the time-bound phenomenon; the choice of sampling strategy then depends on the specifics of the study. With a more occasional phenomenon, the risk increases of insufficient occurrence – from whence the question arises – are some time-bound phenomena too short to use diary method, whether for interval-based or event-based sampling?

This section has set out interlinked factors relating to diary duration which need to be addressed when formulating a diary study. First, there is the distinction between *ongoing phenomena* and *time-bound phenomena*. Linked with this, there is the question of what counts as a *short-term* diary study, and how length of diary study relates to duration of the phenomenon in question. Second, there is the decision between *interval-based* and *event-based* sampling, which is linked to the duration of the phenomenon and the duration of the diary study. Short-term diary studies (of one month and less, as a working definition) face different challenges to the issues of attrition and quality decline faced by longer-term studies – instead, the issues relate to whether a short-term diary study can capture sufficient occurrence of the phenomenon to form a substantial basis for analysis. With a *short-term* diary study of *ongoing phenomenon*, the duration of the diary study is chosen to balance occurrence with participant fatigue; with a *short-term* diary study of a *short-term time-bound phenomenon*, the diary study duration is not chosen by the researcher. The only choice open to the researcher is the choice of *interval-based* or *event-based* sampling, which must balance the feasibility of recording the experience of the phenomenon while also experiencing it. There is, then, a higher risk involved in researching a *short-term, time-bound phenomenon*, which is perhaps why this is a less common form of diary study, and one that is almost entirely neglected in higher education research; it is the aim of this chapter to inspire more researchers to attempt this type of diary research.

'In Two Places at Once' – researching academic-carers at conferences

The 'In Two Places at Once' project is a relatively rare example of a study which used an *event-based* sampling strategy for a *short-term, time-bound phenomenon*: namely, academic conferences. The objective of the study was to relate this specific aspect of academic practice to wider understandings of academia and care (Hook, 2016; Moreau and Robertson, 2017), which tend to encompass ongoing, institutional issues. Furthermore, other studies on the inequalities of conferences have tended to focus on access *to* conferences[2] (i.e. who attends the conference) rather than access *within* (i.e. whether those present can participate fully in the conference) (Henderson, Cao & Mansuy, 2018). The study used diary-interview method (Zimmerman & Wieder, 1977) to capture the minutiae of how academics with caring responsibilities balance their roles as conference delegate and carer when they attend conferences. Each research participant completed a diary for one 'case' conference; the diary gathered information predominantly on communications with caring responsibilities or co-carers. The diary then provided the basis for the post-conference interview, where we discussed the diary in more detail, and also participants were invited to compare experiences of the 'case' conference with their other conference experiences.

The diary took the form of a Word document which included some basic information such as current role and principal caring responsibilities, as well as basic details of the conference (number of days, location). Then there were free-text boxes which asked participants to record any care-related preparation activities they had engaged in before leaving for the conference, and any notes on the journey. For the duration of the conference, a simple grid was provided, in which participants were to record the date and approximate time of an entry, then the type of care-related interactions (i.e. the *events* for *event-based sampling*) in the next column, followed by any notes in the final column (e.g. on emotions, details of the interaction). The following section was again a free-text box to record notes on the journey home and any care-related 'catch-up' activities they engaged in when they returned home. Finally the form included a section asking for any further general thoughts participants wanted to include about the experience. A Word document was chosen as the pilot study found that this suited academics, who could either work on the document on their laptops (including offline) or print it out and keep it in their notebook for the conference. The diary form was not structured in the sense that the data would be statistically analysed to assess how many care events occurred, rather the diary's purpose was to facilitate participants in producing representations of their care-related experiences at conferences. Twenty participants completed the diary-interview study (for further details of the sample and the study, see Henderson, Cao & Mansuy, 2018).

Short-term time-bound diary studies in higher education – troubling the terms

There is something of a dilemma in methodological accounts of diary method, in that the paucity of literature on this method means that the field is in need of typologies and distinctions to develop its legitimacy alongside more developed methods; on the other hand, the necessity of firming up the method also means that to date there has been relatively little critical or analytical engagement with the foundations of diary research. This chapter has already set up binary distinctions – long-term/short-term, ongoing/time-bound, interval-based/event-based – which are doubtless useful terms for developing the precision of diary studies. However in this section I also want to bring a critical angle to this terminology, by showing how, in practice, the binary distinctions of ongoing/time-bound and interval-based/event-based, outlined earlier in the chapter, may be blurred and therefore worked with in a more nuanced manner.

Exploring the boundaries of time-bound phenomena

The 'In Two Places at Once' study focused on academics attending a single conference, which appears to be a clear example of a short-term, time-bound phenomenon, where academics travel to the conference, participate in the conference, and then return home again. The diary form (described above) was also constructed around this three-part process. However, there were two principal ways in which the boundaries of this short-term, time-bound experience were blurred.

First, several participants incorporated other work-related activities in their conference travel. This ranged from combining a conference with collecting data in a nine-day trip, accessing archives for a day before the conference, travelling from a conference to a project meeting and then home again. Two participants travelling to the UK from Australia curated much longer trips (up to more than two months), including seeing family and friends and taking holidays, giving talks and attending at least one conference. This reflects the complexity of academic work and the 'high mobility' (Viry & Kaufmann, 2015) of the profession. Furthermore, this multi-purpose travel is significant in its own right as the participants in the study reflected that they tried to limit the number of trips they took – particularly overnight trips (Henderson, in 2020b) – and therefore tried to combine multiple activities in one packed trip. In these examples, the boundaries of the short-term phenomenon of study were blurred by the extension of the trip, where the conference was nested within the wider phenomenon of short-term academic mobility (Henderson, 2019b).

The second way in which the boundaries of the time-bound phenomenon were blurred was by the revelation that conferences are in some senses an ongoing phenomenon, particularly in relation to care. One of the key findings of the study was that participants engaged in intensive care-related preparation before the conference, and equally intensive aftermath management, and that this fed into an ongoing negotiation with co-carers and caring responsibilities about conference participation past, present and future (Henderson, Cao & Mansuy, 2018). This ongoing negotiation entered into participants' accounts in different ways, most often in the preparation and aftermath stages of the conference travel. One participant referred in her diary to having an argument with her partner when she returned home; I asked her more about this in the interview, which led to her recognition of the 'post-conference argument', a phenomenon which she remembered identifying with another friend at another conference two years before, and which had now fallen into place as a common post-conference 'homecoming', as she expressed it. Participants kept internal logs of which conferences they had missed, which they had left early, which had been ruined, which had left those at home in a tricky situation … The case conferences were clearly situated within the parallel, intertwined strands of home lives and academic career trajectories, thus undermining the significance of the boundaries of the short-term, time-bound case conferences.

Following on from the two ways in which the boundaries of this time-bound phenomenon were blurred, there are further considerations for diary research. First, it is worth considering whether the time-bound phenomenon is fully bounded, or if it is bounded in different ways for different people, or indeed if the study has been designed with assumptions about the shape of the phenomenon (as indeed the 'In Two Places at Once' study held in-built assumptions about the nature of conference travel as a discrete trip). It may be tempting to fix the boundaries in place in order to gain control over the study, but in fact the blurred boundaries may be significant for the topic of the study, as in my study – and diary method in its more flexible forms (Hyers, 2018) can accommodate this blurring.

Second, when researching time-bound phenomena, it is worth considering that a time-bound phenomenon is nested within ongoing lives, and may also be an instance of a longer-term, episodic phenomenon. Conferences are a clear example of this type of episodic phenomenon, with other higher education-related examples being exams, open days, union action or away days. While they appear to be discrete, time-bound phenomena, an individual's experiences of any of these examples will be layered with previous experiences and future expectations. I argue that diary research would be all the richer if researchers acknowledged and further justified the overlapping, complex and blurred nature of the temporalities within which their research phenomena are situated.

The im/possibilities of event-based sampling

Earlier in the chapter, and following on from others who have been instrumental in consolidating diary method as a legitimate form of social sciences research (Alaszewski, 2006; Bartlett & Milligan, 2015; Hyers, 2018), I drew up a clear distinction between interval-based and event-based sampling. Any diary study needs to set out the sampling strategy, and these terms are useful demarcations indeed. However, when examined more closely, the strategies are less fixed; in this section I particularly focus on the slippages which pertain to event-based sampling in a short-term, time-bound study.

Already if event-based sampling has been selected, this is because the researcher is certain that the phenomenon of study will occur several times during the time-bound period. In my study, I knew that academics with caring responsibilities would experience several of the 'events' (here defined as making or receiving contact with co-carers or caring responsibilities, talking or thinking about caring responsibilities) while at the conference. The decision for event-based sampling also implies that there will be enough occurrences of the phenomenon to mean that an ongoing record of the phenomenon is beneficial, as opposed to a post-phenomenon interview. With my study, I knew that care-related events would occur frequently enough, and also potentially be 'quickly forgotten' (Hyers, 2018, 70), that an ongoing record would capture more of a sense of the interweaving of care and conferences (hence 'in two places at once') than a post-conference interview. Indeed the diaries provided invaluable fodder for the interview, both in terms of reminding participants about parts of the conference, but also in terms of legitimising discussions about micro-level issues which had at the time felt extremely significant, but which participants were somewhat sheepish about discussing in the interview. This included a participant who found herself 'in two places at once' as she added an item to the online grocery order during the keynote; the significance of the hamster's water bottle breaking and the participant's partner being unable to fix it; a child's disaster haircut which dominated the conference owing to the ongoing family tensions it provoked. Event-based sampling was particularly important as the diaries tracked these micro-moments more or less as they unfolded, which even a frequent interval-based sampling strategy would not have captured.

While there was a strong argument for event-based sampling, which was indeed borne out in the data, there are challenges associated with this sampling strategy for a diary study of a short-term, intense phenomenon such as a conference. There is already some acknowledgement of the slippage in event-based sampling in the literature. For example, Hyers (2018, p. 97) defines event-based sampling as follows: 'the participant is vigilant for an event to occur, after which, *or as soon as possible after which*, they make an entry about some aspect of the event' (emphasis added). Moreover, Bartlett and Milligan (2015, p. 8) note that 'diary method allows the participant to record [an event or feeling] as it occurs (*or at least closer to the moment that it occurs*)' (emphasis added). In both of these statements, as in my use of the expression 'more or less' in the previous paragraph, there is slippage between the desired almost-simultaneity of living and recording that is a hallmark of diary research, and the recognised challenge of balancing living with recording (see e.g. Waddington, 2005).

This balance is particularly fine in a short-term study where participants are already juggling multiple tasks and responsibilities. Participants in the 'In Two Places at Once' study found multiple ways of engaging with the challenges of event-based sampling, which became clear both in the submitted diaries and in the post-conference interviews. The submitted diaries were in some cases a form of collage, where notes of incidents with vague indications of time were combined with specific time-stamped copy-pasted text messages and even some photos that were sent (e.g. of the venue). One participant included a photo of a drawing, with the note that the drawing was produced by her child when he was upset before she left for the conference, and which she took with her on the trip (see Figure 2.1). Further detail of how participants managed the recording process emerged when some participants asked to schedule the post-conference interview a few days later because they wanted to collate or type up their diaries: some participants jotted down incidents in the margins of their conference notebook as they also took notes on the presentations; these were then collated with digital records of communications. The records were interwoven with their other conference documentation strategies, thus necessitating a further process of collation after the conference. The burden of adding the diary to the existing fragile balance of conference and care was heightened by the need to then produce the final diary during the 'aftermath' stage of the conference.

Figure 2.1 Drawing by a participant's child of a person crying.

It was clear that the nature of this study had necessitated a flexible interpreta-tion of event-based sampling, and this particularly highlighted the importance of the post-conference interview as a space for participants to reflect on their use of the diary to produce a representation of their conference/care experience. Perhaps I could have used a more instantaneous recording system, such as using an instant messaging service, but there was an important process in collating the diary that helped participants to reflect on the conference as a whole and to take 'editorial control' (Bartlett & Milligan, 2015, p. 72). Some of the benefit – as well as the risk – of diary method is that, as noted by Alaszewski (2006, p. 73), 'diarists choose where, when and how to complete their diaries'.

With interval-based and event-based sampling alike, participants find different ways of participating in diary studies (Bartlett, 2012; Chapter 6, this volume). Researchers can be very clear, organised and structured in their instructions and instruments, but embedded within the method is the potential for participants to exercise agency in their recording processes. In the 'In Two Places at Once' study, participants enacted event-based sampling to the best of their abilities, finding ways to capture micro-level details of their experiences of managing care while at a conference. It is important for diary researchers to consider whether they view the diary as an objective, accurate record or a subjective, personalised representation of the phenomenon. In my case, event-based sampling was the underlying principle rather than a strictly defined instruction, which meant that any attempt a participant made to record their conference/care experiences was taken as sufficient and valuable. This is a necessary consideration for a short-term study, where participants may struggle to balance recording with experiencing the phenomenon. There is a further consideration here, which is that the participant group for this study were academics, who are accustomed to handling multiple forms of data and types of software in their everyday lives, which may have enhanced their agency and autonomy in deciding how to represent the conference. Many of the participants were also empirical researchers themselves, which may have led to a more conscientious diary-keeping process; this aspect may be applicable across different higher education participant groups, as was also discussed by students in another study (Cao & Henderson, 2020).

Conclusion

There are many short-term, time-bound phenomena which occur in the domain of higher education, and which may easily become blurred with the ongoing strands of activities involved in working and/or studying in higher education and academia. Some of these are one-off; some are episodic. These phenomena may include attending meetings and away days, participating in union action, submitting or marking assessments, organising or attending open days and outreach activities – and attending conferences. Studying these phenomena is different from researching ongoing phenomena, where the diary duration is chosen by the researcher, or long-term phenomena, where the diary is adapted to maximise the effectiveness of the study over a longer period of time. For short-term, time-bound phenomena, the duration is set by the phenomenon itself. The researcher is obliged to design the study around the question 'how short is too short?', thus ensuring that a diary study is both possible and meaningful for a phenomenon that is measured in days rather than weeks or months. Careful consideration of diary design in combination with the sampling strategy (interval-based or event-based) is crucial for short-term diary studies, given the necessity of ensuring that the participant is able to both experience the phenomenon and record their experiences within a tight time frame. There is a degree of risk in conducting short-term diary studies, as the researcher is reliant on there being sufficient instances of the phenomenon to record – and furthermore the researcher may not be able to give feedback to the participants during the diary-keeping process. However this chapter has demonstrated the potential for diary method (particularly diary-interview method in this study) to produce rich, detailed data from time-bound phenomena in higher education and beyond which have a duration of just one day or a few days.

Beyond setting out key considerations for diary study duration, the chapter has critically explored these considerations, arguing for the need for more methodological critique in diary research. First, the chapter included a discussion of how bounded time-bound phenomena are, and indeed how short short-term phenomena may be. In relation to the 'In Two Places at Once' study, I found that conference travel merged with other travel purposes, so that the boundaries of the conference did not always coincide with the boundaries of the trip; I also found that the case conferences were embedded in long-term, ongoing discussions of how conferences – and academic work more broadly – and care fit together. Second, the chapter queried the slippage in the otherwise clearly defined sampling techniques, particularly pertaining to the notion that diary research captures lived events almost simultaneously to living them (Hyers, 2018; Bartlett & Milligan, 2015). In my short-term diary study using event-based sampling, for instance, participants engaged in different processes of recording whenever this was possible in among the conference activities, and then collated the detail with e.g. online communications before submitting to me, thus blurring the notion of recording the 'event' immediately after its occurrence.

To complement studies of long-term and/or ongoing phenomena in higher education and beyond, using diary method for short-term, time-bound phenomena can serve to capture different facets of participants' lives that, due to their intensity, are marked out from routine everyday life. In conclusion, while many diary studies implicitly or explicitly grapple with the question 'how long is too long?', this chapter has asked, 'how short is too short? – with the answer being that, as long as the phenomenon is suited to diary method and the sampling has been carefully considered, no phenomenon is 'too short' for a diary study.

Acknowledgements

Many thanks to the University of Warwick Research Development Fund and Institute for Advanced Studies for the funding that supported this study. Thanks also to Julie Mansuy and Xuemeng Cao, who provided research support during the project. Finally thanks to my co-editor for this book, Xuemeng Cao, for all the fascinating discussions about diary research.

Notes

1 It should be noted that the concerns relating to longer time-bound phenomena are closely aligned with those relating to ongoing phenomena. Indeed, the dichotomy ceases to hold when we query the boundary between long-term and ongoing, as all ongoing phenomena are to some extent time-bound (e.g. researching how students use their time ends with the end of the qualification).
2 For example, Derudder and Liu (2016), Eden (2016), King, Mackenzie, Tadaki, Cannon, McFarlane, Reid & Koppes (2018), Timperley, Sutherland, Wilson & Hall (2020), Sabharwal, Henderson & Joseph (2020).

References

Alaszewski, A. (2006) *Using diaries for social research*. London: Sage.

Bartlett, R. (2012) Modifying the diary interview method to research the lives of people with dementia. *Qualitative Health Research*, 22, 12: 1717–1726.

Bartlett, R. & Milligan, C. (2015) *What is diary method?* London: Bloomsbury.

Beckers, R., van der Voordt, T. & Dewulf, G. (2016) Why do they study there? Diary research into students' learning space choices in higher education. *Higher Education Research & Development*, 35, 1: 142–157.

Bucarelli, B. & Purdon, C. (2015) A diary study of the phenomenology and persistence of compulsions. *Journal of Behavior Therapy and Experimental Psychiatry*, 49: 209–215.

Cao, X. & Henderson, E. F. (2020) The interweaving of diaries and lives: Diary-keeping behaviour in a diary-interview study of international students' employability management. *Qualitative Research*. DOI: 10.1177/1468794120920260

Chen, H.-Y., Yarnal, C., Hustad, J. T. P. & Sims, D. (2016) Take a selfie of life: A qualitative exploration of college students' self-reflections on free time use and personal values. *Journal of College and Character*, 17, 2: 101–115.

Day, M. & Thatcher, J. (2009) 'I'm really embarrassed that you're going to read this …': Reflections on using diaries in qualitative research. *Qualitative Research in Psychology*, 6, 4: 249–259.

Derudder, B. & Liu, X. (2016) How international is the Annual Meeting of the Association of American Geographers? A social network analysis perspective. *Environment and Planning A*, 48, 2: 309–329.

Eden, D. (2016) Women's participation in academic conferences in Israel. *Journal of Higher Education Policy and Management*, 38, 4: 406–421.

Eidse, N. & Turner, S. (2014) Doing resistance their own way: Counter-narratives of street vending in Hanoi, Vietnam through solicited journaling. *Area*, 46, 3: 242–248.

Furness, P. J. & Garrud, P. (2010) Adaptation after facial surgery: Using the diary as a research tool. *Qualitative Health Research*, 20, 2: 262–272.

Henderson, E. F. (2015) Academic conferences: Representative and resistant sites for higher education research. *Higher Education Research & Development*, 34, 5: 914–925.

Henderson, E. F. (2019a) Academics in two places at once: (Not) managing caring responsibilities at conferences. In R. Finkel, B. Sharp & M. Sweeney (eds), *Accessibility, inclusion, and diversity in critical event studies*. New York: Routledge, pp. 218–229.

Henderson, E. F. (2019b) A PhD in motion: Advancing a critical academic mobilities approach (CAMA) to researching short-term mobility schemes for doctoral students. *Teaching in Higher Education*, 24, 5: 678–693.

Henderson, E. F. (2020a) *Gender, definitional politics and 'live' knowledge production: Contesting concepts at conferences*. New York: Routledge.

Henderson, E. F. (2020b) Sticky care and conference travel: Unpacking care as an explanatory factor for gendered academic immobility. *Higher Education*. DOI: 10.1007/s10734-020-00550-1

Henderson, E. F., Cao, X. & Mansuy, J. (2018) *In two places at once: The impact of caring responsibilities on academics' conference participation*. Final project report. Coventry: Centre for Education Studies, University of Warwick. doi:10.31273/CES.06.2018.001.

Henderson, E. F. & Moreau, M.-P. (2020) Carefree conferences? Academics with caring responsibilities performing mobile academic subjectivities. *Gender and Education*, 32, 1: 70–85.

Hook, G. A. (2016) *Sole parent students and higher education: Gender, policy and widening participation*. Basingstoke: Palgrave Macmillan.

Hyers, L. L. (2018) *Diary methods*. New York: Oxford University Press.

Hyers, L. L., Syphan, J., Cochran, K. & Brown, T. (2012) Disparities in the professional development interactions of university faculty as a function of gender and ethnic underrepresentation. *Journal of Faculty Development*, 26, 1: 18–28.

Jacelon, C. S. & Imperio, K. (2005) Participant diaries as a source of data in research with older adults. *Qualitative Health Research*, 15, 7: 991–997.

Kenten, C. (2010) Narrating oneself: Reflections on the use of solicited diaries with diary interviews. *Forum Qualitative Sozialforschung / Forum: Qualitative Social Research*, 11, 2, article 16. Retrieved from: http://nbn-resolving.de/urn:nbn:de:0114-fqs1002160.

King, L., Mackenzie, L., Tadaki, M., Cannon, S., McFarlane, K., Reid, D. & Koppes, M. (2018) Diversity in geoscience: Participation, behaviour, and the division of scientific labour at a Canadian geoscience conference. *Facets*, 3: 415–440.

Kitterød, R. H. & Pettersen, S. V. (2006) Making up for mothers' employed working hours? Housework and childcare among Norwegian fathers. *Work, Employment and Society*, 20, 3: 473–492.

Moreau, M.-P. & Robertson, M. (2017) *Careers and carers: Career development and access to leadership positions among academic staff with caring responsibilities*. London: Leadership Foundation for Higher Education.

Nicolson, D. J. (2017) *Academic conferences as neoliberal commodities*. Basingstoke: Palgrave Macmillan.

Nonis, S. A., Philhours, M. J. & Hudson, G. I. (2006) Where does the time go? A diary approach to business and marketing students' time use. *Journal of Marketing Education*, 28, 2: 121–134.

Reynolds, B. M., Robles, T. F. & Repetti, R. L. (2016) Measurement reactivity and fatigue effects in daily diary research with families. *Developmental Psychology*, 52, 3: 442–456.

Sabharwal, N. S., Henderson, E. F. & Joseph, R. S. (2020) Hidden social exclusion in Indian academia: Gender, caste and conference participation. *Gender and Education*, 32, 1: 27–42.

Scott, J., Green, P. & Cashmore, A. (2012) Bioscience students' first year perspectives through video diaries: Home, family and student transitions. *Bioscience Education*, 20, 1: 53–67.

Sullivan, O. & Gershuny, J. (2018) Speed-up society? Evidence from the UK 2000 and 2015 time use diary surveys. *Sociology*, 52, 1: 20–38.

Swim, J. K., Hyers, L. L., Cohen, L. L. & Ferguson, M. J. (2001) Everyday sexism: Evidence for its incidence, nature, and psychological impact from three daily diary studies. *Journal of Social Issues*, 57, 1: 31–53.

Timperley, C., Sutherland, K. A., Wilson, M. & Hall, M. (2020) He moana pukepuke: Navigating gender and ethnic inequality in early career academics' conference attendance. *Gender and Education*, 32, 1: 11–26.

Viry, G. & Kaufmann, V. (eds) (2015) *High mobility in Europe: Work and personal life*. Basingstoke: Palgrave Macmillan.

Waddington, K. (2005) Using diaries to explore the characteristics of work-related gossip: Methodological considerations from exploratory multimethod research. *Journal of Occupational and Organizational Psychology*, 78, 2: 221–236.

Williamson, I., Leeming, D., Lyttle, S. & Johnson, S. (2012) 'It should be the most natural thing in the world': Exploring first-time mothers' breastfeeding difficulties in the UK using audio-diaries and interviews. *Maternal & Child Nutrition*, 8, 4: 434–447.

Zimmerman, D. H. & Wieder, D. L. (1977) The diary: Diary-interview method. *Urban Life*, 5, 4: 479–498.

Chapter 3

Audio diaries

A creative research method for higher education studies in the digital age

Dangeni, Dely Lazarte Elliot and Carole MacDiarmid

Introduction

Despite a range of empirical enquiries using diary studies in the higher education (HE) context, there is arguably still a lack of methodological-related understanding with respect to the use of audio diaries. We first provide an overview of diaries and their benefits prior to offering a comprehensive discussion of the utilisation of audio diaries as employed within a longitudinal research design. This chapter is contextualised within a study that tracks and reflects on the Chinese international postgraduate student experience. By reflecting on the entire research process, we share not only our initial experience of implementing audio diaries but, more importantly, elucidate, discuss and highlight a number of associated methodological implications.

The audio diary method in this longitudinal project was conducted with Chinese students studying Master's programmes at two Scottish universities. More specifically, this project aims to gain an in-depth understanding of the learning engagement experience and subsequent conceptual change as experienced by Chinese learners of Teaching English to Speakers of Other Languages (hereafter TESOL). This chapter's focus on utilising audio diaries aims to clarify the rationale behind adopting this research technique. Audio diaries are deemed suitable for flexibly obtaining insightful and enhanced reflection among participants from their day-to-day learning experiences. Contextualised within the HE context and TESOL learning experience, the discussion in this chapter will highlight the strengths and challenges inherent to the use of audio diaries. We will then critically discuss the suitability and potential pitfalls when employing audio diaries in research in this digital age. We argue that audio diaries are valuable tools for research aiming to: (a) enhance researchers' understanding of participants' perceptions of their everyday experiences; (b) encourage greater participant reflection; and (c) harness the technological advancement audio diaries offer to enhance the quality of both the research design and the research data.

Methodological focus: diary studies

Diaries, which we refer to as records of life, are often referred to as the personal records and outlets of experienced thoughts, feelings and ideas, in which diarists write and express their life stories as they live them (Cucu-Oancea, 2013; Travers, 2011). With the ability to capture detailed accounts of everyday processes and routines (Reid, Hunter & Sutton, 2011), diaries have been adopted by researchers from various disciplines, starting with health research, since 1930s to investigate participants' environments and the daily situations characterising their social and psychological processes across different settings (Beckers, van der Voordt & Dewulf, 2016; Travers, 2011). Diaries exist in a variety of forms. According to Cucu-Oancea (2013, p. 234), the three most frequently employed diaries in social research are the 'solicited diary' (participant's thematic record according to the research purpose over a defined period of time), 'solicited log' (periodical inventories focusing on a specific type of behaviour) and 'diary-interview' (a requested diary followed by an in-depth interview for in-depth investigation). Usually, in a more traditional written form, diaries are arguably a valuable means of recording dynamic, complex and rich data to address one's research objectives.

Since the main argument is informed by the first author's longitudinal research employing audio diary studies in the HE context, this chapter seeks to contribute to the methodological knowledge gap regarding this particular type of diary. Before that, however, different types of diary will be briefly reviewed. In a photo diary, a device such as a camera or a notebook is used by participants to help them record visual images that are later used to prompt memories of the events captured (e.g., via interviews), as it is not possible to observe participants at all times (Gabridge, Gaskell & Stout, 2008). Another recent example is an online diary, as facilitated by Google Forms, for instance, where participants document their behaviour and experiences in this format (Haley & Clough, 2017). These two examples are part of the growing methodological explorations in the audio-visual domains and of the kind of creative methods that are beginning to draw attention from researchers.

As visual diaries require participants to film their thoughts to allow the researchers to observe the non-verbal communication, they are an empowering tool for telling life stories. Equally, there are disadvantages to using visual diaries: (a) participants might feel uncomfortable when reflecting in front of a camera (Muir, 2008); and (b) a more detailed set of instructions can limit participants' reflections (Buckingham, 2009). Therefore, researchers have sought alternative approaches to gaining an in-depth understanding from participants while encouraging them to reflect freely without the pressure of standing in front of a camera. Yet, there remains little exploration of the audio diary method, in which participants can record their personal and private voices and experiences using Dictaphones, mobile phone software, or chat apps without the pressure of filming (Worth, 2009). This leads nicely to a discussion of the innovative diary method that takes advantage of increased technological advancement, particularly the use of chat apps (e.g., WhatsApp, WeChat and Viber). Once a connection has been established between two users – in this case, the researcher and the participant – the flexibility offered by these chat apps is extended to the use of text, emojis, photos, voice messaging capabilities, sending audio and video files, as well as making phone calls.

Audio diaries

So, what are audio diaries? What are the advantages of using them? Of the various and unique features offered by technology, including the most recent apps for instant communication, we are particularly interested in them as an innovative means of capturing qualitative data, specifically diary data. Rather than writing down participants' reflections via traditional diary methods, an audio diary allows participants to use an audio recording facility to record their thoughts following reflection on personal aspects of life and stories. Arguably, the ease of recording counteracts the inconvenience typically posed by diary writing that may easily discourage both researchers and participants from implementing a diary method. Potential acquisition of useful research data can otherwise be missed through written or video diaries due to such concerns as convenience, accessibility and flexibility of the recording process (Hislop, Arber, Meadows & Venn, 2005). With the rapid development of technology, such concerns have largely been addressed by giving participants additional options for recording audio files. In this research, instead of carrying a portable recorder customarily used in research interviews, participants were advised to use the recording function of the WeChat app (a chat app popularly used by Chinese students) in their phones. Another crucial feature of these chat apps is that they have the built-in facility to send their reflections directly to the researcher.

Although the benefits and flexibility of audio diaries have been acknowledged, the literature on audio diary methods nevertheless remains somewhat limited, particularly in the HE context. Only a few examples to date of utilising audio diaries (mainly using audio recorders) can be found in the field of medicine (Monrouxe, 2009) and psychology (Crozier & Cassell, 2016). For instance, audio diaries were adopted in work psychology to understand transient working patterns and stress among temporary workers in the UK (Crozier & Cassell, 2016), and also in the exploration of young British people's transition to adulthood (Worth, 2009). Likewise, audio diaries were employed to explore disabled young men's experiences, in which an integrated use of research tools (i.e., with photography and interviews) was employed (Gibson et al., 2013). Due to the fact that these empirical audio diaries studies were mainly conducted in research fields where thoughts and reflections, to some extent, are very personal and are, therefore, typically beyond researchers' reach, it can be argued that this method helps in creatively capturing even these generally 'inaccessible' private experiences. When seeking participants' dynamic and complex personal reflections, these flexible and participant-friendly audio diaries can provide a suitable platform for recording their private experiences over time, and indeed with greater control over what to record (Crozier and Cassell, 2016).

The empirical studies in the HE context, though limited in number, further amplify the strength of this method in terms of its ability to capture real-time experiences in a natural means of communication compared with the written form (Bakker & Bal, 2010; Field & Burton, 2012). Additionally, it can be strongly argued that the audio diary method is particularly valuable for longitudinal research designs. For example, aiming at investigating the nature of medical students' epistemological talk during medical school and their narratives in developing professional medical identities, Monrouxe (2009) employed audio diaries with 15 participants and collected 255 diary entries over 18 months. By focusing on participants' narrative enquiries and structures, audio diaries helped facilitate both the participants and the researcher in gaining new insights into the way they make sense of the world, i.e., medical students' experiences in learning and living in medical schools along with the development of their professional identity. In another study by Collett, Neve and Steven (2017), employing smart phones for data collection, medical students' learning process and their identification of threshold disciplinary concepts were investigated using audio diaries. In both of these studies, audio diaries innovatively assisted in capturing profound insights into participants' development and identity development as part of a longitudinal project. While the *audio* element enabled students with busy schedules to share their stories and experiences with the researcher, the *diary* component facilitated in-depth reflection of their learning and development. Therefore, for HE researchers who are seeking an in-depth understanding of participants' everyday learning experiences and development, the audio diary technique enables such exploration across space and over time with flexibility and operability.

Diaries in the Language Teacher Education context

The TESOL Master's programmes, which are the research context in this project, are a form of language teacher education programme designed for students who aim to gain better professional knowledge and qualifications about English language learning and teaching (Skinner & Abbott, 2013). In the HE and language teacher education context, diaries have been adopted to investigate learning experiences, knowledge processing and language teacher development (Ho & Richards, 1993). Notably, as a tool for collecting feedback on teacher education courses and for gaining perspectives from individual experiences, written reflection is encouraged (Borg, 2006). In particular, the written reflections, where teachers freely express their beliefs, thoughts and attitudes on language learning and teaching, often lead to a sound understanding of the processes underpinning teacher development.

In the field of teacher education, reflective journal writing has unsurprisingly been the most frequently employed tool, including logs (objective record of information), diaries (the log-type recording that primarily focuses on the expression of thoughts, reactions and ideas) and journals (both the objective data of the log and with personal interpretations and expressions of experience) (Holly, 1989, pp. 25–26). Despite terminological differences, the ultimate aim of employing diaries (or journals) in the field of teacher education is to 'make tacit mental processes explicit and hence available for examination' (Borg, 2006, p. 295). To illustrate, in order to understand pre-service teachers' development of teacher cognition during a practicum, written diaries were adopted by researchers, at times in conjunction with data from other sources such as observations and interviews

(Johnson, 1992; Numrich, 1996). No matter which term is employed and which form of reflection is utilised for the research, diaries have been acknowledged for their value in enabling researchers to investigate participants' personal accounts of their thinking and practice over a period of time, e.g., a course, a semester, or as in this empirical study the use of audio diaries for an entire academic year. While written forms of diaries have been widely adopted, the efficiencies and increased accessibility of audio diaries have not yet been harnessed, as indicated by the lack of both practical or methodologically focused literature in the HE context, particularly in language teacher education programmes – a discussion to which we will now turn.

The study

In seeking an in-depth understanding of the learning engagement and conceptual change among Chinese TESOL learners (hereafter CTLs) in Master's programmes at two UK universities, this project utilised audio diaries as part of a longitudinal design. Audio diaries facilitated participants' meaningful reflections on their everyday experiences of learning, engaging and development that emanated from being part of an English language teacher education programme. Investigating their perceptions and approaches to learning engagement is arguably theoretically and practically crucial in facilitating their development effectively and as they transform to become English language teachers.

This research employed a qualitative approach since the notion of student learning engagement is generally viewed as a 'dynamic continuum with different locations (task, classroom, course and institution), and is thus not measurable by surveys but best understood through in-depth qualitative work' (Kahu, 2013, p. 769). A longitudinal design is considered helpful to illuminate Chinese TESOL learners' conceptual change in becoming English language teachers over time (Bryman, 2016). In this respect, the specific research question that this chapter aims to address focuses on the CTLs' perceptions of their experiences of the learning engagement that leads to a conceptual change. It is also worth noting that several methods were embedded in this longitudinal design throughout the academic year to address this research question: (a) document analysis, (b) participant observation, (c) audio diaries, (d) 'river of experience' interviews, and (e) semi-structured interviews with academic staff (see another diary-embedded mixed method study in Chapter 1 of this volume). However, since this chapter aims to address the lack of methodological-related publications on audio diary studies, it will focus only on the audio diaries component. Starting with the rationale for adopting audio diaries in this particular research context, a detailed introduction and explanation of how audio diaries played a strategic role in this research will follow.

Appropriateness of audio diaries

Audio diaries were employed as a major component in this longitudinal design for several related reasons. Firstly, studying in this one-year, intensive Master's programme as international students and future English teachers, participants would be spending a huge amount of their time not only adjusting to a new learning context but also coping with a heavy workload, strategically managing their time. Asking for additional reflection for a research project on a monthly basis would therefore likely increase the pressure on them; the time commitment involved could easily discourage them from taking part in or continuing with this project. Secondly, since they are likely to write reflective journals with course content as a part of their course assessment; any extra written reflection for this project may be perceived to be mere repetition and therefore not an efficient use of their time. The third point addresses the first two, i.e. with the research aiming to understand participants' experience of engagement and conceptual change, audio diaries help to free participants from the extra burden of taking part in written activities. Yet, the flexibility of audio diaries still has the added advantage of encouraging participants to think, speak and reflect on their experiences, and their voices can really be 'heard' with different tones to show their emotions and feelings. Finally, with the study participants' likely familiarity and regular usage of chat apps, specifically WeChat, this facilitated not only efficient communication between the participants and the researcher but also expedited the ease of transfer of the recorded audio diaries. Taken together, participants' research participation entails the use of a novel research technique – audio diaries.

Pilot study

Following approval by the University's Ethics Committee, a pilot study was first conducted with a CTL before the main data collection. The pilot study was intended to help ensure the clarity of audio diary recording instructions, the manageability and feasibility of recording and transferring audio diaries, and give an indication of any monitoring issues that may potentially arise during data collection. Constructive feedback was received and reflected upon. For example, the pilot participant stressed the usefulness of the briefing session in understanding the research aims, and the ease of using WeChat for audio recordings and for sending back the audio diaries. With a choice of either English or Chinese, she tried them respectively in two diary entries and valued both options. Since English is more challenging, she reported that using Chinese enabled her to provide much more reflection without thinking about grammatical rules. Therefore, this pilot study guided the researcher in amending the audio diary instructions to ensure that they clearly offer flexible recordings, with the option to use the student's preferred language.

Data collection

Using purposive sampling (Bryman, 2016), the main criterion for participant recruitment was simply that participants were Chinese TESOL Learners at Scottish universities. From October 2018, the formal collection of audio diaries from twenty-four participating CTLs at two Scottish TESOL programmes started, following ethical approval from the University of Glasgow. The audio diaries collected on a monthly basis provided the longitudinal data for comprehensively understanding CTLs' 'journeys' of engagement and conceptual change. Permission was obtained from programme leaders and face-to-face, and individual briefings with each voluntary participant were arranged. Apart from facilitating participants' understanding of the project in general, briefings also offered the opportunity to build rapport and get to know them. After explaining participants' involvement through the Plain Language Statement and giving them audio diary instructions (see Figures 3.1 and 3.2) and a consent form, the WeChat connection was finally established. For those participants who had never previously used this particular chat app for recording, a step-by-step guide was given during the briefing session.

Aim: Audio-diaries are audio recordings of your thoughts and impressions that are informed by your experience (as a Chinese learner) of participating in a TESOL programme in a British institution. These audio-diaries will be collected on a monthly basis. In these recordings, please reflect on and record your perceptions on the following given themes or any other theme that you encountered in the TESOL programme.

Time: the maximum length of recording is 10 minutes per month.

Recording and collection of audio-diaries: you will be contacted (reminded) by the researcher on a monthly basis via email on sending the recordings back to the researcher via WeChat. (Initial WeChat contact between the researcher and participants will be established for the purposes of this research before the data collection commences.)

If needed, you can contact the researcher with respect to your role and tasks as a research participant via WeChat or email.

Figure 3.1 Audio diary recording instruction.

Audio-diary recordings:
Talk about your role, your learning experience, the activities that you engage with, your understanding of teaching English and being an English teacher and your characteristics as a Chinese TESOL learner. There is no right or wrong answer.

Suggestions:
- your experience on the approaches provided by the programme to facilitate your learning (e.g., reading, writing, teaching practicum, online tools, teaching methods such as lecture, seminar and workshop, group work and micro-teaching)
- any other opportunities available
- any changes through your learning engagement
- any differences or challenges you encountered during your learning engagement
- anything you've learned as a Chinese TESOL learner

Figure 3.2 Recording template for participants.

Participants were advised to use the WeChat app and were given accompanying specific instructions about recording their experiences and thoughts as well as sending the recordings back to the researcher, again via WeChat. It is important to note the potential ethical considerations regarding data security when using an application for data collection. Abiding by the ethics protocols, participants were informed that WeChat would only be used for recording and as a transfer tool for the data collection, but *not* for storing. Once all diary recordings were received, all audio files on the WeChat app are deleted after securely transferring them to the university-protected OneDrive Cloud storage area. It is worth stressing how the flexibility of this technique also contributed to participants' willingness to be involved in this project, as indicated in the first month of audio diary collection:

> I didn't volunteer for another staff [member's] project because her project asks us to reflect in written forms. I didn't have much time to do that as I am so busy with academic tasks. Audio form is something new for me, and I would like to try.
>
> (Louise,[1] October 2018)

Based on Louise's reflection, the ease of the audio diary recording is the main cited reason for her decision to be involved in this study. This further emphasises the benefit of audio diaries compared to their written counterpart; audio diaries make the recording process easier and require a more straightforward input from participants (Crozier & Cassell, 2016).

A total of 187 ten-minute audio diaries were received from participants and were subsequently stored and transcribed (on a monthly basis). Despite two participants dropping out of the research after the first three months of recording because of academic pressure, there was a comparatively high completion rate in terms of the collected audio diary entries, on average 20 entries per month by 22 participants. There was a slight decrease in the number of entries submitted from March to August 2019 in general across the participants; their reflections indicated that this was a busy dissertation period. In terms of the language used in audio diaries, CTLs shifted languages and primarily recorded them in Chinese. Five participants, however, continued to use English throughout as they viewed recording practice as a means of improving their English language competence.

Another point to consider is that participants' depth of reflection and honest accounts of their learning experience with emotions complemented the data generated via documentary analysis and later observations. For example, emerging themes such as the assignment writing and interactions with peers and academic staff members were firstly reflected from the document review (first phase of data collection). However, unlike the first phase of data collection, which focused on the programmes' provision of opportunities for student learning engagement, the audio diary entries allowed for students' own reflections on the opportunities provided by the programme.

I struggled a lot with my assignment writing. Though I had discussed it with my classmates and made an appointment with the course organiser, I still feel very confused.

(Sybil, January 2019)

In this quotation, Sybil not only explained the particular opportunities obtained from assignment writing, but her deep reflection is conveyed through emotion-laden expressions such as 'struggled' and 'confused'. Such emotional engagement can also be heard from audio recordings in that particular month – where her intonation and deep sighs reinforced the intensity of her reflection, intellectual and emotional engagement.

Researcher's reflections

By using audio diaries' with CTLs throughout the one-year Master's programme, the benefits of employing this method were amplified. Firstly, audio diaries promote flexibility in recording. The participants' experiences were characterised by extremely tight schedules with courses on campus and with off-campus self-study. With audio diaries, it was more manageable to record their reflections on their learning and engagement at any time of the day, e.g. during class breaks or even when they were lying on their beds while relaxing in the evenings. This benefit aligns with other researchers who valued the convenience of this technique compared with the written diary format (Hislop et al., 2005; Crozier & Cassell, 2016); this then provided participants with greater control over recordings of their experiences (Bernays et al., 2014). When reviewing the entire data collection process, particularly during the data analysis, such review points to the richness of the acquired data as well as the method's inherent flexibility and accessibility to participants' data. In turn, the long-term use of this method becomes more advantageous for longitudinal-type studies.

Being free from recording constraints, audio diaries enabled both higher completion and participant retention during the data collection. For a longitudinal project requiring one whole academic year, 22 of the 24 participants continuously contributed and reflected passionately on their experiential learning journeys. This can be regarded as an outstanding benefit of audio diaries, particularly for longitudinal projects. Arguably, the innovative and flexible nature of recording enabled and encouraged participants to record and reflect on their thoughts, feelings, and experiences both instantaneously and more effectively (Tian & Lowe, 2013), with support from digital technology. With their increased enjoyment of using audio diaries to record their experiences of learning engagement over time, they were not simply recording their experiences for research purposes; they also used this as the learning tool to construct their understanding of their learning in this recording process (Monrouxe, 2009). Unsurprisingly, they willingly engaged with this audio recording 'journey' to monitor their own growth and development.

As part of a longitudinal research design, the implementation of audio diaries served to complement other research tools to achieve the aim of seeking an in-depth understanding of CTLs' experiences of learning engagement and development over time. Audio diaries are seen as an effective means of data collection, particularly when investigating the 'behind the scenes' aspects of everyday life (Hislop et al., 2005). There were a number of times when CTLs reflected on the challenges they had encountered and their emotional engagement with academic activities, both within and outside the programme. In doing so, audio diaries supported their reflection, e.g. contributory factors to challenging experiences and struggles. These detailed and personal experiences arguably cannot be accessed simply by analysing documents such as their programme handbooks or observing their behavioural engagement in classrooms. After collecting the year-long audio diaries, interview sessions with both CTLs and their lecturers at the end of the academic year were expected to lead to an even more comprehensive appreciation of the participants' learning journeys. This was followed by asking them to 'draw' a summary of their learning experiences – the different research methods employed were strategically utilised to promote and achieve triangulation in this moderately sized but complex research (Bryman, 2016). In summary, these points exemplify several benefits and important considerations for researchers when using audio diaries – from the time they decide on the appropriateness of this method to their research, particularly when audio diaries are intended to be integrated with other research methods (Gibson et al., 2013).

The challenges

At the end of the one-year audio diary collection and data analysis, there are several reflections from the researcher about the challenges encountered by both the participants and the researcher. Firstly, in communicating with and collecting participants' personal accounts of their daily experiences and learning development over time, it is vital to consider the researcher's potential impact on participants throughout the process (Field & Burton, 2012). In this study, after receiving their first monthly reminders via WeChat, there were a few participants who always asked the researcher 'what should I record in this diary?'; on several occasions, some expressed their concern as to whether their reflections were 'right' according to the diary research period. Despite the briefing session, where the researcher provided an explanation concerning participation and recording instructions, these participants were still concerned about whether there were certain expected or 'right' answers in the recording process. The researcher reassured the participants by providing further explanation of the main purpose of the research, and that there were no right or wrong answers; participants should simply consider the guide question and what they regard as crucial when recording their audio diaries. They were not in any way led to respond in a particular way; by contrast, they were encouraged to preserve their ideas as much as possible. This further communication acted as a way of strengthening participants' understanding of the inherent strengths of this research tool (i.e. a flexible tool for recording their everyday experiences of learning, engagement and development throughout their one-year Master's programme).

Making the diary more manageable for participants also has its downsides, i.e. requiring transcription, which potentially makes the process less manageable for the researcher. Whereas collecting hundreds of diary entries for a year may generate rich and valuable data, the analysis that follows in order to acquire an in-depth understanding of the topic also requires being immersed in it, by 'swimming' in the data, so to speak. Data can be overwhelming and can be likened to being 'flooded', particularly during transcription, translation and, eventually, during data analysis. The ease of obtaining data from audio diaries can equally lead to data management issues, particularly if no or little management planning has been put in place for the data analysis and synthesis stages.

However, even though the first author made a data management plan before collecting the audio diaries, the audio files and transcriptions gained from more than twenty participants for one year meant over three hundred files to manage and organise. At times, the CTLs did not reflect on a monthly basis; instead, they preferred to record every two months. Being given the same academic task (such as dissertation writing) for two consecutive months, they had thought that it was not necessary to send separate recordings. On such occasions, a monthly box-ticking data management plan needs to already be in place and needs to be updated and adjusted throughout the entire data collection period. Therefore, having a feasible data management plan in this case means all diary entries and relevant files from participants need to be labelled and organised systematically for later analysis.

Employing the audio diary method longitudinally in contexts such as a TESOL Master's programme can lead to participants producing rich data, including very detailed emotional accounts of their experiences (Crozier & Cassell, 2016). This then necessitates a strategic and well-considered response to deal with the data (see also Chapter 7, this volume). In this study, managing a huge amount of data meant that transcription had to start immediately, even, indeed, when participants were still providing their audio diaries, in order to ease the transcription pressure at the conclusion of the data collection period. Moreover, the transcription task became more manageable when the generated audio diaries were divided into short segments (i.e. with ten small transcription tasks; see Figure 3.3). Despite this challenge, the transcribing process, as expected, also contributed to the researcher's meaning-making process through additional opportunities to listen to participants' reflections.

Conclusion

As identified in the previous studies and literature, and supported by this study, diary studies enable a more in-depth elicitation of reflections of participants' experiences, opinions and circumstances, which is argued to be particularly useful in longitudinal design (Filep et al., 2018). Audio diaries continue the rigour and trustworthiness of diary studies, with the added benefit of capturing emotions and fostering higher

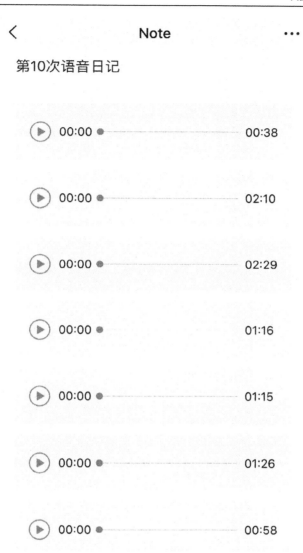

Figure 3.3 An example of audio diaries sent via WeChat – a combination of a participant's short audio diaries on a selected topic.

retention during data collection, especially in longitudinal studies. In the HE context, and in contexts such as this project, i.e. an intensive learning environment with a large number of international students, we argue that audio diaries are particularly suitable, manageable and reliable. Audio diaries serve as a handy, pragmatic tool to contribute to this exploration and understanding of such complex experiences. Audio diaries, as a creative and powerful tool for generating rich research data, can also suitably capture and aid our understanding of complex psychological, emotional and cognitive states through a thoughtful 'observation' of respondents' everyday lives. On the practical side, the ease of transfer via advanced technological tools facilitates communication between the researcher and the researched, which results in more efficient data management. While the use of audio diaries may demand substantial time, effort and commitment from the researcher (as discussed in this chapter), it is equally likely to contribute to the acquisition of a more in-depth and, in turn, more comprehensive understanding of the investigated phenomenon. Using examples from the first author's research project, this chapter intends to offer other researchers useful ideas and warn of potential pitfalls which could assist them in their reflection about what to consider and what to avoid after making the decision to embark on a study that employs audio diaries.

Acknowledgements

We would like to acknowledge the TESOL students and staff members who participated in this project and thank them for their valuable time.

Note

1 All participants were asked to choose their own pseudonyms.

References

Bakker, A. B. & Bal, M. P. (2010) Weekly work engagement and performance: A study among starting teachers. *Journal of Occupational and Organizational Psychology*, 83, 1: 189–206.

Beckers, R., van der Voordt, T. & Dewulf, G. (2016) Why do they study there? Diary research into students' learning space choices in higher education. *Higher Education Research and Development*, 35, 1: 142–157.

Bernays, S., Rhodes, T. & Terzic, K. J. (2014) Embodied accounts of HIV and hope: Using audio diaries with interviews. *Qualitative Health Research*, 24: 629–640.

Borg, S. (2006) *Teacher cognition and language education: Research and practice.* London: Continuum.

Bryman, A. (2016) *Social research methods*, 5th edition. Oxford: Oxford University Press.

Buckingham, D. (2009) 'Creative' visual methods in media research: Possibilities, problems and proposals. *Media, Culture & Society*, 31, 4: 633–652.

Collett, T., Neve, H. & Steven, N. (2017) Using audio diaries to identify threshold concepts in 'softer' disciplines: A focus on medical education. *Practice and Evidence of Scholarship of Teaching and Learning in Higher Education*, 12, 2: 99–117.

Crozier, S. E. & Cassell, C. M. (2016) Methodological considerations in the use of audio diaries in work psychology: Adding to the qualitative toolkit. *Journal of Occupational and Organizational Psychology*, 89, 2: 396–419.

Cucu-Oancea, O. (2013) Using diaries: A real challenge for the social scientist. *Procedia-Social and Behavioral Sciences*, 92: 231–238.

Field, J. & Burton, J. (2012) Oral reflective journals. In R. Barnard & A. Burns (eds), *Researching language teacher cognition and practice: International case studies*, Bristol: Multilingual Matters, pp. 162–179.

Filep, C. V., Turner, S., Eidse, N., Thompson-Fawcett, M. & Fitzsimons, S. (2018) Advancing rigour in solicited diary research. *Qualitative Research*, 18, 4: 451–470.

Gabridge, T., Gaskell, M. & Stout, A. (2008) Information seeking through students' eyes: The MIT photo diary study. *College and Research Libraries*, 69, 6: 510–523.

Gibson, B. E., Mistry, B., Smith, B., Yoshida, K. K., Abbott, D., Lindsay, S. & Hamdani, Y. (2013) The integrated use of audio diaries, photography, and interviews in research with disabled young men. *International Journal of Qualitative Methods*, 12, 1: 382–402.

Haley, A. N. & Clough, P. (2017) Affective experiences of international and home students during the information search process. *New Review of Academic Librarianship*, 23, 4: 396–420.

Hislop, J., Arber, S., Meadows, R. & Venn, S. (2005) Narratives of the night: The use of audio diaries in researching sleep. *Sociological Research Online*, 10, 4: 1–13.

Ho, B. & Richards, J. C. (1993) Reflective thinking through teacher journal writing: Myths and realities, *Perspectives*, 5, 2: 25–40.

Holly, M. L. (1989) *Writing to grow: Keeping a personal-professional journal*. Portsmouth, NH: Heinemann.

Johnson, K. E. (1992) Learning to teach: Instructional actions and decisions of preservice ESL teachers. *TESOL Quarterly*, 26, 3: 507–535.

Kahu, E. R. (2013) Framing student engagement in higher education. *Studies in Higher Education*, 38, 5: 758–773.

Monrouxe, L. V. (2009) Solicited audio diaries in longitudinal narrative research: A view from inside. *Qualitative Research*, 9, 1: 81–103.

Muir, S. (2008) Participant produced video: giving participants camcorders as a social research method. http://eprints.ncrm.ac.uk/541/1/2008-07-toolkit-camcorders.pdf (accessed 18 December 2019).

Numrich, C. (1996) On becoming a language teacher: Insights from diary studies. *TESOL Quarterly*, 30, 1: 131–153.

Reid, L., Hunter, C. & Sutton, P. W. (2011) Rising to the challenge of environmental behaviour change: Developing a reflexive diary approach. *Geoforum*, 42, 6: 720–730.

Skinner, B. & Abbott, L. (2013) An exploration of differences in cultural values in teacher education pedagogy: Chinese English language teacher trainees' perceptions of effective teaching practice review. *Teacher Development*, 17, 2: 228–245.

Tian, M. & Lowe, J. (2013) The role of feedback in cross-cultural learning: A case study of Chinese taught postgraduate students in a UK university. *Assessment and Evaluation in Higher Education*, 38, 5: 580–598.

Travers, C. (2011) Unveiling a reflective diary methodology for exploring the lived experiences of stress and coping. *Journal of Vocational Behavior*, 79, 1: 204–216.

Worth, N. (2009) Making use of audio diaries in research with young people: Examining narrative, participation and audience. *Sociological Research Online*, 14, 4: 1–11.

Chapter 4

Broadening the normative and evaluative space for assessing the impact of photo diary research in higher education

A capabilities approach

Mikateko Mathebula and Carmen Martinez-Vargas

Introduction

The use of photo diaries and other participatory visual methods in higher education research can be partially attributed to the 'participatory' turn in the social sciences, in response to feminist, postcolonial and postmodern critiques against positivist conceptions of objectivity (Gubrium & Harper, 2013). In particular, research that is based on photographs taken by participants is said to shift the power dynamic in the researcher/participant relationship that typically privileges the researcher, thus empowering participants (Mitchell, de Lange & Moletsane, 2017). Claims about empowerment are also made due to the idea that researchers empower participants by privileging participant knowledge and experience throughout the research process, allowing participants to construct meaning from the photographs they take, unconfined by the researcher's preconceptions (Clark, 2010). However, as Pauwels (2015) points out, participatory visual methods are based mainly on undisclosed assumptions, often advocated on the grounds of their intended outcomes, but lack empirical evidence or methodologies for arriving at proposed outcomes. While some studies do encourage critical reflections on the potential to empower participants through participatory visual methods and suggest different ways of understanding empowerment in development contexts (see Mikhailovich, Pamphilon & Chambers, 2015) – none propose alternative evaluation criteria for assessing the impact of these methods.

This chapter proposes a framing and extension of the evaluation of the impact of photo diary research, drawing on data from a project that used a photovoice approach to research the university experiences of low-income youth from rural and township areas in South Africa. Using the capabilities approach (Sen, 1999) as a normative and evaluative framework to make a judgment on the value and impact of our photovoice approach in the context of higher education research, we propose that photovoice approaches, understood here as an extension of photo diary methods, be assessed according to three criteria. Namely, the extent to which they enhance opportunities for (a) epistemic contribution, (b) well-being achievement and (c) collective agency. We argue that these criteria broaden the evaluative space for assessing what constitutes justice in knowledge-making and knowledge-sharing processes in photo diary research, and that this matters particularly in Global South contexts, where participatory visual research methods are often used to interrogate structural inequalities that prevent marginalised groups from enjoying certain freedoms. We see the proposed evaluative framework as applicable to participatory visual research methods more broadly, but to diary methods in particular.

The chapter begins with a discussion of various methods that incorporate photographs, focusing on photo diary research and photovoice approaches with an emphasis on their similarities and differences, as well an explanation of how we see photovoice as producing photo diaries. Thereafter, we briefly discuss literature on the use of photovoice as a higher education research method in the South African context. Following this, we discuss the theoretical foundations of our proposed evaluative framework. We then describe the photovoice project upon which we base our reflections, before elaborating on and justifying our argument on the broadening of the evaluation criteria of photo diary research. This is then followed by the conclusion.

Different approaches in photography research: understanding photo diaries and photovoice

Photography methods in a variety of forms e.g. photo elicitation (Harper, 2002; Leonard & McKnight, 2015; Chapters 6 and 8, this volume) photo diary (Swallow, Petrie, Power & Edwards, 2015; Chapter 10, this volume) photo novella (Wang & Burris, 1994; 1997) or photovoice (Wang, 1999, 2006) emerged as a turn from documentary photography to more reflexive and participatory approaches (Mikhailovich et al., 2015). Used as a method in social research (e.g. in areas of healthcare, homelessness and education), photographs are usually used to elicit information to inform research and as tools to stimulate self-reflection and interactions with others (Liebenberg, 2018; Mikhailovich et al., 2015). Used as a method in higher education research, photographs can be used for the same purposes mentioned above, but also to create a visual record of the 'everyday context' of one's life, thus creating a photo diary (see Baker, 2020). Depending on the aim of the research, participants may be asked to make a diary entry by taking a photograph every time a particular event takes place, or to do so periodically, according to a predetermined amount of time that an entry ought to be made, regardless of the event that may be taking place. This could be done, for example, to gather a longitudinal narrative picture of participants' educational decision-making and choices (see Baker, 2020) or of how their personal values change while they are at university (see Chen, Yarnal, Hustad & Sims, 2016). When used this way, photo diaries are particularly useful for documenting changes within a person over a period of time (Milligan & Bartlett 2019).

Similarly, photovoice also facilitates the creation of a narrative picture based on photographs that are taken by participants. However, in photovoice, participants usually take photographs over a shorter period, with the photographs being more symbolic and based on reflections about an issue or problem that a community seeks to have addressed. As conceptualised by Wang (1999) photovoice is intended to galvanise communities, to get them gathered around a particular cause and to collect evidence that can help to make a case for that cause, ultimately leading to some action that supports that cause. The key difference then between photo diaries and photovoice, is that the former typically requires participants to take photographs of the actual event under exploration, or to take photographs at particular moments or set intervals, while the latter usually requires participants to take photographs that convey a specific message or story that the participants have constructed beforehand.

Photo diaries and photovoice therefore have important similarities; they are clearly interrelated and can inform each other well (Bartlett & Rhynas, 2016). That is, they are both examples of how photography can be incorporated into research, they both have participatory elements, especially because the photographs are taken by participants, not researchers (this is not necessarily the case in photo elicitation) and they both enable the creation of a narrative picture of an aspect of people's lives. As such, in both cases, photographs are not necessarily objects of analysis in the research, but entry points to discussions and a basis for developing situated, storied constructions of participants' social realities. For these reasons, we acknowledge them as distinct participatory visual research approaches, but consider photovoice as a mode of producing photo diaries, even though the photographs taken by participants of photovoice projects are not captured as and when a particular event occurs on a day to day basis.

Before we proceed to the discussion of our proposed evaluation criteria and the theory that underpins them, we contextualise and locate this chapter within contemporary South African higher education literature that uses participatory visual methods in the next section. We do this not only to locate this chapter in this literature, but also to highlight the political dimension of photovoice, particularly in South African higher education research. We return to this point in the conclusion to discuss how this aspect of photovoice may complement other photo diary methods.

Using photovoice as a political instrument: photography and social justice in South African universities

Within the South African higher education research space, photovoice is the most commonly used method that intersects verbal discussion, visual (photographic) depiction or photo diaries. Although it is a relatively new research approach in this context, it is gaining traction. This is evident in recent literature based on empirical research that covers a wide range of topics. Most of this literature can be located in the growing body of work that explores how race and gender influence experiences of belonging and alienation in South African universities. For example, Cornell and Kessi (2015, 2017) studied black students' experiences of transformation at the University of Cape Town (previously a 'white only' institution) using photovoice to develop photo stories that reflect the negative stereotypes the students encounter but also the strategies they use to resist discourses of black inferiority. The research process began with focus group discussions on the meaning of transformation in higher education. Participants were then asked to write a short personal reflection on their own understanding and experiences of transformation. Finally, the participants were trained by professional photographers, given cameras for a month, and asked to construct photo stories of 'transformation'.

Other studies that focus on similar issues include research on narratives of black queer students and their negotiations of identity at an historically white university (Boonzaier & Mhkize, 2018). Boonzaier and Mhkize's (2018) research procedure began with individual interviews. The researchers were interested in hearing about how participants spoke about their gendered/sexual identities and how these identities were negotiated in the spaces they occupied. After the initial interview, participants were given cameras and taught how to use them. Participants were then asked to take photographs that represented their lives as queer black students at the University of Cape Town. They had the cameras for about three weeks (see Boonzaier & Mhkize, 2018).

Photovoice has also been used to study narratives on gender and sexuality (Ngabaza, Shefer & Clowes, 2018) or how gender, citizenship, race and class intersect with other categories of students' identities to affect their perception and experience of un/belonging and un/safety at an the University of the Western Cape (Ngabaza et al., 2015). In this study, participants were asked to identify and take photographs of places where they felt safe or unsafe on campus. The photographs were accompanied by a narrative that explained why the students felt the way they did in those particular spaces. Different to the aforementioned literature, and located closer to this chapter in scope, in their study, Martinez-Vargas, Walker and Mkwananzi (2019) reflect on the value of a photovoice project on access to higher education in South Africa, and argue that photovoice creates space for producing contextually relevant knowledge, while challenging epistemic barriers and fostering human development among the research participants. During the course of about five weeks, research participants were involved in various workshops, including photography training and group reflections which culminated in the production of individual photo-essays about different aspects of 'access' to university (see Martinez-Vargas et al., 2019).

Interestingly, all these studies are connected to political discussions and demands through participants' involvement in the process of knowledge generation. They all explore and address contemporary issues that remind us that South Africa continues to grapple with the consequences of colonialism and apartheid, and that higher education institutions, but universities in particular, are important sites for discussion about unfair discrimination and social and epistemic in/justice. It is also clear that these studies employ photovoice as a narrative tool for decolonisation (Kessi, 2018) within the South African higher education space.

As pointed out earlier, participatory visual research methods like photovoice are usually promoted on the grounds that they empower participants or create opportunities for social change. However, the literature reviewed here seems to promote the use of photovoice based on its intended outcomes, and does not elaborate on how researchers have gone about evaluating the photovoice process. Our chapter deviates from this literature, by offering critical reflections on the evaluation of the strengths and weaknesses of photo diary research in a higher education context, focusing on photovoice as an example of a research approach that produces photo diaries. We see photovoice as an extension of photo diary methods in the sense that it has more politicised use, which offers possibilities for designing innovative, more inclusive diary methods that involve participants more deeply in knowledge-making and knowledge-sharing processes.

This involvement, therefore, is not only to generate knowledge from a more bottom-up approach that centres on participants' own reflections and perceptions in the process of creating their photo diaries, but a normative statement about the importance of participants' active involvement in knowledge generation as an example of more socially just research methods. Hence, it can be said that photovoice shifts photography methods towards a more politicised agenda of research which can inform more 'traditional' uses of photo diaries particularly for researchers seeking to embrace a decolonial ethics (Dunford, 2017) in their approach to research. The point is not to encourage the transformation of all photo diary research into more engaged and politicised methods, but to provide an innovative assessment lens to explore genuinely how such photo diary methods may impact research participants. We suggest a capabilities (Sen, 1999) informed assessment, because of the emphasis in this approach on the importance of enhancing individuals' well-being through the expansion of their valued freedoms.

Evaluating photovoice through a capabilities lens

The interpretative lens that we use in this chapter is based on Amartya Sen's capabilities approach (Sen, 1999). As a normative framework for human development, the capabilities approach tells us that what matters when assessing the impact of any process that has a bearing on human lives are individuals' freedoms, their well-being, what they have reason to value in and for their lives and whether or not they can exercise agency to achieve their aspirations (Sen, 1999). It differentiates between capabilities – real freedoms that individuals have, and functionings – the achievement of what they have reason to value (Robeyns, 2017). Therefore, as an evaluative framework, the approach is often used to identify situations in which individuals are constrained in their capability sets but also in the use of their agency (Sen, 1999). As such, it encourages us to consider differences between individuals, but also among groups, by directing our attention to societal structures, to consider how they impact people's ability to convert freedoms into valued functionings and to exercise their reasoned agency in doing so (Crocker, 2008; Robeyns, 2005).

Using the capabilities approach as an evaluative framework for photovoice, we argue that it is important to assess the value of the research practice by looking at the extent to which participants are better off in their opportunity sets and agency after their involvement in a photovoice project, compared to before its implementation. This has implications for social justice, as the capabilities approach maintains that, in order to advance towards social justice, we need to remove injustices that leave individuals with unreasonably limited opportunities or choices (Sen, 2009). Therefore we argue that expanding the choices and freedoms of individuals who are unfairly deprived (in the case of our project, low-income rural and township youth who are deprived of opportunities for equitable access and participation in universities) advances progress towards a more socially just higher education space. Applied to photo diary research more broadly then, expanding the choices and freedoms of research participants advances more socially just research practices.

In brief, the capabilities approach encourages us to think about the opportunities and freedoms people effectively have, in our assessment of their well-being, or in our evaluation of whether or not they are better off because of a particular process. From a capabilities lens then, the value of photovoice as a method in higher education research could be assessed according to three criteria: the extent to which it enhances research participants' opportunities for (a) epistemic contributions, (b) well-being achievement and (c) collective agency. If these criteria frame the evaluative space for assessing the impact of photovoice, instead of solely focusing on the concept of empowerment or social change, we might make better judgments about what constitutes justice in knowledge-making and knowledge-sharing processes in photo diary research more broadly.

We now briefly describe our photovoice project and how we implemented it, and reflect on a few excerpts drawing from students' feedback about the photovoice process.

The photovoice project

For our photovoice project, we worked with 19 volunteers out of the 65 students involved in the broader Miratho project, which investigates the achieved higher education learning outcomes for low-income rural and township youth in South Africa, who are located across three provinces in South Africa at five different universities. Because the students were enrolled in a variety of disciplines and widely dispersed, we designed the process within the bounds of this context and the limited time we spent in two of the three different locations.

The widely applied programme consisted of an intense six day schedule, in which day 0 would be done remotely by the participants before meeting with us and days 1, 2 and 3 would be implemented during the workshops or contact sessions with the students. Days 4 and 5 were used for the collective data analysis and the photovoice exhibition respectively.

Each day was carefully thought through, and arranged around activities and reflective exercises aimed at assisting students to articulate their experiences of being at university through photo diaries that were 'converted' into photo stories. Olivier, Wood and De Lange (2009) define four central pillars to guide this procedure, which we generally followed: (1) conceptualisation of the project; (2) introduction to the methodology; (3) discussion of the prompt to guide photo taking; and (4) training on the use of the cameras (also see Sutton-Brown, 2014). As Simmonds, Roux and ter Avest (2015) assert, it is essential for the participants to reflect on the given prompt to arrive at a clear understanding of what they are required to do. Hence, our prompt was: take photographs that reflect your daily experience at university, with a focus on situations that make or made you feel included or excluded at your university. We then discussed examples and dimensions or processes of material and symbolic inclusion and exclusion and brainstormed what kind of images could reflect these issues.

Students participated in reflexive exercises throughout the workshops, like the River of Life (a drawing of a river that is symbolic of one's life - including for example boulders or rapids to represent obstacles or struggles, or bridges and stepping stones to represent support or opportunities) and developing storyboards, before taking any photographs. Once they had received photography training, they were issued with digital cameras and had three days to take photographs guided by our prompt, but also in alignment with the storyboards they had developed. Having selected a maximum of six photographs from their photo diaries to convert into a photo story, the students captioned each photograph and gave a title to their stories, sharing their stories and talking us all through each photograph and narrating its significance through presentations and group discussions during the workshops. As such, the various activities at the photovoice workshops facilitated the explicit structuring of the photo diaries in three ways: (1) around past events to stimulate retrospective reflection, (2) around current experiences to stimulate mindfulness and (3) around aspirations to stimulate reflections on possible future trajectories. The activities were also aimed at building a community of practice where students assume their roles as co-researchers on the photovoice project.

Following the three-day workshops held at the two 'away' university sites, a joint workshop was arranged for all students who were part of the photo voice project at the 'base' university site. 15 of the 19 students spent a weekend in the province where the base university is located, spending much of this time engaged in group discussions about the significance of each other's photo stories and experiences. They also worked together in small groups to identify common themes across the stories and produced some general conclusions and recommendations for changes that ought to be made for universities to be more inclusive or supportive in enabling valued capabilities and functionings for low-income youth. These recommendations are summarised in an Inclusion Charter which the students drafted, and the research team assisted in consolidating.

Subsequent to the collective analysis, the exhibition was held in a large hall, with each photo story printed on high quality paper and mounted on separate sections on the walls to allow ample space for each story to stand out. Before inviting the public to view and engage with the students about the stories, a short introduction about the broader Miratho project was provided by the research team, before four of the students – one from each of the four out of five universities – spoke to the audience, briefly telling their stories individually. This was an important part of the process, as visual participatory methods not only aim to create data from a bottom-up approach but also to have the data analysed and disseminated by the participants (Rowel et al., 2017). Our strategies of dissemination to the public were done in different ways besides the exhibition: through the production of short video clips with the students telling their stories, the production of photobooks containing all 19 individual stories, plus a common book titled *The Bitter Truth of Success*, which students compiled using selected photographs from the 19 photo stories. Additionally, we have a project website (www.ufs.ac.za/miratho) and twitter account (@MirathoP) where some of these data can be accessed by the public.

As such, there were many strategies to stimulate public discussion and thus impact the university context, however, our data highlight that more than engaging university leaders or influencing policy makers, the project had a substantial impact on the research participants, with significant expansion of their epistemic contribution capability. While we cannot say with certainty that participating in the photovoice project has improved the well-being of students, or inspired them to exercise their agency collectively, we do think that the enhancement of any of these dimensions of impact has positive or multiplier effects on other capabilities that research participants may value.

Broadening the evaluative space for assessing the impact of photo diary research

Photovoice methodology implicitly assumes that community priorities will be communicated to policy makers who have the influence and power to bring about desired change. We did not achieve this through our photovoice project, and this is probably due to two reasons. First, the project design did not allow substantive engagement with higher education policy makers at the institutional or national level in the knowledge mobilisation process. Second, although we have been working with the same group of students for four years now, our engagement with students during the photovoice workshops was limited to three days of working on developing their photo stories, plus two days (about six months after the workshops) during the analysis and exhibition period. This constrained our ability to explore and implement more effective methods of public engagement, or to build on the positive effects the project had in establishing a community of trust and friendship among the 15 students who came together for the exhibition.

Although our project has not enabled students to reach policy makers, we believe that the process has enhanced students' opportunities to be advocates in their own lives and communities, through gaining powerful and credible skills related to telling their stories and sharing their knowledge. This is evident in their written feedback on the photovoice project, where students expressed their appreciation for having a safe space to share their stories, reflect on their life and university experiences as well as having follow up opportunities to have their stories heard and acknowledged at the exhibition:

> [When I participated in the PV I felt ...] safe which led to being able to narrate my story without fear. That I was not alone.
>
> (Bongeka[1])

> [When I participated in the PV I felt ...] connected and free to express my feelings. Inspired, motivated and encouraged to reach my goals. Responsible for my actions. Appreciative, hopeful, purposeful and grateful.
>
> (Anathi)

It was important for our approach to be encouraging and supportive, and to position students as the experts on their lives while challenging them to think about what they can do, but also what universities ought to be doing to improve their university experiences and the experiences of students who will face similar challenges through their higher education journeys. Meaningful engagement on our part as facilitators meant not just listening to but also affirming students' stories and recognising them as having an important role to play in countering and reforming dominant, uncontested discourses that often do not position students from rural and township communities as trusted testifiers or credible knowers. Through its process, our photovoice approach enabled students, through sharing stories and experiences with others, and feeling affirmed by the commonality of some experiences, to begin to acknowledge themselves as members of a community of knowers and tellers:

> I felt part of something big and life changing. Being able to share my life story with someone to help them have it better than I did. To be able to share my events in order to change how the education structure should work is extremely profound than I could ever express.
>
> (Dumisani)

Therefore, we see the value of our photovoice project mostly lying in its potential to create opportunities for epistemic contribution (Fricker, 2015) through storytelling that is informed by critical reflections on one's own life as it relates to the lives of others. Fricker (2015, p. 6) defines epistemic contribution as the effective opportunity to 'contribute to the pool of shared epistemic materials – materials for knowledge, understanding, and very often for practical deliberation'. Fricker (2015) also argues that there are societal structures in place that impede individuals from becoming valuable epistemic contributors or givers and takers of shared social and academic knowledge, through two unfair social dynamics: testimonial and hermeneutical injustices.

We believe that both forms of injustices are generally exercised together when people are denied their freedom to contribute to knowledge, and this is clear in our case of working with low-income undergraduate students. In our project, the capability approach points to constraints in students' freedom to function as epistemic contributors. This constraint is a result of the structural inequalities that limit equitable access and distribution of the language, knowledge, skills and world views that are valued in university settings. That is, students who come from low-income households situated in rural and township areas in South Africa experience testimonial injustices in university spaces (Mathebula, 2019) due to the many prejudices and negative stereotypes that lectures and other students may have towards them. Moreover, this is accentuated by their low chances of accessing quality primary and secondary schools that allow them to acquire hermeneutical intelligibility for the university context. Building from this line of thought then, to advance towards social justice, we need to pay attention to historical and persistent epistemic injustices against excluded collectives and individuals (De Sousa Santos, 2015).

Therefore, instead of 'empowerment' we think it is more helpful to look for evidence of change in individuals taking specific actions to achieve goals that they have reason to value. And instead of looking for evidence of social change (which is scarce in photovoice literature) we think it is more helpful to ask whether or not individuals are better off because of their involvement in a photovoice project. We believe that these are more appropriate criteria to evaluate the impact of photovoice projects, and that they are more achievable goals for related methods, than the objective to empower participants or achieve significant social change. We think the students we worked with are better off in terms of recognising themselves as credible testifiers and trusted knowers, which we see as having potential multiplier effects on enabling collective agency and/or individual well-being.

Because we consider photovoice as producing photo diaries, we think that photo diary research can benefit from this capabilities-informed assessment of impact. Both photovoice and photo diary methods require participants' collaboration and active involvement in the process of knowledge generation – despite their methodological differences – this is an opportunity to question and investigate how such processes impact participants. We have proposed a three-fold assessment based on whether photovoice expands opportunities for (a) epistemic contribution, (b) well-being achievement and (c) collective agency. However, it is important to emphasise that using the capabilities approach to explore the impact of photo diary methods offers opportunities for other evaluation criteria to be identified. This could create new opportunities for photo diaries to not only generate visual data, but to do so with some consideration of the ways in which research conducted this way may enhance capabilities that participants have reason to value and consequently, contribute towards more critically engaged and genuinely participatory methods.

Conclusion

We have argued that, instead of promoting the use of photo diary-based methods in higher education research on the grounds that they lead to empowerment and social change, it is more appropriate to promote them because they have great potential to enhance participants' opportunities to recognise themselves, be seen and act as epistemic contributors. We came to this conclusion through applying the capabilities approach to understand the value of our photovoice project, which we see as an extension of photo diary research. Using the capabilities approach to understand the impact of photo diary research means looking for evidence of enhanced valued freedoms. This implies that any assessment about the value of diary research more broadly should include questions about what the participants have reason to value about the process. For our project, we concluded that epistemic contribution capabilities were enhanced for students who participated in the photovoice project; and that it is a capability that is a likely multiplier of other valued capabilities. Importantly, evaluating our photovoice project through a capabilities lens illuminated valued freedoms that may have gone unrecognised, had we used assessment criteria based on photovoice principles alone. These criteria usually ask us to look for evidence of social change or empowerment. However, in the context of higher education, we cannot talk about empowerment without talking about the freedom to learn, know and tell; the freedom to be recognised as a credible testifier and trusted knower. In this context, it is also not possible to talk about empowerment in the absence of the effective freedom to act in order to dismantle (albeit incrementally) structural inequalities that limit individuals' valued freedoms. For these reasons, we proposed alternative criteria for making judgments about impact, and argued that researchers should instead look for evidence of epistemic contribution, well-being achievement and collective agency.

This evaluation can be extended to other participatory visual methods, as all of them build knowledge from photographs, drawings, videos etc. that are captured by participants. We believe that by increasing participants' involvement in visual methods in general, researchers are able not only to generate rich and compelling data but also to enhance participants' freedoms and articulation of different functionings that are related to making epistemic contributions. This happens when participants are not only asked to take photographs of their daily experiences, as typically done in photo diary or photo elicitation methods, but when they also engage in the analysis of their photo diaries or make meaning of visual representations of their lived experiences; and share this knowledge publicly, as done in photovoice projects.

The normative and evaluative framework provided in this chapter can inform innovative and more inclusive alternatives to implementing photo diary research, so that participants have effective opportunities to achieve functionings that they have reason to value, thus facilitating more socially just research practices in capabilities terms.

Acknowledgements

Our thanks to everyone who was involved in the Miratho Project and the photovoice workshops and exhibition. We especially thank Melanie Walker. Gratitude is also due to the project funders: the ESRC (grant number ES/N010094/1) and the NRF (grant number 86540).

Note

1 All names are pseudonyms.

References

Baker, Z. (2020) The vocational/academic divide in widening participation: the higher education decision making of further education students. *Journal of Further and Higher Education*, 44, 6: 766–780.

Bartlett, R. & Rhynas, S. (2016) When methods meet: Diary methods and photovoice. Retrieved from www.sgsss.ac.uk/methods-resource/diary-methods-and-photovoice (accessed 30 March 2020).

Boonzaier, F. & Mhkize, L. (2018) Bodies out of place: Black queer students negotiating identity at the University of Cape Town. *South African Journal of Higher Education*, 32, 3: 81–100.

Chen, H. Y., Yarnal, C., Hustad, J. & Sims, D. (2016) Take a selfie of life: A qualitative exploration of college students' self-reflections on free time use and personal values. *Journal of College and Character*, 17, 2: 101–115.

Clark, A. (2010) Young children as protagonists and the role of participatory, visual methods in engaging multiple perspectives. *American Journal of Community Psychology*, 4, 1–2: 115–123.

Cornell, J. & Kessi, S. (2015) Coming to UCT: Black students, transformation and discourses of race. *Journal of Student Affairs in Africa*, 3, 2: 1–16.

Cornell, J. & Kessi, S. (2017) Black students' experiences of transformation at a previously 'white only' South African university: A photovoice study. *Ethnic and Racial Studies*, 40, 11: 1882–1899.

Crocker, D. A. (2008) *Ethics of global development: Agency, capability, and deliberative democracy*. Cambridge: Cambridge University Press.

De Sousa Santos, B. (2015) *Epistemologies of the South: Justice against epistemicide*. London: Routledge.

Dunford, R. (2017) Toward a decolonial global ethics. *Journal of Global Ethics*, 13, 3, 380–397.

Fricker, M. 2015. Epistemic contribution as a central human capability. In G. Hull (ed.), *The equal society*. London: Lexington Books, pp. 73–91.

Gubrium, A. & Harper, K. (2013) *Participatory visual and digital methods*. Walnut Creek, CA: Left Coast Press.

Harper, D. (2002) Talking about pictures: A case for photo elicitation. *Visual Studies*, 17, 1: 13–26.

Kessi, S. (2018) Photovoice as a narrative tool for decolonization: Black women and LGBT student experiences at UCT. *South African Journal of Higher Education*, 32, 3: 101–117.

Leonard, M. & McKnight, M. (2015) Look and tell: using photo-elicitation methods with teenagers. *Children's Geographies*, 13, 6: 629–642.

Liebenberg, L. (2018) Thinking critically about photovoice: Achieving empowerment and social change. *International Journal of Qualitative Methods*, 17: 1–9.

Martinez-Vargas, C., Walker, M. & Mkwananzi, F. (2019) Access to higher education in South Africa: expanding capabilities in and through an undergraduate photovoice project. *Educational Action Research*, 28, 3: 427–442.

Mathebula, M. (2019) Recognising poor black youth from rural communities in South Africa as epistemic contributors. *Critical Studies in Teaching and Leaning*, 7, 1: 64–85.

Mikhailovich, K., Pamphilon, B. & Chambers, B. (2015) Participatory visual research with subsistence farmers in Papua New Guinea. *Development in Practice* 25, 7: 997–1010.

Milligan C. & Bartlett R. (2019) Solicited diary methods. In P. Liamputtong (ed.), *Handbook of research methods in health social sciences*. Singapore: Springer, pp. 1447–1464.

Mitchell, C., de Lange, N. & Moletsane, R. (2017) *Participatory visual methodologies: Social change, community and policy*. London: Sage.

Ngabaza, S., Bojarczuk, E., Masuku, M. & Roelfse, R. (2015). Empowering young people in advocacy for transformation: A photovoice exploration of safe and unsafe spaces on a university campus. *African Safety Promotion*, 13, 1: 30–48.

Ngabaza, S., Shefer, T. & Clowes, L. (2018) Students' narratives on gender and sexuality in the project of social justice and belonging in higher education. *South African Journal of Higher Education*, 32, 3: 139–153.

Olivier, T., Wood, L. & De Lange, N. (2009) *Picturing hope in the face of poverty, as seen through the eyes of teachers: Photo Voice – a research methodology*. Cape Town: Juta and Company.

Pauwels, L. (2015) 'Participatory' visual research revisited: A critical-constructive assessment of epistemological, methodological and social activist tenets. *Ethnography*, 16, 1: 95–117.

Robeyns, I. (2005) The capability approach: a theoretical survey. *Journal of Human Development*, 6, 1: 93–117.

Robeyns, I. (2017) *Wellbeing, freedom and social justice: The capability approach re-examined*. Open Book Publishers.

Rowell, L. L., Bruce, C. D., Shosh, J. M. & Riel, M. M. (eds). (2017). *The Palgrave international handbook of action research*. Basingstoke: Palgrave Macmillan.

Sen, A. (1999) *Development as freedom*. New York: Oxford University Press.

Sen, A. K. (2009) *The idea of justice*. Cambridge, MA: Harvard University Press.

Simmonds, S., Roux, C. & ter Avest, I. (2015) Blurring the boundaries between photovoice and narrative inquiry: A narrative photovoice methodology for gender based research. *The International Journal of Qualitative Methods* 14, 3: 33–49.

Sutton-Brown, C. A. (2014) Photovoice: A methodological guide. *Photography and Culture*, 7, 2: 169–185.

Swallow, D., Petrie, H., Power, C. & Edwards, A. (2015) *Using photo diaries to elicit user requirements from older adults: A case study on mobility barriers*. 15th Human–Computer Interaction (INTERACT), September, Bamberg, Germany.

Wang, C. C. (1999) Photovoice: A participatory action research strategy applied to women's health. *Journal of Women's Health*, 8, 2: 185–192.

Wang, C. C. (2006) Youth participation in photovoice as a strategy for community change. *Journal of Community Practice*, 14, 1–2: 147–161.

Wang, C. C. & Burris, M. A. (1997) Photovoice: Concept, methodology, and use for participatory needs assessment. *Health Education and Behavior*, 24: 369–387.

Wang, C. C. & Burris, M. A. (1994) Empowerment through photo novella: Portraits of participation. *Health, Education and Behaviour*, 21, 2: 171–186.

Part II

Exploring the nuances of the diary research process

Chapter 5

Researcher–participant 'win–win' in diary research

Participant recruitment and retention in a longitudinal diary-interview study on employability management

Xuemeng Cao

Introduction

Solicited diaries, defined as 'an account produced specifically at the researcher's request, by an informant or informants' (Bell, 1998, p. 72), have been acknowledged to be an effective method facilitating a researcher (or a research group) to explore the same group of people across time and across contexts (Breakwell, 2006; Milligan, Bingley & Gatrell, 2005). However solicited diaries have also been argued to be a method that carries a considerable risk of preventing people from signing up to participate, considering the associated commitment of the greater time and effort involved in providing data than many other research methods (Bedwell, McGowan & Lavender, 2012). Moreover, diary research studies, longitudinal ones in particular, require participants to produce diary data on a regular basis according to the researchers' guidelines, which can easily result in respondent fatigue and participant attrition (Okami, 2012). Higher education (HE) research is not an exception in being faced with these methodological concerns when the diary method is adopted. Although the players in the HE domain usually have sufficient literacy to complete diary entries, they may feel overburdened when participating in this type of research, given that they are already busy with their own work. This chapter explores the efforts researchers could make to succeed in recruiting and maintaining participants during longitudinal diary research studies. Previous research has highlighted participant recruitment and retention as the main challenges to undertaking diary research (Toms & Duff, 2002); few articles, however, have specifically focused on this topic, which may partly due to the paucity of methodological literature on the diary method (Bartlett & Milligan, 2015; Hyers 2018; Cao & Henderson, 2020). Furthermore, articles presenting the empirical results of diary studies tend not to elaborate on the process of sampling and participant maintenance. This chapter, as such, contributes to developing the existing knowledge of this method. The principal aim of this chapter is to articulate the key issues in relation to working with participants at every stage of longitudinal diary data collection in order to provide a reference for researchers' practices in conducting diary research studies.

The study that this chapter is based on embraced a nine-month diary element together with two rounds of interviews, which constituted an 'interview–diary–interview' format. The research study explored the employability management of Chinese international students who were enrolled on social sciences taught Master's programmes in a UK university over one academic year (2017/18). The challenges that existed were in recruiting a sufficient number of participants within a limited timeframe and, of course, retaining them while they were otherwise engaged in an intensive (and overseas) learning effort. Successfully recruiting 33 participants within one month and losing only one during the entire year of research, this chapter highlights the significance of a participant-friendly research design and the supportive role of the researcher in cooperating with participants during diary research. In this chapter, following a literature review on how participant recruitment and retention in diary research has hitherto been investigated, the empirical study is introduced. The chapter then elaborates on the specific practices that the researcher engaged in regarding researcher–participant cooperation in the research process, and concludes with suggested further work related to this topic. The core argument is that desirable results of participant recruitment and retention can be achieved via longitudinal diary studies in HE area by taking advantage of the features of the HE context, making a participant-friendly research design and establishing a participant–researcher rapport. Diary researchers in HE and beyond are suggested to keep participants' circumstances and needs in mind while designing and undertaking diary research so as to achieve a 'win–win' for both researcher(s) and participants in the research cooperation.

Participant recruitment and retention in diary research

Participant recruitment and retention are significant challenges to any diary research (Toms & Duff, 2002). People with physical disabilities (e.g. visual impairment) or low literacy may be excluded from diary research (Meth, 2003), though taking other formats of diaries such as photographs, audio and video (digital abilities are required for these types of diary tasks) could make it more inclusive to some extent. Diary research studies employing any tools demand that participants dedicate a certain time and vigour to data provision; longitudinal studies that adopt a qualitative analysis purpose are extremely onerous, and are more likely to cause respondent fatigue, and lead to incomplete diaries and significant participant attrition (Dwyer et al., 2013; Eidse & Turner, 2014; Scott, Green & Cashmore, 2012). Moreover, diary keeping, which is culturally regarded as intimate and confessional behaviour (Hyers, 2018), may make people feel awkward when writing diary entries as they have a clear awareness that their narratives will be read and evaluated.

Using diary method in HE research, the most apparent feasibility is that research objects usually have the desired literacy to complete diary tasks, notwithstanding the ability of written expression varies from person to person even in the senior intellectual group. However, it could be difficult for diary research studies with a high associated commitment to recruit and retain people in the HE area who are already busy with their own work (Hyers et al., 2012; Scott, Green & Cashmore, 2012), compared to those targeted at elderly people or patients who may enjoy more free time. The diary method can facilitate participant recruitment in HE research since reflective writing has been demonstrated to be an effective means of academic development (Vinjamuri, Warde & Kolb, 2017; Wallin & Adawi, 2018), and indeed participants are sometimes interested in the novelty of under-used diary formats such as audio diaries (Worth 2009). Nonetheless, the diary method may rule people out of HE research due to ethical concerns, that is, their diary entries would be with a teacher/colleague-as-reader (Cao & Henderson, 2020).

Few articles have specifically explored the participant recruitment and retention practices in diary research, which is surprising considering that the diary method is so highly participant-dependent. Alongside a paucity of methodologically oriented literature on the diary method itself, a potential reason for the associated lack of discussion on participant engagement is that many diary studies I have accessed either involved a small sample size (e.g. five participants in Furman, Coyne & Negi, 2008; ten participants in Jacelon and Imperio, 2005; eight participants in Lewis, Sligo & Massey, 2005) and/or lasted for only a short duration of data collection (e.g. one week in Beckers, van der Voordt & Dewulf, 2016; ten days in Bedwell, McGowan & Lavender, 2012; one week in Lewis, Sligo & Massey, 2005), which removed the participant-related concerns. The difficulty of recruiting participants for diary research can also be mediated when it is conducted as a part of or a follow-up to a larger research project (e.g. Dietrich, Kracke & Nurmi, 2011; Kaur, Saukko & Lumsden, 2018; Martinez-Vargas, Walker & Mkwananzi, 2019) which already had a participant pool. Otherwise, considerable effort is needed from researchers to achieve their desired sample size for diary studies.

The previous literature reflected the fact that researchers tended to use a variety of methods to expose their research to the target population. For example, Bates (2013) advertised her diary research via websites, email lists and personal contacts; Heng (2017) disseminated her study through international students' offices, friends, social media websites, flyers, and bulletin board postings. Almost no research rejected volunteering diarists as long as they met the criteria of being involved in the sample group, with snowball sampling employed by many such studies (e.g. Heng, 2017; Reid, Hunter & Sutton, 2011) to enlarge sample sizes. Moreover, researchers usually introduced the diary tasks at the data collection stage prior to the diary research (e.g. pre-diary interviews in Eidse & Turner, 2014; also in Jacelon & Imperio, 2005) or specifically conducted pre-diary events (e.g. kick-off sessions in Beckers, van der Voordt & Dewulf, 2016; private face-to-face meetings in Kaur, Saukko & Lumsden, 2018) to explain the diary method and sometimes give diary-keeping training (Martinez-Vargas, Walker & Mkwananzi, 2019; Reynolds, Robles & Repetti, 2016; Chapter 4, this volume) in order to make the diary tasks clear to participants, including how to use diary-keeping tools, and how much effort they may need to contribute.

Exploring the participant recruitment of diary research in HE studies, a unique phenomenon is that researchers embedded diary research into the curricula they delivered as teachers, with some of them allowing students to engage in this voluntarily (Chen et al., 2016), while others made diary-keeping a compulsory part of the module (Travers, 2011). Curriculum-conjunct diary research suffered little difficulty in participant recruitment, but this challenge is still met by many HE researchers where participation is more optional in nature.

Comparing to the participant recruitment process which is sometimes detailed by researchers in the sampling section of articles, researchers' efforts regarding participant retention were less elaborated upon in the previous literature, except for some longitudinal diary research that emphasised the significance of establishing trust and rapport with participants by pre-diary visits and revisits during data collection (Eidse & Turner, 2014; Lewis, Sligo & Massey, 2005; Thomas, 2007), making timely responses to participants' inquiries (Boz & Okumus, 2017; Eidse and Turner, 2014), and giving regular feedback to participants' diary works (Monrouxe, 2009; Travers, 2011). However, it is noteworthy that considerations of participant retention are always implied in diary research design. For instance, diary keeping tools were designed to be *as simple as possible* to shorten the completion time (Hyers et al., 2012; Kenten, 2010); the duration of diary keeping was minimised under the premise of ensuring the sufficiency of the data (Jacelon & Imperio, 2005); and event-contingent approaches have been used to replace everyday diary keeping (Day & Thatcher, 2009) to reduce the burden on the participants.

The above participant retention strategies used by diary studies in general can also be found in the HE area. An interesting point to be noted is that some HE researchers (Martinez-Vargas, Walker & Mkwananzi, 2019; Schmitz & Wiese, 2006) issued a certificate to participants who completed diary research to attract and maintain participants, which is different to others (e.g. Eidse & Turner, 2014; Reynolds, Robles & Repetti, 2016; Swim et al., 2003) who used monetary incentives, though the effectiveness of incentives for encouraging the participation of qualitative research has been criticised (Head, 2009).

In relation to participant recruitment and retention strategies, another issue worth discussing is the participant–researcher relationship in diary studies, longitudinal ones in particular, considering researchers' insider roles during the research process. Previous discussions (e.g. Filep et al., 2018; Heller et al., 2011; Monrouxe, 2009) focused more on how the positionality of the researchers affected the rigour of diary data, which is particularly significant. However, few articles have explored how the participant–researcher relationship worked in terms of participant engagement in diary research, except that of Eidse and Turner's (2014, p. 245) diary research on Vietnamese street vendors which reflected that their participants felt 'obliged' to engage in the research, even though the diary work was 'too tiring and difficult' for them because the rapport had been cultivated between the participants and researchers (and the research assistant).

Based on my literature review, I did not find a diary study in the HE domain that elaborated upon the impact of researcher's role(s) in participant engagement, which effectively presents a gap to fill, especially when some diary research was conducted by a researcher who had no existing power relationship with the participants.

Employability management of Chinese international students: the study

The present study researched the process of how Chinese students managed their employability during the period of studying social sciences taught Master's programmes in the UK. Employability in this research is interpreted as being a complex concept, embracing both personal abilities that make individuals more employable and multifaceted contextual factors that impact one's employment outcomes and long-term career prospects (Walker & Fongwa, 2017). Employability management, as such, is believed to be a dynamic process that permeates individuals' everyday experiences which are impossible for the researcher to fully access via cross-sectional data collection techniques such as questionnaires or single-round interviews. Therefore, the diary-interview method (Zimmerman & Wieder, 1977), which enables the researcher to enter into participants' lived lives based on their almost-simultaneous reflections, was regarded as the most suitable method for this longitudinal study of employability management. The data collection involved two rounds of semi-structured interviews at the start and end of the course and nine months of solicited diary keeping. In order to ensure participants' experiences could be traced longitudinally while occupying less of the participants' time with diary keeping, for each month, one week was chosen as the diary week (usually the third week where possible).

This study is qualitative in nature; the principle of sampling for qualitative studies has been argued to be one of choosing participants who fit into the research topic rather than achieving a statistical sample size (Cucu-Oancea, 2013). However, this research was expected to show both shared and distinctive measures that participants took to manage their employability, and thus anticipated a relatively large sample size of around 25. Moreover, aiming to trace the process of participants' employability management while receiving overseas HE, the data collection was designed to continue throughout the entire one-year course, which required high loyalty on the part of the participants to the research engagement. This study, as such, met significant challenges in terms of participant recruitment and retention. Owing to a series of efforts made by both the researcher and the participants, this research involved 33 participants in the sample group, with 32 of them completing the entire process of data provision.

Sharing my experience of conducting diary research in different events, I found that lots of researchers hesitated to use the diary method due to a lack of confidence in good participant engagement, and they were interested in the specific strategies which can facilitate researcher–participant cooperation. This chapter is therefore inspired to discuss how to effectively work with diarists based on my substantial experience in conducting longitudinal solicited diary research. For the purposes of this chapter, I reviewed the notes I made during the study in relation to participant recruitment and retention, for example, the ways of advertising the study, texts introducing the study to potential participants, participant-related considerations in the research design, and reflections on my roles during the study, and then compared my practices with those of previous researchers. In addition, I returned to the second-round interviews, which had included a specific discussion of the diary research participation, to explore participants' accounts of why they decided to engage in, and maintained their involvement, in this research. The following section presents these participant-related methodological thoughts alongside the research process.

Working with diarists

Recruiting participants within a limited time

The first participant-related challenge met by this study was to recruit a sufficient number of participants from an otherwise small-scale cohort within a limited time-frame. I recruited participants from Chinese students in a single UK university who met two criteria: (1) they had completed an undergraduate course in mainland China, and (2) they were enrolled on a social sciences taught Master's programme in the 2017/18 academic year. The majority of these students could only be accessed after they arrived the university at the end of September 2017, though with some enrolled on pre-course language sessions being reachable in July or August depending on the duration of their language sessions. As this study included long-itudinal diary research, the pre-diary interviews needed to be completed by the end of October 2017 so as to leave enough time for participants' diary keeping. As such, there was only one month available to access the target students and persuade them to join in the research, notwithstanding three participants who had been recruited in August 2017 from an online forum for Chinese international students, where an advertisement about this research had been posted.

From the time the newcomer registration began, several methods were adopted to advertise the research, for example bulletin board postings (see also Heng, 2017), distributing flyers (see also Reynolds, Robles & Repetti, 2016), and messaging WeChat (an social APP widely used among Chinese students) groups for Chinese newcomers. However, these strategies, which had worked effectively in previous research, were less effective in recruiting participants in this instance. Only two participants were recruited at this stage, possibly because the new students were understandably busy with their settling-in issues at that time.

A boost in participant numbers was seen in the welcome week when I was given the opportunity to advertise my research at a workshop for newcomers, through which nine participants were recruited. Moreover, the sampling process was also assisted by administrative officers in five departments of the social sciences faculty who mailed new Chinese taught Master's students about this research, with ten of them agreeing to join. In addition, snowball sampling (see also Heng, 2017; Reid,

Hunter & Sutton, 2011) was also employed to enlarge the sample size, with nine more students accepting the invitation from their peers who had been the sample group members. The effectiveness of these three approaches to participant recruitment were then interpreted by the participants in the follow-up interviews. They were willing to join this research because they felt it to be 'authorised' (Participant 27, Interview 2) when teachers, administrative staff or classmates introduced it to them. In total, 33 participants were successfully recruited. The sample size was larger than I had anticipated (approx. 25 was originally intended), but none of them were excluded in case subsequent participant attrition was high.

Demonstrating the attractiveness of the research participation

As many researchers (Bates, 2013; Kaur, Saukko & Lumsden, 2018) suggested, I arranged individual pre-research meetings with each participant to explain the research process. What was found to be important in the research introduction is to inform participants about the *benefits* they can achieve by engaging in the study, in addition to emphasising the significance of the study itself. In the case of this research, the importance of employability management during the one-year taught Master's course, a relatively intensive overseas HE programme, was discussed with the participants in order to ensure they realised the *close relation* between this research topic and their overseas experiences. More importantly, diary keeping, which might prevent already busy students from participating in this research, was introduced as an invaluable opportunity to simultaneously reflect on one's gains and losses over studying abroad, with the completed diaries emphasised as a reference for participants' preparation for Curriculum Vitae and employment interviews. Many participants reported in the second-round interviews that their acknowledgement to the values of recording the employability-related experiences 'defeated their worries about conducting long-term diary tasks' (Participant 6, Interview 2). Further, participants felt they were 'self-motivated to persist in the diary keeping and treat it seriously' (Participant 15, Interview 2). The internal motivation of diary research participation not only positively contributes to the quality of diary data (Day & Thatcher, 2009), but also 'enhances participants' ability of self-reflection' (Participant 18, Interview 2).

When introducing a diary method study to potential participants, incentives have often been used to attract them (Meth, 2003). This particular research provided no monetary incentives because participants were expected to be involved in the research out of their own intrinsic motivations rather than any external profit. However, in order to reward participants' contributions, in the pre-research meetings I promised to share employment information and employability-related events on WeChat, providing an informal consultation service about PhD course and scholarship applications, and allowed participants to have face-to-face meetings with me when they had enquiries or needed emotional support. These non-monetary incentives proved to be extremely attractive to participants who were new to the overseas education context, where 'a senior played an important role in [their] establishment of social support system' (Participant 25, Interview 2). Although the degree of rapport developed with the researcher varied from participant to participant throughout the course of the research, incentives that meet participants' needs proved to be effective both in terms of participant recruitment and retention in this longitudinal diary study.

Participant-friendly research design

Conducting a diary study with extensive commitment demands, it is important to have a participant-friendly research design in order to achieve the balance between obtaining the desired data collection outcomes and reducing participants' burden in terms of data provision. The most innovative design of this diary study was to ask participants to keep employability diaries for *one week of each month* throughout the academic year (November 2017 to July 2018), which can rarely be found in previous literature as an approach, with the only known exception being a study on stroke survivors (Alaszewski & Wilkinson, 2015). The fact of the length of time of the diary research ensured that participants' experiences could be traced longitudinally, while the reduced frequency of diary entries mediated respondent fatigue and lessened incidences of repeated data.

The diary workloads were further alleviated by the event-contingent approach (Hyers, 2018). Participants were not requested to write entries every day, but rather complete a semi-structured recording form when each employability-related experience occurred. The form was in Microsoft Word format, which was more convenient than a handwritten one for participants who always worked on laptops. Also, this Word-based form allowed participants to decide on the quantity of data they would like, or were prepared, to provide – they needed neither to shorten the length of entries due to the limitation of reserved space, nor feel embarrassed for giving short narratives. Moreover, participants were allowed to freely choose the language (Chinese or English) of diary writing, in case their expression was restricted by their English proficiency. To assist participants in their diary keeping, broad guidelines (see also Eidse & Turner, 2014) were provided alongside recording forms, since the concept of employability was new to some participants. In addition, participants also received a sample entry (see also Bartlett, 2012) which demonstrated the diary keeping format required using the recording form. Although providing sample entries has been criticised for perceived intervention in participants' diary keeping (e.g. Kenten, 2010), this strategy was suggested by pilot participants to ensure the effective use of the recording form. Reviewing the nine-month diary keeping in the second-round interview, the majority of participants reported that they were not overburdened by the diary tasks since 'writing entries in the sampled weeks was manageable' (Participant 5, Interview 2) and 'the recording form was easy to use' (Participant 23, Interview 2).

To achieve the participant-friendly research design, in addition to referencing the strategies used by other researchers, an approach worthy of note is that I participated in the pilot study to test the diary method. I kept an employability diary for five successive weeks. This experience, which enabled me to inspect the research process from the standpoint of the actual participants, significantly contributed to the improvement of the research design. The feasibility and effectiveness of this approach was due to the shared experience of the researcher and participants in the HE context, but it might not be a valid approach for use in other research areas, for example a healthcare study whose participants are patients while the researchers are not.

Researcher's roles

During the one year of data collection, I kept in touch with my participants by playing different roles. As a researcher, I sent recording forms to each participant separately by email on the Sunday prior to each sampled diary week, and informed them of the same on WeChat in case of a problem with the email or the internet. Participants were asked to return the completed diaries on the Sunday of every diary week. The regular diary collection positively contributed to participant retention since it gave participants a 'rhythm' of diary tasks rather than leaving them a long time without any formal contact with the researcher. Moreover, I gave feedback to participants based on their entries. Some feedback was closely related to the data providing (see also Boz & Okumus, 2017; Travers, 2011) regarding their use of the recording form (especially in the first diary week), while in other cases it was more conversational, for instance when they mentioned experiences that particularly interested me. These research-specific contacts are important for informing participants that their contributions have been acknowledged and by encouraging their continued involvement in the study (Monrouxe, 2009).

In addition to the research-related contacts, I had many personal connections with my participants. As a researcher, but also a senior student, participants regarded me as an information provider about issues relating to daily life (e.g. where to buy Chinese ingredients) and an adviser for study (e.g. module selection, PhD applications). I responded to their inquiries in as timely a manner as possible, not only because they were my participants but also because I understood their situations as newcomers to an overseas education context. Moreover, as promised in the pre-research meetings, I proactively shared employment information and interesting events with my participants on WeChat to make them feel more included in the research.

Meanwhile, many participants asked for emotional support from me, especially in the early stages of data collection, which was also the initial period of their overseas lives. Since all of my participants had no or very limited previous overseas experience, connecting with me gave them a sense of security in an unfamiliar environment. Although the number of participants who frequently contacted me for emotional support declined as time passed, possibly because their social support system in the UK became better-established, which reduced their dependence on me, I became good friends with some participants.

The research-participant rapport can trigger ethical issues, especially when participants rely on the researcher's emotional support with mental health. It is risky for both participants and the researcher since the researcher is not a psychological consultant or psychotherapist. Responding to this, I, on the one hand, lent these participants a sympathetic ear and provided support where possible; on the other hand, I reminded them to keep a watchful eye on their mental health and suggested they seek professional help if they felt they were at risk.

The researcher's efforts with regard to providing support in and out of the research were acknowledged by participants when they reviewed their research participation in the follow-up interviews. Similar to the participants in Eidse and Turner's research, who felt 'obliged' to complete the data providing due to the researcher–participant rapport (Eidse & Turner, 2014), many participants in this research reported that they never thought about dropping out of this research. They had a sense of responsibility to help me complete my research because I was a friend, a listener, an adviser, and an emotional supporter during their very difficult time in the UK. Furthermore, participants, as researchers of their own studies, deeply understood the researcher's dedication to participant retention and much of the other work involved in such a longitudinal study. As such, they self-motivated to be the participants responsible for their data providing. This obviously reflects an advantage of conducting diary research (and other participant-effort-demanded research) in the HE area, where participants share empathy with the researcher with regard to the hardship of conducting academic research.

Conclusion

The principal aim of this chapter was to discuss the challenges and strategies for participant recruitment and retention in longitudinal qualitative diary research studies. I argue that participant engagement should be centred by researchers when planning and conducting diary studies, considering its significance to data quantity and quality. In the chapter, I reviewed how participant recruitment and retention in diary research have been explored by the existing literature, and specifically how these issues are featured in HE diary research. Based on this, I discussed how my research practices have spoken to the literature, and what unique strategies adopted by my research can contribute to the methodological development of diary research.

In considering participant recruitment and retention for a longitudinal diary study, I argue that six elements can be addressed: (i) exposing the research to the target population through multiple media can be helpful for recruiting participants, especially within a limited timeframe; (ii) advertising the research via specific groups or persons related to the target population (e.g. administrative staff in this study) can be highly effective in participant recruitment; (iii) making potential participants aware of the *benefits* they can gain from the diary research participation is significant in terms of encouraging participants' engagement with and persistence in the study; (iv) incentives that inspire participants' self-motivation to engage in the diary study positively work for participant recruitment and retention; (v) it is vital to have a participant-friendly research design to minimise the burden of participants' diary tasks, with the duration, frequency, diary data collection tool, guidelines and sample entries requiring sophisticated design; and (vi) the researcher–participant relationship significantly impacts participant retention – researchers can enhance the rapport with participants by playing supportive roles both in and outside the research.

Moreover, I argue that there are some strategies for participant recruitment and retention that are specifically effective in HE diary research, which may also be enlightening for researchers in other domains: (i) embedding diary research into curricula can effectively diminish the challenge of participant recruitment and retention; (ii) advertising the research via departments or other university-based societies and organisations can give the research engagement the impression of an authorised activity to target population, so that they are more likely to get involved; (iii) non-monetary incentives such as a certificate of research participation, information/event sharing, and network opportunities can work effectively in attracting HE players' diary research participation; (iv) researchers who share similar experiences with the target participants can engage with the pilot study themselves to achieve a participant-friendly diary research design; and, finally, (v) researchers may find it easier to recruit and maintain participants within their own HE community given the associated geographic accessibility; however, ethical issues are worth careful consideration when collecting participants' well-round data by means of a diary (Malone, 2003).

From the exploration of participant recruitment and retention in general diary studies and with respect to HE research specifically, many gaps are apparent that could be addressed to further these discussions. For instance, the researcher–participant power relationship is worth further exploration regarding the ethical issues underlying participants' decisions to engage in a study conducted by a senior or a teacher (see Chapter 9, this volume). It would also be meaningful to discuss the extent to which the success in participant retention is positively associated with better quality of diary data, considering some participants may remain in the sample group until the end of research but lose the passion to do so midway through the research. Finally, ethical issues in relation to diary researchers are also worth exploring further in terms of how they deal with participants' requirements (sometimes unreasonable) when they try to be supportive to their participants. This chapter has addressed the key issues relating to the practices of participant recruitment and retention in longitudinal diary research studies, and calls for increased attention and discussion in this area.

Acknowledgements

This article is based on doctoral research funded by the China Scholarship Council. Many thanks to the China Scholarship Council for funding this study. Thanks to my co-editor for this book, Emily Henderson, for all the fabulous ideas about diary research and the efforts for the editing work.

References

Alaszewski, A. & Wilkinson, I. (2015) The paradox of hope for working age adults recovering from stroke. *Health*, 19, 2: 172–187.

Bartlett, R. & Milligan, C. (2015) *What is diary method?* London: Bloomsbury.

Bates, C. (2013) Video diaries: Audio-visual research methods and the elusive body, *Visual Studies*, 28, 1: 29–37.

Beckers, R., van der Voordt, T. & Dewulf, G. (2016) Why do they study there? Diary research into students' learning space choices in higher education. *Higher Education Research & Development*, 35, 1: 142–157.

Bedwell, C., McGowan, L. & Lavender, T. (2012) Using diaries to explore midwives' experiences in intrapartum care: An evaluation of the method in a phenomenological study. *Midwifery*, 28, 2: 150–155.

Bell, L. (1998) Public and private meanings in diaries: Researching family and childcare. In J. Ribbens & R. Edwards (eds), *Feminist dilemmas in qualitative research: Public knowledge and private lives*. London: Sage, pp.72–86.

Boz, I. & Okumus, H. (2017) The 'everything about the existence' experiences of Turkish women with infertility: Solicited diaries in qualitative research. *Journal of Nursing Research*, 25, 4: 268–275.

Breakwell, G. M. (2006) Using self-recording: diary and narrative methods. In G. M. Breakwell, S. Hommond, C. Fife-Schaw & J. A. Smith (eds), *Research methods in psychology*, 3rd edition. London: Sage, pp. 255–272.

Cao, X. & Henderson, E. F. (2020) The interweaving of diaries and lives: diary-keeping behaviour in a diary-interview study of international students' employability management. *Qualitative Research*. DOI: 10.1177/1468794120920260

Chen, H. Y., Yarnal, C., Hustad, J. T. & Sims, D. (2016) Take a selfie of life: A qualitative exploration of college students' self-reflections on free time use and personal values. *Journal of College and Character*, 17, 2: 101–115.

Cucu-Oancea, O. (2013) Using diaries: A real challenge for the social scientist. *Procedia-Social and Behavioral Sciences*, 92: 231–238.

Day, M. & Thatcher, J. (2009) 'I'm really embarrassed that you're going to read this ...': Reflections on using diaries in qualitative research. *Qualitative Research in Psychology*, 6, 4: 249–259.

Dietrich, J., Kracke, B. & Nurmi, J. E. (2011) Parents' role in adolescents' decision on a college major: A weekly diary study. *Journal of Vocational Behavior*, 79, 1: 134–144.

Dwyer, S., Piquette, N., Buckle, J. & McCaslin, E. (2013) Women gamblers write a voice: Exploring journaling as an effective counseling and research tool. *Journal of Groups in Addiction & Recovery*, 8, 1: 36–50.

Eidse, N. & Turner, S. (2014) Doing resistance their own way: Counter-narratives of street vending in Hanoi, Vietnam through solicited journaling. *Area*, 46, 3: 242–248.

Filep, C. V., Turner, S., Eidse, N., Thompson-Fawcett, M. & Fitzsimons, S. (2018) Advancing rigour in solicited diary research. *Qualitative Research*, 18, 4: 451–470.

Furman, R., Coyne, A. & Negi, N. J. (2008) An international experience for social work students: Self-reflection through poetry and journal writing exercises. *Journal of Teaching in Social Work*, 28, 1–2:71–85.

Head, E. (2009) The ethics and implications of paying participants in qualitative research. *International Journal of Social Research Methodology*, 12, 4: 335–344.

Heller, E., Christensen, J., Long, L., Mackenzie, C. A., Osano, P. M., Ricker, B. & Turner, S. (2011) Dear diary: Early career geographers collectively reflect on their qualitative field research experiences. *Journal of Geography in Higher Education*, 35, 1: 67–83.

Heng, T. T. (2017) Voices of Chinese international students in USA colleges: 'I want to tell them that …'. *Studies in Higher Education*, 42, 5: 833–850.

Hyers, L. L. (2018) *Diary methods.* New York: Oxford University Press.

Hyers, L. L., Syphan, J., Cochran, K. & Brown, T. (2012) Disparities in the professional development interactions of university faculty as a function of gender and ethnic under-representation. *The Journal of Faculty Development*, 26, 1: 18–28.

Jacelon, C. S. & Imperio, K. (2005) Participant diaries as a source of data in research with older adults. *Qualitative Health Research*, 15, 7: 991–997.

Kaur, H., Saukko, P. & Lumsden, K. (2018) Rhythms of moving in and between digital media: A study on video diaries of young people with physical disabilities. *Mobilities*, 13, 3: 397–410.

Kenten, C. (2010) Narrating oneself: Reflections on the use of solicited diaries with diary interviews. *Forum Qualitative Sozialforschung/Forum: Qualitative Social Research*, May, 11, 2.

Lewis, K., Sligo, F. & Massey, C. (2005) Observe, record, then beyond: Facilitating participant reflection via research diaries. *Qualitative Research in Accounting & Management*, 2, 2: 216–229.

Malone, S. (2003) Ethics at home: Informed consent in your own backyard. *Qualitative Studies in Education*, 16, 6: 797–815.

Martinez-Vargas, C., Walker, M. & Mkwananzi, F. (2019) Access to higher education in South Africa: Expanding capabilities in and through an undergraduate photovoice project. *Educational Action Research*, May: 1–16.

Meth, P. (2003) Entries and omissions: Using solicited diaries in geographical research. *Area*, 35, 2: 195–205.

Milligan, C., Bingley, A. & Gatrell, A. (2005) Digging deep: Using diary techniques to explore the place of health and well-being amongst older people. *Social Science & Medicine*, 61: 1882–2892.

Monrouxe, L.V. (2009) Solicited audio diaries in longitudinal narrative research: A view from inside. *Qualitative research*, 9, 1: 81–103.

Okami, P. (2012) Dear Diary: A useful but imperfect method. In M. W. Wiederman & B. E. Whitley Jr (eds), *Handbook for conducting research on human sexuality.* Hillsdale, NJ: Psychology Press, pp. 195–208.

Reid, L., Hunter, C. & Sutton, P. W. (2011) Rising to the challenge of environmental behaviour change: Developing a reflexive diary approach. *Geoforum*, 42, 6: 720–730.

Reynolds, B. M., Robles, T. F. & Repetti, R. L. (2016) Measurement reactivity and fatigue effects in daily diary research with families. *Developmental Psychology*, 52, 3: 442–456.

Schmitz, B. & Wiese, B. S. (2006) New perspectives for the evaluation of training sessions in self-regulated learning: Time-series analyses of diary data. *Contemporary Educational Psychology*, 31, 1: 64–96.

Scott, J., Green, P. & Cashmore, A. (2012) Bioscience students' first year perspectives through video diaries: Home, family and student transitions. *Bioscience Education*, 20, 1: 53–67.

Swim, J. K., Hyers, L. L., Cohen, L. L., Fitzgerald, D. C. & Bylsma, W. H. (2003) African American college students' experiences with everyday racism: Characteristics of and responses to these incidents. *Journal of Black Psychology*, 29, 1: 38–67.

Thomas, F. (2007) Eliciting emotions in HIV/AIDS research: A diary-based approach. *Area*, 39: 74–82.

Toms, E. G. & Duff, W. (2002) I spent 1½ hours sifting through one large box ...: Diaries as information behaviour of the archives user: Lessons learned. *Journal of the American Society for Information Science and Technology*, 53, 14: 1232–1238.

Travers, C. (2011) Unveiling a reflective diary methodology for exploring the lived experiences of stress and coping. *Journal of Vocational Behavior*, 79, 1: 204–216.

Vinjamuri, M., Warde, B. & Kolb, P. (2017) The reflective diary: An experiential tool for enhancing social work students' research learning. *Social Work Education*, 36, 8: 933–945.

Walker, M. & Fongwa, S. (2017) *Universities, employability and human development*. London: Springer.

Wallin, P. & Adawi, T. (2018) The reflective diary as a method for the formative assessment of self-regulated learning. *European Journal of Engineering Education*, 43, 4: 507–521.

Worth, N. (2009). Making use of audio diaries in research with young people: Examining narrative, participation and audience. *Sociological Research Online*, 14, 4, 77–87.

Zimmerman, D. & Wieder, D. (1977) The diary-interview method. *Urban Life*, 5: 479–497.

Chapter 6

'I'm not really sure why I took that!'

Exploring the forms of diarying present in the participant-generated photo-elicitation method

Michael Keenan

Introduction

While recent years have seen an increase in research exploring LGBTQ issues and experiences, research in the higher education context has often been 'broad-brush', focusing on the umbrella term 'LGBTQ' and utilising methods which are reflective of key moments and over-arching feelings rather than accessing the detail of everyday experiences. The overgeneralisation present in the use of the umbrella term of LGBTQ is particularly an issue which has been raised and acknowledged in research literature, in areas such as the experiences of young people (Wagaman, 2016), and in health provision (Bosse & Chiodo, 2016). Within the higher education setting Formby's (2015) report on LGBTQ university experiences and perspectives illustrates the diversity of LGBTQ experience, highlighting specific experiences of those who identify as lesbian, bisexual and trans. Indeed, bisexual and trans narratives have particularly been singled out as being under-represented in LGBTQ research. Heath (2005) for example discusses the silent B, and MacFarlane, Grieves and Zwiers (2014) the silent T in research which groups together LGBTQ experiences, illustrating the need for research to recognise and reflect this diversity and detail.

Alongside this need for detail and depth, reflections on equality discourses and policies have drawn attention to the distance between policy and practice in the discussion of and the experience of equality and inclusive practice (see Ahmed, 2007). Such research illustrates that policy focused on developing and maintaining inclusivity can often be seen very differently as it plays out in everyday practice and does not necessarily achieve the desired inclusive goals. It is therefore important for research to be able to access and reflect on everyday experiences in order to speak to and reflect upon higher education policy and institutional practice.

The higher education context also requires a reflection on and engagement with its diversity. The higher education experience is both specific and varied. It is recognised as a site of change and transition (Balloo, Pauli & Worrell, 2017), often discussed in its specificness as a 'university bubble' which is separate from and qualitatively different from experiences outside of the university context (Anderson & Green, 2012). This specificity of location however is further complicated by the diverse spaces and contexts which may be included within the university experience. The classroom is a very different space from the student union or the sports field, the interaction with friends very different from the interaction with coursemates, academic staff or student services. While research has emerged exploring specific aspects of the university experience, even these put boundaries upon what the researcher and therefore the research may view as the university experience – or relevant to higher education research.

For these reasons the research discussed here sought to take an approach that allowed access to the diverse aspects of student life, everyday experiences, the influence of wider policy and the opportunity for students to document student life as they saw it without the influence of boundaries that the research might be seen to place on it. This required an approach which allowed for the incorporation of diverse moments, contexts and experiences, as well as space for reflection and discussion of meaning. Participant-generated photo-elicitation was seen to be a method which allowed this engagement, offering an opportunity for depth of exploration, access to everyday university experience, and giving participants a degree of power to shape the research boundaries.

Understanding photo-elicitation's relevance to diary research

Photo-elicitation is a method of interviewing which uses photographs as the basis for and the focus of the interview (Richard & Lahman, 2015). While photo-elicitation is used and developed in diverse ways by studies, it is generally seen as taking two forms: interviewing based on photographs provided by the participant (participant generated; see Chapter 10, this volume), or interviews based upon photographs provided by the researcher (researcher generated) (see Allen, 2012; Mathison, 2012). Key advantages seen to be offered by the method in general include that the combination of the use of photographs and interviewing allow research to access depth (Meo, 2010), to offer access into other people's everyday worlds (Samuels, 2004), and to challenge expectations or perspectives (Harper, 2002). The focus of this chapter is primarily on the diary-like qualities of participant generated photo-elicitation (see also Chapter 8, this volume), such qualities can be drawn out from a reflection on three recognised advantages – accessing depth, the everyday and alternative perspectives.

The depth of access offered by photo-elicitation is drawn out well by Harper (2002). In his overview of the method across its uses in anthropology and sociology Harper discusses how he sees photo methods having particular benefits for encouraging deep reflection. He writes:

> I believe photo elicitation mines deeper shafts into a different part of human consciousness than do words-alone interviews. It is partly due to how remembering is enlarged by photographs and partly due to the particular quality of the photograph itself. Photographs appear to capture the impossible: a person gone; an event past. That extraordinary sense of seeming to

retrieve something that has disappeared belongs alone to the photograph, and it leads to deep and interesting talk.

(Harper, 2002, pp. 22–23)

Harper's reflections here emphasise not just the depth of reflection which photo-elicitation makes possible, but also the specificity of that depth in encouraging reflection on a specific site, scene, object or time, encouraged by the position photography has in our cultural practice.

The research benefits of photography were also identified by Meo (2010) who emphasised the cultural location of photography by reflecting upon the way in which we use, discuss and reminisce over photographs, which in turn allows photo-based research to access and engage with such responses to photography to elicit narratives of depth and meaning. Here there is a clear comparison to more specifically 'diary'-focussed methods as seen in Harvey's (2011) discussions of reflection in private diaries, and Milligan, Bingley and Gatrell's (2005) reflection on the benefits of the diary as a site of both recording and reflecting.

Existing research has further reflected on how, when used for appropriate studies, photo-elicitation allows research to build and develop upon existing knowledge. One example of this is Silver and Reavey's (2010) study of body dysmorphia wherein they argue that the visual nature of the issue under discussion was a clear reason for the importance of including visuals in the study, developing research knowledge by more fully representing the experiences of participants. Similarly, Metcalfe (2016) argues that visual methods in higher education research allow for a fuller and more developed engagement with a context which is many textured and particularly can be argued to be increasingly visual. Indeed, while so many issues studied in social sciences include visuals, smells, tastes and feelings, the study of them through text and speech alone have required translations which move the description and discussion of experience away from the 'sensuousness' (Marks, 2002) of the everyday. The variation in textures and materials present in photo-elicitation research therefore allows for such depth and reflection, and is increasingly being recognised in diary and diary-like studies which incorporate the visual (Garcia et al., 2016; Daum et al., 2019).

'Everydayness' was another positive of the photo-elicitation method which reflected diarying. Accessing everyday experiences has been identified as a reason for seeking out diary approaches (Gunthert & Wenze, 2012), and the everyday focus of diaries is seen to change perspectives allowing research to access otherwise less obvious interactions – including 'mundane experiences' (Hyers et al., 2006). Photography has the potential to further engage and develop such everyday research. The recognition of the method as an everyday practice, and the focus on the everyday that the method gives research are both important factors.

Contemporary photo-elicitation studies benefit from the everydayness of the process of documenting and indeed sharing one's life through photography, due to the pervasive nature of smartphones in contemporary society (Schreiber, 2015). By incorporating smartphone photography, photo-elicitation studies are able to both remove the suspect presence of the camera and embrace participants' familiarity with the process.

When photo-elicitation studies ask participants to specifically take photographs for the purpose of the study, they introduce a particular everydayness. Drawing attention to a moment or context experienced and captured specifically with the project in mind, in the moment of experience (or remembering). This was particularly clear in Samuels' (2004) photo-elicitation research with young Buddhist monks. Samuels argues that the presence of the photos within the research kept conversations grounded in the everyday, encouraging discussions of mundane everyday experiences and practices and drawing out these realities within the research. Similarly, Guell and Ogilvie's (2015) photo study of commuting practice illustrates how by capturing everyday life photo-elicitation draws attention to the mundane and encourages alternative and detailed reflections – thus such us of photo-elicitation reflects and extends the potential of diary-based research. Instant reporting is an area of development in diary research, illustrated by technological developments in pain reporting (Lalloo et al., 2015) and time-use recording (Daum et al., 2019), photo-elicitation, as discussed above highlights the relevance and importance of such instant recording to accessing lived experience.

Photo-elicitation also has the power to change the way we look at things. Mannay (2010) for example makes use of the very descriptive phrase of 'making the familiar strange'. This is illustrated in Harper's (2002) discussion of the use of aerial photography in interviews with farmers; using such visuals literally changed farmers' perspectives on their farms and allowed the interview to challenge expected views and encourage participants to look again at their lives. Harper refers to this as a process of 'breaking the frame', presenting the familiar in a new way, breaking established frames of reference. Alongside this, Samuels (2004) argues that engaging participants in taking and collating photographs for interview was not only a way of being able to access and engage with unfamiliar lives, but also allowed the research to break the frame, or challenge the expectation of the researcher. Thus photo-elicitation has the power to break the frame of both the researcher and the participant, opening up the unexpected and challenging expected borders of relevance.

Across the literature on both researcher-generated and participant-generated photo-elicitation, there is discussion of how the use of the method can lead to the emergence of the unexpected. Van Auken, Frisvoll and Stewart (2010) suggest that the process of photo-elicitation allows for the tapping of unconscious reflections. Continuing with the idea of 'breaking the frame', they discuss how turning the camera on everyday things encourages the noticing of detail which can lead to unexpected discussion. Such 'unexpected' narrative emerging in response to photographs was also clear in the researcher generated photo-elicitation present in the work of Leonard and McKnight (2015). The study used photographs in group interviews to explore young people's views of life in Belfast. In reflecting on the way young people responded to a picture of a shopping centre, the researchers were surprised to find that the young people were more focused on the presence of a plastic bag in the picture rather than the expected focus of the shopping centre. Here then reflection on photography in photo-elicitation reflects but also extends the potential of diary-like research to capture the unexpected. While diary research changes perspectives, and promotes the mundane to being worthy of reflection, this literature reflects photo-elicitation's potential to take this to new spaces by emphasising the unexpected and engaging participants in reflecting on imagery – including their own in the case of participant generated photo-elicitation – from various perspectives, allowing the emergent conversation to access the everyday, capture reflection and challenge expectations – to go to places other diary methods may not.

With reference to the higher education context, the 'episodic' diarying nature of photo-elicitation – allowing diverse scenes and contexts to be included – clearly speaks to the nature of university life discussed above. Further, the many textures and aspects of the reality of higher education are done a disservice by research limiting itself to text and speech; as the incorporation of the visual allows research to engage more fully and engagingly with the higher education context (Metcalfe, 2016). While the use of visual research and specifically photo-elicitation remains under-utilised in the higher education research context, existing studies have recognised its benefits for accessing seldom-told experiences in higher education, particularly in terms of diarying gender and sexuality. Joy and Numer (2017) for example, used photo-elicitation by asking participants to record LGBTQ group events, and Witcomb, Brophy and McDermott (2019) asked participants to use photography to document moments where they experienced affiliation and disaffiliation as gender non-conforming university students.

The above section has drawn out some reasons why the diarying nature of photo-elicitation offers research the ability to access depth, everyday experience and unexpected content. These aspects are identified as being particularly relevant to the higher education experience, and specifically relevant to discussion of sexual and gender identity in higher education contexts. Going forward, the chapter highlights the issue of the unexpected and the presence of various perspectives in participant generated photo-elicitation to illustrate the co-existence of two aspects of diarying within the project – engagement with the everyday and in-depth reflection. In doing so, the chapter presents three examples of images which were introduced by participants as images they were not sure why they included. These 'unexpected' images show the power of photo-elicitation to 'diary', and extend diarying, as they access a depth of discussion and everyday insight through participants' dual roles in the research process as creators and interpreters of the study data.

Diarying the research design

The project aimed to explore the everyday experiences of undergraduate students who identified as either bisexual or trans; these identities were understood to encapsulate diverse self-identifications, including (but not limited to) pansexual and non-binary identities. The project asked participants to use their smartphones to take pictures which reflected and documented their university experiences as bisexual or trans identifying undergraduate students. Participants were then asked to forward these photographs to the researcher, and interviews were arranged. The provided photographs formed the basis of these interviews which used the photographs as a structure for a conversational interview style. Interviews followed the episodic, diary-like nature of the photographs provided by exploring episode by episode the experiences documented.

Recruitment to the project occurred via a variety of primarily online approaches. The project was publicised widely via social media and email – particularly via university LGBTQ societies and associations. Contacts for LGBTQ societies were sought out via online information and social media locations. Potential institutions were identified from HEFCE (Higher Education Funding Council for England – dissolved in 2018) listings of English higher education institutions. The project also utilised personal contacts to access universities and LGBTQ societies offline. Further, the project utilised snowballing to encourage further participation through the networks of those who took part.

In total 15 students completed the photography and interview parts of the project. These 15 respondents were from across 11 higher education institutions in England. Of the 15 students who took part, 11 participants expressed an identification as trans or non-binary and 10 students expressed an identification as bisexual or pansexual. Although students were asked to take a maximum of 20 photographs, this was clearly communicated as a maximum, not an expectation and the final submitted amount of photographs ranged from 4 to 15. Participants were encouraged to complete the photography task within a two-week period. The interviews took place in an appropriate location of the participant's choosing – these ranged from place of residence, to different locations on their home campus, or in their local area; and lasted between 50 and 120 minutes. The project was approved by the Nottingham Trent University College of Business, Law and Social Sciences College Ethics Committee, and was undertaken with reference to the British Sociological Association's ethical guidance.

In terms of information and guidance, participants were provided with a brief information sheet following their first contact, which outlined the aims of the study and the photograph and interview methods; this was followed up with photography guidelines when participants agreed to take part. Photography guidelines were left as brief as possible to encourage diversity in the photography; however specific guidelines which were included were to discourage the inclusion of other people in photos, to emphasise that photos should only be taken in situations which felt safe, and to only include information which the participants were comfortable with and were willing to reflect upon. Suggestions on what to photograph included, but did not limit participants to, reflections of everyday experiences, photographs which represented a particular incident, or which were representative of wider reflections on university life.

While this approach meant that an everyday 'diarying' was only part of the focus of the photography, the reminiscing present in other photography engaged with everyday experiences and reflected the desire of the project to draw out the reflexive and storytelling aspects of diarying.

As well as meeting the aims of the project in terms of accessing the everyday and the reflective, photo-elicitation was also seen to be appropriate to exploring the context of university experiences. This form of photo-elicitation used a medium that was familiar to potential respondents – mobile phone photography – which is pervasive on university campuses. This allowed access and engagement with the various locations and spaces which may be viewed to be included in 'the university context'. While certain locations might be more difficult to represent (e.g. the university classroom), the use of mobile phone photography meant that pictures could be taken without arousing suspicion or excessive concern and these locations were present in the data.

Illustrating the diarying potential of photo-elicitation

The chapter now illustrates how the use of photo-elicitation in this project engaged participants in acts of diarying – both in terms of recording and reflexively interpreting everyday life. With reference to three photographs the chapter illustrates the co-existence of intimacy and distance in the method. In reflecting upon these examples, the dual role of the participant as creator (intimately connected) and interpreter (reflexive from a distance) is drawn out. These examples illustrate how photo-elicitation accessed the above-mentioned diary-like aspects of depth, the everyday, alternative perspectives and unexpected connections. Pseudonyms are used throughout.

The examples also illustrate how photo-elicitation allows an episodic diary-like telling. Two of the three photographs presented are from the same participant. Their presentation illustrates how photo-elicitation, by its episodic nature, allowed 'a big story to be told in small parts'.

It is impossible to do justice to the intricacies of the emergent narratives elicited by the method in the space available, but I hope that the following reflections on three photographs illustrate the purpose and potential of photo-elicitation diarying in higher education research.

From house to 'home'

This first image (see Figure 6.1) illustrates the potential of the photo-elicitation method to encourage self-reflection and detail, and to elicit unexpected connections. The picture was taken by Joe, who identified as a trans man. The picture showed the back of a three-storey house (Joe's student house) backing onto unkempt grass and bushes, and illustrated the house's aging paint, including a line across the building above the back door where the paint gave way to bare plaster. Introducing the picture, Joe said, 'I'm not really sure why I took this.' However, he continued to reflect on the image, saying, 'I don't think I ever considered how tall the house actually was.' The response then continued as follows, as Joe latched onto a meaning in the image:

Figure 6.1 Joe's house.

I feel like I know why I took it because this line here, I saw it as this is a sort of level of my personality that never really leaves the house … so I have like the surface levels of me that go out and go function and then because this is the basement so this is where we all get really drunk and really loud and rowdy… Yes, I rarely leave the house because I am so fond of my house mates.

These reflections illustrate the 'can-opening' potential of photo-elicitation, discussed by Leonard and McKnight (2015), and the importance of reflecting on the mundane – so well established in diary-research (Allen, 2012). Here the combination of self-taken mundane image and reflective interview drew out a deep narrative, which focused on the symbolic content of the picture, taking the discussion further and deeper. This journey through description to reflection was possible due to the dual role of creator and interpreter that participant generated photo-elicitation allows, a dual role which is to some extent recognised in diary research – for example in Milligan, Bingley and Gatrell's (2005) reflection on the diary as a place of record and reflection. Here, however the duality of intimate and distant is particularly clear. Joe identifies the image as picturing his life as it was created/taken by him, but it is through the interpretation of the image as a more distant observer, distanced from the memory of the initial stimulus for the image's creation, but remaining connected to it as an illustration of lived experience, that the intimate meaning of home and friendship emerges.

This emergent narrative from house to the experience of home and friendship developed across the interview but emerged initially in response to this image. The episodic emergence of a connected narrative is seen in Joe's response to the next, seemingly unconnected picture.

Unexpected flows

Joe's second photograph (see Figure 6.2) is an everyday picture of nature and includes a stream and five small swans swimming between two larger swans. This time Joe began his response to the image by suggesting that its inclusion may have been a mistake and not meant for inclusion in the submission. However, he reflected upon the natural imagery in the photo, and discussed how it may have been taken to sum up the way he feels about being at university in a place that is commonly viewed as picturesque, accessing the kind of everyday mundane experience which Kenten (2010) identifies solicited diaries as accessing. Once again Joe latched on to symbolic content. He said:

> I think this was just a reflection on the whole sort of family unit, and I feel like the one at the back is very reflective of my dad, who is not quite there with the whole transition thing. He's just not. Like on Father's Day I was still getting texts from him saying 'she' and 'her' and calling me that name.

This photo and the resultant discussion re-engage with the idea of unexpected connections. While there is a clear everyday diarying present in this example as discussed above, the diarying most present is the reflexive narrative that emerges from the photo. This narrative flows through discussions of mistaken inclusion, through the beauty of the local area, and into a deeper reflection on the experience of difference and distance from family. While experiences with family may often be present in research around LGBTQ lives, this example was clearly

Figure 6.2 Joe's swan picture.

emergent from, and encouraged by, the symbolism of the photograph, and Joe's reflections upon it. Such reflection is widely recognised in diary and diary-interview research, Lewis, Sligo and Massey (2005) for example draw out how the diary-interview approach encourages a form of reflection on experience not always accessible to other methods. For Harvey (2011) the diary-interview has a confessional quality – encouraging deeper telling through reflection. Joe's reflections illustrate a similar deepening narrative in response to his images.

Joe's reflections are also interesting here in the way they challenge and expand expectations around the boundaries of 'the higher education experience', Joe draws in the importance and relevance of both the surrounding area, and the impact of family relationships on his higher education experience – emphasising the importance of centring student experience and reflection in discussions of the higher education experience. Joe's narrative also illustrates the relevance of diarying as a way of more holistically understanding the higher education experience.

It is also important to recognise the interconnections of the episodic nature of the photo-elicitation method which this example reflects. Joe's discussions of his distance from family, which emerged from this photograph, led to Joe again emphasising the importance of his close friendships which had previously been discussed in response to the photograph of his student house.

The above example illustrates the power of photo-based research to see meaning in everyday detail and to take research to places it may not otherwise reach (Van Auken, Frisvoll & Stewart, 2010). It also illustrates the diverse potential of images (Leonard & McKnight, 2015), and the flexibility of boundaries (here in terms of the higher education context). These reflections also emphasise the importance of the interview aspect of elicitation research because, as discussed by Samuels (2004), these discussions allow participants to reflect upon *their* lives and draw out *their* readings of the images *they* have taken.

Meaning through distance

The final image (see Figure 6.3) analysed here is one which centralises the co-presence of intimacy and distance in the photo-elicitation method. In doing so it once again reflects upon the importance of giving space to reflections on everyday contexts, things and experiences (Kenten, 2010). The image was a picture of Shaun's (a trans man) room in university accommodation. Again, the photograph was introduced as one that had been forgotten. Shaun said, 'I don't know why I took a picture of it ...', illustrating his dual presence as creator and observer. Shaun recognises his image, and his life, but he is revisiting it as a more distant observer. Shaun continued, saying:

> It looks like my sanctuary a little bit. Oh, yes, I'm guessing here ... You know, the place where I can sit in my pyjamas and read a book ... My bed for some

Figure 6.3 Shaun's room.

reason is my sanctuary ... It's nice and comfortable and you can snuggle up in there ... It's like a special place but also on a bad day it can be like a prison, which is very sad.

Looking as an observer into the space which is recognised as his own leads Shaun to reflect deeply on the meaning of the space for the self that took the picture. The narrative is presented at a distance by using the language of 'guessing', but in doing so includes claimed experiences (sanctuary and prison) which reflect the extremes of the potential meaning of the space – perhaps the inherent distance making such confession more accessible and expressible. The recognition of the dual role of the participant as creator and interpreter also draws to the fore Harper's (2002) and Samuels's (2004) discussions of 'breaking the frame'. The framing of the room present in the picture (a forgotten framing), allows for Shaun to reframe his reflections, to look from a different perspective – differentiated by time and context. Again, we can see the diary-like quality of photo-elicitation. Here this self-reflection is reminiscent of the experiences reported by Lewis, Sligo and Massey (2005) and Harvey (2011), however here there is something specifically enabling about the recognised symbolic power of the image (something Harrington and Schibik (2003) emphasise in their discussion of freshman experience) – encouraging the symbolic turn in Shaun's reflections.

Shaun's discussions illustrate how the research accessed the everyday through the intimacy of the visual, but also allowed the distance of time and context to facilitate depth of discussion. They also illustrate the ability of the form to access challenging and difficult experiences by using photographs to encourage and develop such discussions (Joy & Numer, 2017; Witcomb, Brophy & McDermott, 2019).

Concluding thoughts

The discussion in this chapter has drawn together reflections from literature and experience to explore the benefits of participant-generated photo-elicitation to higher education research. In so doing, the chapter sought to add to contributions elsewhere in this volume by reflecting on these benefits in terms of 'diarying'. The chapter argued that participant generated photo-elicitation in the form undertaken was a method which allowed participants to diary their experiences. Specifically, this diarying can be seen in the way the method allowed access to the everyday – similar to the representations of everyday lives found in time-use diaries, and reflective narratives – similar to those accessed by the reflexive diaries. Photo-elicitation also develops such diarying with the inclusion of the visual, bringing varied mediums into research to more appropriately reflect the various textures of everyday life, and to encourage reflection and reminiscing.

Specific to the context of higher education, the example images included show the ability of photo-elicitation to access the diverse everyday contexts of higher education experiences, and to elicit narratives which are deep, varied and personal. From the first image's emergent narrative of self and friendship, through the discussion of family and the need for space in relation to the second image, into the third image's reflection on the varied and extreme meanings of personal space, the discussions highlight the power of photo-elicitation to engage with and develop the reach of higher education research. These possibilities – present due to the co-existence of the roles of creator of the image (presenting everyday experience), and interpreter of the image (reflexively narrating and interpreting the image), allowed for unexpected flows to emerge.

Despite the clear benefits of diary methods generally, and here participant generated photo-elicitation particularly, the methods remain underutilised in higher education research. It is hoped the contributions in this volume, and the reflections in this chapter, can encourage researchers to consider diary methods in order to allow the everyday and the personal to continue to be present and to emerge more fully in discussions of higher education.

Acknowledgements

Michael Keenan would like to thank the Society for Research into Higher Education for their generous funding of the research project 'Exploring LGBTQ Diversity in Higher Education: Extending Research into LGBTQ Student Experience' (Annual Award 2016) which is the basis for the included chapter. Michael would also like to thank all the participants in this research for their engagement, time, effort and creativity. Finally, Michael would like to thank the editors of this volume for their encouragement and helpful comments.

References

Ahmed, S. (2007) 'You end up doing the document rather than doing the doing': Diversity, race equality and the politics of documentation. *Ethnic and Racial Studies*, 30, 4: 590–609.

Allen, L. (2012) 'Picture this': Using photo-methods in research on sexualities and schooling. *Qualitative Research*, 11, 5: 487–504.

Anderson, P. & Green, P. (2012) Beyond CV building: The communal benefits of student volunteering. *Voluntary Sector Review*, 3, 2: 247–256.

Balloo, K., Pauli, R. & Worrell, M. (2017) Undergraduates' personal circumstances, expectations and reasons for attending university. *Studies in Higher Education*, 42, 8: 1373–1384.

Bosse, J. D. & Chiodo, L. (2016) It is complicated: Gender and sexual orientation identity in LGBTQ youth. *Journal of Clinical Nursing*, 25, 23–24: 3665–3675.

Daum, T., Buchwald, H., Gerlicher, A. & Birner, R. (2019) Times have changed: Using a pictorial smartphone app to collect time-use data in rural Zambia. *Field Methods*, 31, 1: 3–22.

Formby, E. (2015) # *FreshersToFinals: From freshers' week to finals: Understanding LGBT+ perspectives on, and experiences of, higher education*. Sheffield: Sheffield Hallam University.

Garcia, B., Welford, J. & Smith, B. (2016) Using a smartphone app in qualitative research: The good, the bad and the ugly. *Qualitative Research*, 16, 5: 508–525.

Guell, C. & Ogilvie, D. (2015) Picturing commuting: Photovoice and seeking well-being in everyday travel. *Qualitative Research*, 15, 2: 201–218.

Gunthert, K. C. & Wenze, S. J. (2012) Daily diary methods. In M. R. Mehl & T. S. Conner (eds), *Handbook of research methods for studying daily life*. Guilford: The Guilford Press, pp. 144–159.

Harper, D. (2002) Talking about pictures: A case for photo elicitation. *Visual Studies*, 17, 1: 13–26.

Harvey, L. (2011) Intimate reflections: Private diaries in qualitative research. *Qualitative Research*, 11, 6: 664–682.

Heath, M. A. (2005) Pronouncing the silent 'B' (in GLBTTIQ). *Gay and Lesbian Issues and Psychology Review*, 1, 3: 88–92.

Harrington, C. E. & Schibik, T. J. (2003) Reflexive photography as an alternative method for the study of the freshman year experience. *NASPA Journal*, 41, 1: 23–40.

Hyers, L. L., Swim, J. K. & Mallett, R. K. (2006) The personal is political: Using daily diaries to examine everyday prejudice-related experiences. In S. N. Hesse-Biber & P. Leavy (eds), *Emergent methods in social research*. London: Sage, pp. 313–329.

Joy, P. & Numer, M. (2017) The use of photo elicitation to explore the benefits of queer student advocacy groups in university. *Journal of LGBT Youth*, 14, 1: 31–50.

Kenten, C. (2010) Narrating oneself: Reflections on the use of solicited diaries with diary interviews. *Forum: Qualitative Social Research*, 11, 2: article 16.

Lalloo, C., Jibb, L. A., Rivera, J., Agarwal, A. & Stinson, J. N. (2015) There's a pain app for that. *The Clinical Journal of Pain*, 31, 6: 557–563.

Leonard, M. & McKnight, M. (2015) Look and tell: Using photo-elicitation methods with teenagers. *Children's Geographies*, 13, 6: 629–642.

Lewis, K., Sligo, F. & Massey, C. (2005) Observe, record, then beyond: Facilitating participant reflection via research diaries. *Qualitative Research in Accounting & Management*, 2, 2: 216–229.

MacFarlane, D., Grieves, L. & Zwiers, A. (2014) One step at a time: Moving trans activism forward in a large bureaucracy. In D. Irving & R. Raj (eds), *Trans activism in Canada: A reader*. Toronto: Canadian Scholars Press, pp. 195–207.

Mannay, D. (2010) Making the familiar strange: Can visual research methods render the familiar setting more perceptible? *Qualitative Research*, 10, 1: 91–111.

Marks, L. (2002) *Touch: Sensuous theory and multisensory media*. Minnesota, MN: University of Minnesota Press.

Mathison, S. (2012) Seeing is believing: The credibility of image-based research and evaluation. In J. Hughes (eds), *Sage visual methods*, volume 2, London: Sage, pp. 181–196.

Meo, A. I. (2010) Picturing students' habitus: The advantages and limitations of photo-elicitation interviewing in a qualitative study in the city of Buenos Aires. *International Journal of Qualitative Methods*, 9, 2: 149–171.

Metcalfe, A. S. (2016) Visual methods in higher education. In F. Stage & K. Manning (eds), *Research in the college context: Approaches and methods*, 2nd edition. Abingdon: Routledge, pp. 111–127.

Milligan, C., Bingley, A. & Gatrell, A. (2005) Digging deep: Using diary techniques to explore the place of health and well-being amongst older people. *Social Science & Medicine*, 61, 9: 1882–1892.

Richard, V. M. & Lahman, M. K. (2015) Photo-elicitation: Reflexivity on method, analysis, and graphic portraits. *International Journal of Research & Method in Education*, 38, 1: 3–22.

Samuels, J. (2004) Breaking the ethnographer's frames: Reflections on the use of photo elicitation in understanding Sri Lankan monastic culture. *American Behavioral Scientist*, 47, 12: 1528–1550.

Schreiber, M. (2015) 'The smartphone is my constant companion': Digital photographic practices and the elderly. In L. Krampet al. (eds), *Journalism, representation and the public sphere*. Bremen: Edition Luminaire, pp. 105–115.

Silver, J. & Reavey, P. (2010) 'He's a good-looking chap ain't he?': Narrative and visualisations of self in body dysmorphic disorder. *Social Science & Medicine*, 70, 10: 1641–1647.

Van Auken, P. M., Frisvoll, S. J. & Stewart, S. I. (2010) Visualising community: Using participant-driven photo-elicitation for research and application. *Local Environment*, 15, 4: 373–388.

Wagaman, M. A. (2016) Self-definition as resistance: Understanding identities among LGBTQ emerging adults. *Journal of LGBT Youth*, 13, 3: 207–230.

Witcomb, G. L., Brophy, H. & McDermott, H. (2019) More than meets the eye: A photo-elicitation study of gender (dis) affirmation in seven gender non-conforming university students. *Psychology*, 10, 12: 1599–1614.

Chapter 7

Reactivity, rationality, emotion and self-protection

Critical reflections on the use and potential of diaries in research on higher education choice and decision-making

Zoe Baker

Introduction

Drawing on data from an Economic and Social Research Council (ESRC) funded study on Further Education (FE) students' higher education (HE) decision-making and choice trajectories, this chapter critically reflects on the use of event-based diary methods in this context. Over the past 10 years, there has been increased political attention paid to students' HE choices in England. The release of the 'Students at the Heart of the System White Paper' (BIS, 2011) by the Coalition government not only trebled the tuition fee cap to £9000, but also heightened attention to the types of information available to prospective students to aid them in making their HE choices and decisions. This brought about the introduction of Key Information Sets (KIS) (HEFCE, 2012) – information documents made available online for each HE course (Unistats.gov, 2012[1]); these provide statistical information on student satisfaction, the destinations of graduates and expected future salaries. Commentators have suggested that these developments frame students as rational 'consumers' (Hart, 2013; Molesworth et al., 2011), who are expected to make their HE decisions and choices based on this information alone. This chapter shows how this political context shaped participants' diary entries, with instances of 'reactivity' emerging in how they presented their choice and decision making processes, framing these as 'rational' in line with political representations of the 'student chooser'.

The chapter also considers that such demonstrations of reactivity in participant diaries appeared to overshadow the role of 'emotion' in their HE choices and decision-making. This is particularly important, as emotional responses to HE institutions have been noted to play an important role in these processes; they can aid prospective students to understand whether they 'fit' into an institutional environment (Allen, 2002; Diamond et al., 2012), which can subsequently reduce the risk of drop-out later (Thomas, 2002). Moreover, one commonly cited strength of the diary method is its ability to incite more emotive accounts from participants than what may be shared in interview (Braun et al., 2017; Day & Thatcher, 2009). Yet, reactivity may negate this strength.

Finally, the chapter considers the ethical implications of tracking decisions and choices over time using the event-based diary method, particularly when emotional investment in HE plans increased over time. Recording HE decisions and choices over time in a format where prior hopes and plans can be revisited and reflected upon at will led some participants to demonstrate psychosocial processes of self-protection when these were later not realised (Alicke and Sedikides, 2009). The relationship between the diary method and such psychosocial responses is relatively under researched; this is reflected upon at the end of the chapter when considering the potential value of the diary method in other areas of HE research.

Recording HE decision-making and choice processes: reflecting on 'reactivity', emotion and ethics in diary methods

Before critically reflecting on the event-based diary method in the context of this research, it is important to consider how 'reactivity' may occur, how this has implications for the presentation of emotion in diary entries, and finally, how emotional responses raise questions around research ethics, with reference to the literature. Reactivity involves participants 'doing what they think the researcher expects them to do or what will please the researcher' (Given, 2008, p. 730). While the research itself did not provide analytical attention to 'reactivity', it is notable to discuss whether requesting participants to focus on, and record decisions and choices in a diary, could in itself influence such processes. This could potentially affect their decisions and choices in unique ways that may not have occurred if participants were experiencing these processes 'organically' (i.e. not keeping a continuous account of each decision and choice that could then be revisited and reflected on at will).

There has been relatively little work on the reactive impacts on individuals documented in diary research. Yet, levels of impact may be associated with the amount of structure provided to participants in diary keeping. In literature reviewed by Reis and Gosling (2010), they conclude that diary methods pose little to no risk of reactivity arising. However, the highly structured format of the diaries in the studies they reviewed may have dampened the effects of reactivity; these consisted of quantitative mood rating forms (Thomas & Diener, 1990), and structured 'logs' to record alcohol addiction relapse (Litt et al., 1998). Hence, these studies employed a highly structured diary format; 'logging' or 'rating' rather than *reflecting* may decrease the intensity of reactivity, as there is less space to contemplate events and experiences along with their implications and impacts.

Reactivity in terms of participant perceptions, and positive behaviour change is evident in some studies adopting more 'open' diary formats which encourage reflection. For example, in Merrilees et al.'s (2008) study on marital conflict which involved participants completing event-based diaries – requiring 'participants to provide reports at every instance that meets the researcher's pre-established definition' (Bolger et al., 2003, 590) – they identified changes in husbands' perceptions of marital quality over time. Furthermore, Stopka et al.'s (2004) study of syringe access and HIV risk among drug users resulted in positive behaviour changes among participants, with a reduction in drug use being noted alongside their daily, qualitative diary-keeping. Therefore, there is an apparent link between diaries that encourage *reflection* via more unstructured formats, and changes in behaviour as a result of this reflection (Reid et al., 2011).

Reflecting on the above literature and considering the use of qualitative event-based diaries (Bolger et al., 2003; Chapter 2, this volume) in the context of HE decision-making and choice research, there may be greater potential for reactivity to be initiated due to the level of reflection required. Documenting decisions and choices involves recounting reflexive processes (Archer, 2003) which can lead to (a) more questioning of them, and (b) attempts to adhere to 'rational' decision-making processes which can subsequently suppress the role of emotion and affective 'gut' feelings. Additionally, the process of diarising decisions and choices is likely to create more 'awareness' of these among participants (Merrilees et al., 2008) which could lead to changes in behaviour (Reid et al., 2011). In asking that participants record events, experiences and thoughts related to their decision-making in a space that is (for the duration of the research) private to them, and able to be reflected on and revisited at will, this may work to shape decisions in a way that may not have occurred had the diary method not been adopted.

In providing increased attention and focus to their HE choice and decision-making processes, as well as attempting to articulate these in diary form, it is possible that participants may represent these as more 'rational'. Consequently, as noted above, this could result in emotional aspects of these processes being downplayed. This is necessary to consider for a number of reasons. First, a frequently reported strength of the diary method in qualitative inquiry is that this can elicit more emotional accounts from participants (Braun et al., 2017; Day, 2016); this is thought to be a result of the sense of 'privacy' that diaries can create, meaning that participants feel more comfortable recording feelings and experiences that they could find difficult to disclose in interview (Day & Thatcher, 2009; Chapter 11, this volume). Second, research into HE decision-making and choice has highlighted that this process is strongly influenced by emotion. To briefly summarise, scholars have found that emotional investment in particular HE institutions is necessary for prospective students to understand how likely they are to 'fit' in to these environments before committing to apply (Allen, 2002; Diamond et al., 2012). The way that reactivity could potentially overshadow emotion in choice and decision-making processes could therefore negate the strengths of the diary method, and reduce opportunities for the multifaceted nature of these processes to be captured.

It is also essential to consider the potential negative impacts of documenting emotions in diaries from an ethical standpoint. Literature has reported that diarising emotions in research can lead to positive outcomes, such as changes in behaviour and benefits to physical and mental health (Stopka et al., 2004). Others, however, have found that writing about emotions can cause distress, though, this is short-lived (Smyth, 1998). Yet, in considering the diary method in the context of choice

and decision-making research, a more specific ethical concern is the potential negative emotional consequences of being able to reflect on intended decisions and
choices that were ultimately not realised. This is possibly a more pronounced risk in
research utilising the diary method, as participants have the ability to easily access
their past accounts and reflect on these. There are limited insights into this idea in the
methods literature. Though drawing on concepts from the field of social psychology,
specifically those exploring psychological 'self-defence' processes (Alicke & Sedikides,
2009; Schüz & Schüz, 2017), is particularly fruitful in exploring how being able to
revisit unfulfilled plans can affect participants' well-being and perceptions of the self
(Sherman & Cohen, 2006; Steele, 1988).

Capturing HE decision-making and choice narratives through event-based diaries

The focus of this study was, in part, inspired by changes to the English HE sector
in 2012, which led to policy discourses that positioned students as making indivi-
dualised, rational, and consumer-driven educational choices (Molesworth et al.,
2011). The research empirically and conceptually explored 16–19-year-old English
Further Education students' HE decision-making and choices over the duration of
their post-16 studies. The study hoped to identify students' reasons and influences
informing their decisions to progress, or not to progress to HE, as well as their
choice of HE institution and degree course. Conceptually, the research sought to
explore to what extent these choice and decision-making processes were propelled
by agency and constrained by structure. A qualitative longitudinal narrative inquiry
approach was taken to capture how FE students' HE choices and decisions were
made, how they changed over time, and what had influenced such changes. Two
methods were employed to explore participants' narratives; semi-structured interviews and focus groups were conducted, on average, once every three months over
an 18-month period (April 2014 to October 2015), and event-based diaries
(Bolger et al., 2003) were completed alongside these. Participants' event-based
diaries were handed in at the end of the data collection period for analysis after
taking part in their final interview/focus group.

Event-based (or 'event-contingent') diaries were deemed to be the most fitting
approach to diary-keeping in line with the research focus. As noted earlier, an
event-based schedule requires 'participants to provide reports at every instance
that meets the researcher's pre-established definition' (Bolger et al., 2003, p. 590);
the 'pre-established definition' here consisted of participants' plans, decisions,
choices and thoughts about life after FE, as well as any experiences or influences
that led to these. As the diaries were intended to capture qualitative accounts of
thoughts and experiences in relation to participants' HE decision-making and
choices, these were ideally aligned to an event-based schedule. Both written and
audio diary formats were offered to participants to increase accessibility (Worth,
2009). Yet, only 4 of the 13 participants accepted the offer of an audio diary, and
just one was returned completed. The diaries worked to provide a continuous

narrative picture of participants' decision-making and choices *over time*, as entries were able to be made in between periodic interviews and focus groups.

Diaries were returned at the end of the data collection period, and were empirically and conceptually analysed. When diaries were retrieved from participants, an analytical 'cut' was made at every three-month point, where possible, in order to mimic the analysis of the interview and focus group transcripts. A 'cut' involved grouping three consecutive months of each participants' diary entries together for analysis, separating them from the following three-month period and so forth. This resonates with Archer's (2010) work, as she contends that temporality is an essential part of the reflexive process. In light of this, she explains that an 'analytical cut' in time is required to allow analysis to take place, asserting that '[i]t is only by separating them in this way that the influences of the past upon the present can be identified and the effects of the present upon the future can be determined' (Archer, 2010, p. 4). In making this quarterly 'cut', the diary entries provide progressive 'snapshots' of how participants deliberated their HE decision-making and choices over time.

Reactivity, rationality, emotion and ethics

Having reflected on the literature to provide insights into how the event-based diary method may have implications for reactivity, emotion and ethics, specifically in the context of HE choice and decision-making research, the remainder of this chapter draws on diary data to consider these themes in more depth. First, the relationship between reactivity and 'rational' HE decision-making in participants' diaries is explored. Following this, the effectiveness of adopting the diary method longitudinally to capture emotion, and potentially 'override' reactivity, is discussed. Finally, the ethical implications of utilising event-based diaries to capture participants' decision-making and choices over time are considered. This discussion focuses on how the ability for participants to reflect on ideal choices and decisions that are sometimes later unfulfilled can lead to 'self-protection' responses, indicating threats to participants' sense of well-being.

Reactivity and 'rational' higher education decision-making

Utilising an event-based diary method to explore HE decision-making and choices in a context where policy discourse portrays these as 'rational' may lead participants to represent them in line with these. As previously discussed, the present study was undertaken in a context where HE policy positioned students as rational consumers (Molesworth et al., 2011); students are framed as having the ability to make rational HE decisions based on the information provided by KIS (Hart, 2013), and other forms of 'cold knowledge' (Ball & Vincent, 1998) – that is, information obtained via prospectuses, websites and league tables instead of direct experience (or 'hot knowledge'). Interestingly, participants' diaries reflected more 'rational' choice and decision-making processes in the early stages of the data collection period; this was presented in participants' diaries by them weighing up 'pros and cons' of various HE institutions and degree programmes, and identifying 'cold knowledge' as playing an especially large role in their initial choices.

The similarities between participants' HE choice and decision-making narratives, and policy representations of students as rational consumers based on the provision of 'cold' knowledge (such as KIS and Unistats), may potentially be indicative of reactivity. Participants may have thought that this approach to their HE choice and decision-making was what others 'expected' of them, leading them to convey these processes as 'rational' and instrumental.

Another interpretation that is notable to consider is that this could evidence how macro-level discourses manifest at the local level of individual experience. Yet, even this interpretation could be an outcome of reactivity in this context; policy representations of the rational student chooser could certainly influence what is perceived as the 'right' way to make HE decisions and choices among students. As detailed earlier in this chapter, the KIS and the host website for this (Unistats) emerged as a result of the Students at the Heart of the System White Paper (BIS, 2011). Thus, the availability of such a tool could reasonably lead students to conclude that this is essential to use. Both of these interpretations though could indeed be mutually reinforcing; if reactivity influenced students to make their decisions and choices in this 'rational' way, it is the policy context which created the conditions for this. This policy context then positions the 'rational' approach as the 'right' approach. Hence, reactivity may act as a means of facilitating macro-level discourses to emerge at the local level. This would be especially beneficial to inquiry that seeks to explore relationships between individuals, society, culture and context.

If reactivity then acted as a means of facilitating students to employ the 'rational' HE decision-making and choice approaches espoused in policy, a danger of this is the impact this could have on downplaying or suppressing the role of emotion in these processes. While it is beyond of the scope of this chapter to present an in-depth discussion of the role of emotion in decision-making and choices, it is important to highlight that despite emotions traditionally being viewed as negatively interfering with decisions (Vohs et al., 2007), they have since been concluded to be beneficial in making *complex* decisions (Mikels et al., 2011).

Reactivity as reducing the space for diarising emotions

As discussed earlier, emotion has been cited in HE choice and decision-making research as playing an important role in this process, providing prospective students an indication of how well they 'fit' with institutional cultures and environments (Allen, 2002; Diamond et al., 2012). In the context of the present study, engaging with rational-focused choice and decision-making may subsequently cast emotions aside, leading to a less than ideal outcome. Interestingly though, emotion became increasingly more prevalent in participants' diaries *after* they had submitted their Universities and Colleges Admissions Service (UCAS) applications. This was represented by entries where participants considered whether they could 'see themselves' at the institutions they had applied to, and presented this as an affective experience (see Baker, 2019a).

The way that emotion featured in participants' diaries more frequently over time adds further weight to the proposal that 'rational' depictions of HE decision-making and choice are an outcome of reactivity. Given (2008, p. 730) explains that over time, 'habituation' occurs as a result of the 'development of rapport and trust between participants and the researcher', leading to a reduction in reactive behaviour. Hence, this shift from rational to emotional accounts of decision-making and choice may then be a result of increased rapport and trust between the participants and myself. This, however, has implications for validity, or rather, 'truthfulness' – as is typically used as an alternative criterion for appraising qualitative research (Lincoln & Guba, 1985). What may appear as 'reactivity' here may be social desirability arising from a lack of familiarity with the researcher (Polkinghorne, 2007). Yet, when reflecting on the issue of 'truthfulness' in qualitative research, Sikes (2000, p. 267) concludes that 'our data were true in that it reflected our informants' perspectives at the time they told their stories'. The presence of more 'rational' accounts of HE decision-making and choice could well have been the participants' 'truth' in the earlier stages of these journeys; in making these educational decisions for the first time in their lives, their initial approach could understandably have been heavily influenced by policy representations of 'student choosers', who compare and contrast information sources (such as KIS) in a rational and instrumental manner.

The longitudinal approach taken in this research provided the opportunity for the emotional aspects of participants' HE choices and decision-making to emerge; it therefore enabled multifaceted experiences of these processes to be captured. Had the research taken a cross-sectional approach, for example, it would have presented a more limited picture of the participants' choice and decision-making journeys. The sharing of emotional responses to their choices and decision-making later on was not only reflected in participants' diaries, but also voiced in interviews and focus-groups too. Longitudinal approaches could therefore help to overcome 'reactivity' generally, and provide the space to achieve a more 'truthful' picture overall. This is not to say that participants were intentionally 'deceitful' when presenting rational approaches to their HE choices and decision-making at the outset of the research. Rather, if these 'rational' accounts were an example of reactivity caused by social desirability, *or* a subconscious process whereby participants reflected macro-level policy discourses in their everyday choice and decision-making practices, the longitudinal approach resulted in this 'balancing out' by providing the time and space for a more intricate picture of these processes to emerge.

Diarising ideal choices and realised decisions: ethics, 'damage control' and outcomes

When considering the event-based diary method in the context of decision-making and choices, it is necessary to reflect on the ethical implications of requesting participants to keep a record of their hoped for or 'ideal' choices in a medium that they can revisit at will – particularly in cases where these were subsequently not realised. For a number of participants, there was a disconnection between these ideal choices and actual outcomes. This tended to occur when participants encountered structural constraints, namely financial, that prevented them from accessing their ideal choices. Being reminded of these ideal choices in cases where these were not realised could lead to distress (Baker, 2019b). It is important to note that while a number of ethical issues concerning diary completion were considered prior to undertaking the research, the specific issue of participant responses to 'ideal plans' and 'unrealised outcomes' was not anticipated in advance.

Participants reported that they revisited their prior diary entries, though they did not indicate that this was a negative experience; rather, they commented that it was useful to be reminded of when they had made particular decisions and choices. Yet, there was some evidence of 'self-protection' responses (Alicke & Sedikides, 2009) when ideal choices were not realised. 'Self-protection' – a concept in motivational psychology – is a means of individuals 'defending themselves against negative self-views' (ibid., p. 2). This is a psychological mechanism that arises when we do not have primary control – that is, the ability to change 'an objective state of affairs by taking effective or instrumental action' (ibid., p. 6). Self-protection occurs as a form of 'secondary control' where we may 'exaggerate the favourability of an event or characteristic, or to minimise its negativity' (ibid., p. 13). Participants who experienced structural constraints to the extent where this prevented them from pursuing their original HE choices tended to convey 'self-protection' through exaggerating the positive aspects of their final destinations; this is consistent with self-protection as a means of exerting secondary control. For instance, two participants – Sofia and John[2] – both had chosen to study at institutions abroad initially, and had noted this in their diaries:

I'm thinking of applying to [Australian institution] in [city] ... I would like to study adult or mental health nursing.

(John, diary entry, September 2014)

It's been a while, but a lot has happened since I have written last. Firstly I have picked 4 out of 7 choices they are:

- (London drama school)
- (Spanish Arts Institution) ...(Sofia, diary entry, October 2014)

However, financial constraints made this impossible for the participants to pursue. Following this realisation, John presented remaining in the UK to undertake his HE studies as a positive outcome, reasoning that this was 'nice and simple' in comparison to his initial 'ideal' choice of studying in Australia:

It was like 12 grand, 12 thousand dollars. That's a year, just for the course ... it'd be travelling into (Australian city) and finding my way around it was just, like, not bothered doing all that. Just, no, I'd rather just stay here where it's nice and simple.

(Interview, January 2015)

Similarly Sofia, who had hoped to study in Spain, encountered a limited set of HE options in the UK and was less than thrilled with the institution she was due to progress to. In response, she begins to emphasise the positive aspects of studying at this particular HE institution:[3]

I didn't know how to feel at first … but I've kind of warmed up to the idea so. I like where I'm living though, where I'm living is really nice so … like the people my mum knows who's been there, like they've said it's like absolutely amazing. Like they give you so many opportunities.

(Focus group, May 2015)

Literature in the field of social psychology regards such 'self-protection' measures as a form of damage control to enable individuals to maintain their sense of self-integrity and self-worth (Alicke & Sedikides, 2009; Steele, 1988). Although this may appear to perform a positive function on the surface, it has been noted that self-protection does not appear to bolster well-being (Schüz & Schüz, 2017).

The way that self-protection performs little function beyond 'damage control' is noteworthy when considering the ethical implications of the diary method. For instance, it can be questioned as to whether such psychological mechanisms would arise in the absence of a tool (the diary) which allows individuals to reflect back on unrealised ideal choices. Could repeat interviews utilised without the diary method result in similar responses? It is beyond the scope of this research to provide a definitive answer to this question. Though, there were some indications in the data that information disclosed in interview was more susceptible to being modified by memory in relation to participants' decision-making outcomes when these were not consistent with initial ideal choices. During an interview, John – who was studying a Business and Technology Education Council (BTEC) qualification in Health and Social Care – rejected the idea of pursuing a career in social work over nursing as he did not wish to work with children:

JOHN: I wanted to be a social worker when I first started this course.
ZB: Did you?
JOHN: And then I was just like 'I'd rather not'. Working with kids … it's more working with kids that have no respect for their elders or respect for authority.

(Interview, October 2014)

However, during a final follow-up phase of the research after participants had completed their FE courses, John (who was now employed as a Support Worker), explained that he was considering a career in social work. Interestingly, he states that he had mentioned this as a 'plan B' earlier in the research:

I recently had another interview for another job and after working with them for 12 months (children up to 18 with mental health issues and supporting them) they will put me in for a Social Worker degree which if I recall I mentioned as a plan B.

(Email follow-up, October 2015)

John had not included his original rejection of a career in social work in his diary. With this account only being shared during interview, it is plausible that it is more susceptible to being modified by memory. Such a modification in memory may mean that psychological damage control responses might not be triggered; rather, this could be more likely to occur when individuals are directly presented with a past narrative in a space (such as a diary) that is incompatible with their current perceptions, causing cognitive dissonance (Festinger, 1957) to arise.

The present study offers some insights into the potential of pursuing a line of inquiry focusing on such ethical implications of the event-based diary method. It would be insightful for future research to propose how discomfort at reflecting on 'ideal plans' that were unfulfilled could be ethically responded to by researchers. In this study, many of these tensions between 'ideal' and 'unrealised' plans were not identified until the analysis phase of the research, as participants were asked to hand in their diaries at the *end* of the data collection period. This meant that while verbal accounts of their HE decision-making and choices were being collected regularly, participants' diary entries were not seen by the researcher until data collection had been concluded. Hence, instances of 'self-protection' and modifications to memory could not be recognised and subsequently responded to while the research was ongoing. Nevertheless, what has been presented in this final section of the chapter positions the diary method as a useful means of data collection for areas of HE research that are likely to capture changes over time, and potentially pose contradictions; these may include explorations of 'aspirations' and 'transitions', and/or interdisciplinary inquiry integrating social psychology into educational research.

Concluding reflections: the value of the event-based diary method in HE research

Throughout this chapter, various aspects of using the event-based diary method have been reflected upon in the context of HE decision-making and choice research, and a number of insights have been put forward. These have consisted of diaries as a means of facilitating reactivity, a way of capturing emotion and finally, a potential cause of 'self-protection' responses and the ethical implications of this. Here, these are summarised, and key takeaways are provided on the value of utilising event-based diaries in HE research more broadly.

The reflections provided on 'reactivity' have suggested that this could be beneficial in some respects. As has been shown, reactivity can offer insights into how macro-level policy discourses are represented at the micro-level of everyday experiences. This is more likely to be accomplished, however, with diary methods that are more unstructured – such as event-based diaries – as opposed to highly structured logs and/or records. Macro-micro relationships cannot be captured without attention being provided to context when analysing diary data, and more unstructured formats can allow the level of detail needed to provide analytical attention to this. Employing both a more unstructured diary format, and considerations of context, can result in the diary acting as a means of facilitating reactivity. The identification of reactivity then offers opportunities to witness macro-micro level relationships. This is valuable for HE research that seeks to explore and understand macro-level impacts on micro-level experiences; this may include studies in the field of the sociology of education, and HE policy.

The data presented in this chapter has also highlighted how diaries can act as a useful tool for capturing emotion. This is more likely to be accomplished in research that adopts a longitudinal approach, as there are more opportunities to build a high level of rapport and trust between the researcher and participants. Gathering such data can assist in capturing complexity and depth in social phenomena, which is necessary for qualitative inquiry. In this research, being able to gather emotion-focused accounts worked to present a more complex picture of HE decision-making and choices. In the context of HE research more broadly though, there are a number of areas where emotion can influence action outside of decision-making and choices. For instance, explorations of student and/or staff experiences of HE cultures and environments. Hence, there is potential for the event-based diary method to be utilised in qualitative inquiry within the HE field where insights into emotion would be welcome.

Finally, ethical questions have been raised concerning the impact of diary keeping on participants' well-being. These concern the psychosocial consequences of participants being able to directly access and reflect upon past events, thoughts, and plans via their diaries. This has opened up some interesting insights into the applicability of the event-based diary method to future research in HE contexts. This includes studies on aspiration and transitions, where capturing changes in participants' plans and situations over time, as well as the impacts this may have on their thought processes and perceptions, may offer interesting interdisciplinary contributions to knowledge. These reflections have also highlighted another avenue for future research more generally; for instance, studies on the ethical implications of reflecting on the past in diary spaces would work to expand our understandings of best practice in utilising the diary method.

Acknowledgements

This study was carried out thanks to the financial support of the Economic and Social Research Council (grant reference: ES/J500215/1).

Notes

1 As of September 2019, Unistats has been replaced by 'Discover Uni' (OfS, 2019).
2 Pseudonyms have been assigned to all participants to maintain anonymity.
3 These aspects of John and Sofia's narratives are explored in more depth in Baker (2019b).

References

Alicke, M. C. & Sedikides, C. (2009) Self-enhancement and self-protection: What they are and what they do. *European Review of Social Psychology*, 20, 1: 1–48.

Allen, D. E. (2002) Toward a theory of consumer choice as sociohistorically shaped practical experience: The Fits-Like-A-Glove (FLAG) framework. *Journal of Consumer Research*, 28: 515–532.

Archer, M. S. (2003) *Structure, agency and the internal conversation.* Cambridge: Cambridge University Press.

Archer, M. S. (2010) Morphogenesis versus structuration: On combining structure and action. *The British Journal of Sociology*, 61, 1: 225–252.

Baker, Z. (2019a). The vocational/academic divide in widening participation: The higher education decision-making of further education students. *Journal of Further and Higher Education*, 44, 6: 766–780.

Baker, Z. (2019b) Priced out: The renegotiation of aspirations and individualized HE 'choices' in England. *International Studies in Sociology of Education*, 28, 3–4: 299–325.

Ball, S. J. & Vincent, C. (1998) I heard it on the grapevine: 'Hot' knowledge and school choice. *British Journal of Sociology of Education*, 19, 3: 377–400.

BIS (2011) *Higher education: Students at the heart of the system.* London: HMSO.

Bolger, N., Davis, A. & Rafaeli, E. (2003) Diary methods: Capturing life as it is lived. *Annual Review of Psychology*, 54, 1: 579–616.

Braun, V., Clarke, V. & Gray, D. (2017) *Collecting qualitative data: A practical guide to textual, media and virtual techniques.* Cambridge: Cambridge University Press.

Day, M. (2016) Documents of life: From diaries to autobiographies to biographical objects. In B. Smith & A. C. Sparkes (eds), *Routledge handbook of qualitative research in sports and exercise.* London: Routledge, pp. 177–188.

Day, M. & Thatcher, J. (2009) 'I'm really embarrassed that you're going to read this …': Reflections on using diaries in qualitative research. *Qualitative Research in Psychology*, 6, 4: 249–259.

Diamond, A., Vorley, T., Roberts, J. & Jones, S. (2012) *Behavioural approaches to understanding student choice.* York: The Higher Education Academy.

Festinger, L. (1957) *A theory of cognitive dissonance.* Stanford, CA: Stanford University Press.

Given, L. M. (2008) *The Sage encyclopaedia of qualitative research methods.* London: Sage.

Hart, C. S. (2013) *Aspirations, education and social justice: Applying Sen and Bourdieu.* London: Continuum International Publishing Group.

HEFCE (2012) Key information sets. Retrieved from www.hefce.ac.uk/whatwedo/lt/publicinfo/kis (accessed 7 August 2013).

Lincoln, Y. S. & Guba, E. G. (1985) *Naturalistic inquiry.* London: Sage.

Litt, M. D., Morse, P. & Cooney, N. L. (1998) Ecological momentary assessment (EMA) with treated alcoholics: Methodological problems and potential solutions. *Health Psychology*, 17, 1: 48–52.

Merrilees, C. E., Goeke-Morey, M. & Cummings, E. M. (2008) Do event-contingent diaries about marital conflict change marital interactions? *Behaviour Research and Therapy*, 46, 2: 253–262.

Mikels, J. A., Maglio, S. J., Reed, A. E. & Kaplowitz, L. J. (2011) Should I go with my gut? Investigating the benefits of emotion-focused decision-making. *American Psychological Association*, 11, 4: 743–753.

Molesworth, M., Scullion, R. & Nixon, E. (2011) *The marketization of higher education and the student as consumer*. Abingdon: Routledge.

OfS (2019) Discover Uni and Unistats. Retrieved from www.officeforstudents.org.uk/a dvice-and-guidance/student-information-and-data/discover-uni-and-unistats (accessed 31 December 2019).

Polkinghorne, D. E. (2007) Validity issues in narrative research. *Qualitative Inquiry*, 13, 4: 471–486.

Reid, L., Hunter, C. & Sutton, P. W. (2011) Rising to the challenge of environmental behaviour change: Developing a reflexive diary approach. *Geoforum*, 42: 720–730.

Reis, H. T. & Gosling, S. D. (2010) Social psychological methods outside the laboratory. In S. T. Fiske, D. T. Gilbert & G. Lindzey (eds), *Handbook of social psychology*. Hoboken, NJ: John Wiley & Sons, pp. 82–114.

Schüz, N. & Schüz, B. (2017) Self-affirmation: Protecting the self and protecting subjective well-being. In M. D. Robinson & M. Eid (eds), *The happy mind: Cognitive contributions to well-being*. Cham: Springer, pp. 291–310.

Sherman, D. K. & Cohen, G. L. (2006) The psychology of self-defense: Self-Affirmation theory. *Advances in Experimental Social Psychology*, 38: 183–242.

Sikes, P. (2000) 'Truth' and 'Lies' Revisited, *British Educational Research Journal*, 26, 2: 257–270.

Smyth, J. M. (1998) Written emotional expression: Effect sizes, outcome types, and moderating variables. *Journal of Consulting and Clinical Psychology*, 66: 174–184.

Steele, C. M. (1988) The psychology of self-affirmation: Sustaining the integrity of the self. *Advances in Experimental Social Psychology*, 21: 261–302.

Stopka, T. J., Springer, K. W., Khoshnood, K., Shaw, S. & Singer, M. (2004) Writing about risk: Use of daily diaries in understanding drug-user risk behaviours. *AIDS and Behaviour*, 8, 1: 73–85.

Thomas, L. (2002) Student retention in higher education: The role of institutional habitus. *Journal of Education Policy*, 17, 4: 423–432.

Thomas, D. & Diener, E. (1990) Memory accuracy in the recall of emotions. *Journal of Personality and Social Psychology*, 59, 2: 291–297.

Unistats.gov (2012) The official website for comparing UK higher education course data. Retrieved from https://unistats.direct.gov.uk (accessed 8 October 2013).

Vohs, K. D., Baumeister, R. F. & Loewenstein, G. (2007) *Do emotions help or hurt decision-making? A Hedgefoxian perspective*. New York: Russell Sage Foundation.

Worth, N. (2009) Making use of audio diaries in research with young people: Examining narrative, participation and audience. *Sociological Research Online*, 14, 4.

Chapter 8

Telling their own story in their own way

Negotiating the ethics of a diary-like photo-elicitation method to capture faith and belief from students' own starting point

Sarah Lawther

Introduction

A participant-generated diary has the benefit of allowing mundane, everyday experiences to be collected in a day-to-day setting that may not be recalled using other research methods that involve retrospective reflection on experiences such as surveys and focus groups (Hyers et al., 2006). Diary method has the potential to encourage deep self-reflection (Chen et al., 2016) and to capture the everyday lives of participants that may otherwise be difficult to access (Hyers, 2018). It can therefore be particularly helpful to capture regular activities, and has been effectively used within higher education to gain a better understanding of students' behaviours: what they do, where and why (Beckers et al., 2016). Diary-like methods can also be useful to capture the complexity and intersectionality of the lives of young people as found by Taylor who used diary exercises as one method (among others) to capture 'insights into the everyday lives, practices, and identities of queer religious youth' (Taylor, 2016, p. 15). It offers the potential, argue Scott et al. (2012), to capture immediate and particular feelings and experiences from the students' own perspective including aspects of their life beyond university life.

This chapter focuses on a research project that used a diary-like photo-elicitation method that invited students to take photographs that capture their everyday beliefs and practices to explore religion and belief in higher education. The strength of this method is that it would allow the students to describe their experience from their own starting point. However, due to the visual nature of the method, there was an ethical tension between giving students that may feel unheard and invisible a voice and my responsibility as a researcher to protect the participants, particularly those that may feel conscious of their visibility and those that wish to keep their religious identity hidden. This ethical dimension, which largely centred around whether to anonymise the photographs in the dissemination of the findings, is explored in this chapter. What was seen is that students negotiated their own way through the research, creating and sharing their photographs on their own terms, ranging from the inclusion of selfies, to self-censored selfies, to withholding photographs altogether.

Contributing to existing research on religion and belief in higher education

Universities are increasingly striving to attract, retain and ensure good outcomes for, a diverse body of students and this is in part due to the competitive nature of higher education within England and its regulation by the Office for Students. Reflecting this, there is a growing amount of sector research to better understand what is working to support the retention, engagement and success of all students and it is recommended here that further attention needs to be paid to students' religion and belief and its impact on student engagement and success (Advance HE, 2018).

Large-scale research in this area has primarily focused on students and provision affiliated to a religious organisation (such as Guest et al., 2013; Aune, Guest and Law, 2019) but recent figures suggest that the religious landscape on campus is more diverse than this. When UK students were asked to declare their religious identity almost a third of those that responded answered 'no religion or belief' (31.1%), over a third (35.6%) refused this information or left this question blank, and those that declared a religious identity were as follows: Christian (23.1%), Muslim (5.2%), Hindu (1.3%), 'any other religion or belief' (1.2%), Spiritual (0.9%), Buddhist (0.9%), Sikh (0.5%) and Jewish (0.3%) (Advance HE, 2018, p. 12). Given this diversity it is recommended that universities consider their support for a range of religious identities, such as those with minority or non-religious beliefs (Advance HE, 2018).

However, focusing only on affiliation to a religion (or not) is just part of the picture. A 'lived religion' approach argues that focusing on those affiliated to a religion does not capture the less visible, individual and idiosyncratic nature of religious identity (Woodhead, 2012) nor the complexity of everyday experience and practice (McGuire, 2008). Individuals, for example, may not agree with the institutional beliefs of the religion that they are affiliated to, they may choose to engage with more than one religion, and their engagement with religion may change over time (McGuire, 2008). It does not capture, for example, that many young people are more likely to believe in the people and relationships around them, finding meaning and happiness from the everyday and the social (Day, 2010), nor does it capture activities such as gardening or meditation that may be seen as spiritual or religious by those engaged in them, even if they would not be defined as such by others (Ammerman, 2014). A lived religion approach therefore focuses on understanding individual's religion as experienced, expressed and practised in everyday life (McGuire, 2008). It is important then that universities *also* consider this breadth of individual experience and practice and how this fits in with students' university life.

This research study aimed to contribute here by starting from the students' individual experience rather than affiliation, to capture meaning-making as described by the students themselves, and takes a research approach that does not privilege any forms of meaning-making over others. The term 'meaning-making' (as used by

Guest, 2017) is used in this research to describe this breadth of experience that includes students' religion, belief, their everyday practices and where they find meaning. This study was particularly interested in understanding students' meaning-making practices, what they *do*, to capture and share these in order to inform policy and practice about how best to support students in their everyday lives.

Drawing upon diary research and photo-elicitation

The method drew upon both diary research and photo-elicitation in order to address several challenges in the design that arose due to the nature and context of the research. Changes in technology have allowed the development of diary-like digital methods that may appear to be very different to a traditional written diary, but this diary-like method can provide instant access to participant experience and voice (Hyers, 2018). In this study, students were invited to take between five and twelve photographs on their mobile phone, or more if they would like to, over a fortnight that captured their everyday beliefs and practices, how these relate to their student life, and what, if anything, these bring to their student experience. These were then discussed in a follow up interview. Hyers (2018) advises that the timing of solicited diary entries needs to take into account the goals of the study, the length of the project, and to balance these with the likelihood of participant attrition. It was decided that a two-week period would be sufficient to capture students' specific meaning-making activities, what they do on a daily basis, and that giving flexibility within this time would allow students to fit the research within their busy student lives. Photographs were chosen because taking and dis-cussing photographs involves a reflective process that has not only been found to be 'particularly helpful to uncover everyday taken for granted things in their research participants' lives' but also to encourage participants to articulate that which may 'usually remain implicit' (Rose, 2016, p. 316). It was hoped that this would therefore help to address the challenge that students may not be familiar with thinking about, or talking about, their meaning-making and that they may find this difficult to articulate because, as Woodhead (2012) argues, words have not kept up with the changing religious landscape, religion as it is lived today.

This method also offered the potential for students to be more in control of their participation in the research within the scope of this PhD project where there were not resources for a more participatory method such as photovoice (e.g. Martinez-Vargas et al., 2019; Chapter 4, this volume). This element of control was felt to be particularly important in a higher education context where students may feel exclu-ded and invisible, and that their voices need to be heard, 'their religious identity frequently unknown and unacknowledged on campus' as found by Stevenson (2017, p. 63). Bartlett, for example, found that using a diary interview method combined with participant observation to research people with Dementia allowed individuals 'control over the process and pace of data collection' (Bartlett, 2012, p. 1718). In the interview itself, the participant becomes the 'expert' rather than the researcher as they discuss their photographs (Rose, 2016). This method also has the potential to offer a voice for those that want to be seen and heard in the dissemination of the photographs that they have taken such as the 'Look at Me! Images of Women & Ageing Project' cited by Clark (2012). However, research has found that religious students can *also* feel highly visible on campus, 'under surveillance and positioned as potential threats' at the same time as being seen as 'both potential victims of violence and responsible for it' (Stevenson, 2017, p. 4) and the research design needed to be sensitive to this. Students may have experienced, or be fearful of, a hate incident because of their religious identity (NUS, 2012) and because universities are required to adhere to the Prevent duty which has been developed as part of the UK's counter terrorism strategy, religion and belief is often discussed in deficit terms, such as dealing with extremism on campus (Stevenson, 2017). The design also aimed to be sensitive to those students who may be choosing to keep their religious identity hidden from others, including their peers, while at university as found by Stevenson (2013) and Guest (2017).

Ethics in diary research

'The uniqueness of diary research', argues Hyers, 'raises equally unique ethical considerations' as it is potentially more intrusive given the personal and intimate nature of a diary, and consideration needs to be given to practical issues of where and how a diary is kept secure (Hyers, 2018, p. 163; see also Chapter 7, this volume). In this study, using photographs gave the participants a choice about how revealing they wanted their contribution to be: students were asked only to take photographs that they were comfortable having on their phone and had the option of taking pictures of places, objects and symbols rather than photographs of themselves. However, while using photographs in a diary avoids the difficulty of anonymising the 'thick description' of a written diary (Hyers, 2018, p. 167) it presents an ethical dilemma in cases where participants choose to take identifiable photographs.

An ethical dilemma

In this study the ethical dilemma largely centred around whether to anonymise the photographs in the dissemination of the findings: whether to give voice to the participants by showing their identifiable photographs or anonymising these in order to protect them. Here, the project drew upon visual research ethics in order to resolve this. While it has been argued that visual data is no more personal than textual data (Allen, 2015) it is the 'immediacy of visual data that raises particular challenges' (Wiles et al., 2012, p. 51). This issue of anonymity has been identified as the key issue within visual research ethics that currently 'remains contested and unresolved' (Wiles et al., 2012, p. 44). Plummer (2000) recommends that hearing others stories about how they have dealt with, as Punch (1994, p. 94) describes, the ethical 'swamp' of ethics within qualitative research that as yet has no map, can prove to be helpful in navigating one's own path through it. In this chapter then I will tell my story, how the ethical dilemma within this research was negotiated by myself in the research design, and then by the students who navigated this path in their own way.

At the heart of current debates within visual ethics is the view that ethical guidelines and frameworks originally derived from positivist, objectivist research may not be appropriate for visual research methods and indeed may limit the advantages of using such an approach (Clark, 2012). It has, argues Allen (2015), become assumed by ethics committees as the norm that anonymisation will be given in order to protect participants and any deviation from this is expected to be justified. Researchers may be less likely to be innovative in research design in order to gain ethical approval which may then compromise data collection and the potential knowledge gained from the research (ibid.). This 'ethics creep', the increasing regulation of ethics, as discussed by Allen is used to protect institutions from litigation and as well as stifling innovation can also lead to censorship in dissemination (ibid.).

Alongside this debate are those that address the practical challenges of conducting visual research ethically such as the issues surrounding informed consent, confidentiality and anonymity (Clark, 2012). Pragmatically, these needed to be negotiated in order to achieve the aims of the project and gain ethical approval while remaining sensitive to the experiences of the students. I first turned to the International Visual Sociology Association (IVSA) Code of Research Ethics and Guidelines which states as its primary goal the welfare and protection of participants. It also states that it supports the 'freedoms and integrity of research that uses visual media and images' (Papademas and the IVSA, 2009, p. 252) and that anonymity is not required in some cases such as participatory research where there is consent from individuals to use identifying information such as their names and visual representations (ibid.). There are, however, conflicting debates within visual research about whether to offer the choice for identification of images and how to protect participants here if consent is given.

Wiles et al. (2012) explored these differing views about how to manage ethical challenges within visual research (they term this 'visual ethics') in practice with experienced visual researchers. The disadvantage of not anonymising images, they argue, is that participants who consent to identifiable images being used may not fully understand what they are consenting to even if the research is fully explained to them and while it is the researcher's responsibility to make the participants aware of the short and long term risks of taking part, the researcher may not be able to predict all the consequences of their involvement (ibid.). This is particularly the case in visual research because the contexts in which images may be seen and interpreted may not always be within researcher's control, especially once images are available online (ibid). Once online the way that an image is used and seen cannot be controlled, and it may be taken out of context (Rose, 2016, p. 365). Anonymisation in this case would help to protect and 'future proof' participants from technologies such as face recognition software (Wiles et al., 2012). Participants may also change their mind about participation in the future and once published it becomes very difficult to remove images (ibid.).

If it is decided to anonymise images, thought needs to be given about how images are rendered unidentifiable. The association of using pixellation or a black bar across the face with criminality can result in what may have been a well-intentioned strategy to protect the participant 'being a form of "violation" or "violence", with a resultant objectification of respondents' (Wiles et al., 2012, p. 45). However, not including identifiable images at all means that the reader is reliant on the researcher's description alone and this, argues Allen (2015) reduces the integrity of the research as the researcher's analysis cannot be contested. Anonymisation also reduces the opportunity to experience the 'sense' of the photograph, and a compromise has been found of using the 'impressionist' blurring function in PowerPoint to give a sense of the image while concealing identity (Nolas, 2018) and which also avoids the issue of anonymising only faces.

Anonymising photographs, however, limits the potential for the participants to be seen, and this potential to offer visibility is one of the benefits of visual research. It may be that in the context where students may feel invisible and that their voices need to be heard that some students would choose to be seen and to take away this choice for identification would be unethical in itself (Wiles et al., 2012). It is argued here that the risks of using identifiable images have been overstated, and that to take away this choice disregards the autonomy of the participants who are not seen as equals with the capacity to give consent, and this can harm the participants' dignity and well-being (ibid.). Choosing to be identifiable in images can empower those involved and so offering this visibility may be particularly important for young people and stigmatised groups (ibid.) and a refusal to grant a participants request for identification can result in the silencing of their voice (Clark, Prosser and Wiles, 2010). It may also be the case that participants would choose to be identifiable because this is commonplace in their everyday life: to share and have their images seen and shared online. As Rose argues, ethical concerns of the visual researcher may be very different to ethical codes used in practice by the participants in their daily lives (Rose, 2016).

A situated ethics approach

Given these competing views and my dilemma about whether to offer the option of identification of the photographs to the participants I took a situated approach to ethics. This takes the approach that there is no one right way to making ethical decisions, rather that they should be determined according to each individual case (Clark, 2012). In this case, ethical decisions were made as part of an ongoing process of reflection that considered students' current experience within higher education, the research aim, and the purpose of the research, that is, to inform change that would benefit students.

As part of this reflective process two feed-forward interviews were conducted with undergraduate students while planning the research method in which I explained the ethical dilemma and asked for their views on this (one of these students went on to take part in the research). While both students believed that participants should be able to give consent for identifiable images to be used, their rationale reflecting much of the discussions above, one of the students who was conducting research himself also reflected that he could understand why this option may not be given:

> People are putting selfies on social media with no ethics and it is completely online, so they haven't got a problem putting it on Facebook or Instagram. Why would they have a problem putting it on a research project that they know will be for a target audience? ... But then ethics-wise I completely understand why we couldn't.

Given the context of the research in which students may be at risk of (and may be fearful of) discrimination, and that they may wish to keep their meaning-making hidden from their peers, it was decided that the priority was to protect the students so choice wasn't offered for identification in the overall dissemination of the findings. This also guarded against the risk that students may change their mind about participation in the future, and that their photographs may be taken out of context online. In order for the students' voices to be heard and to effectively 're-represent' the meanings intended by the participants direct quotations from the interviews will be used where possible to describe the photographs as recommended by Filep et al. (2017). It was also decided not to offer identification because anonymisation is particularly recommended in cases where sensitive data is discussed alongside images at an individual level as there is a greater potential of harm to participants' well-being than when description is at the higher level of overall themes (Wiles et al., 2012). In this case being able to illustrate what individual students do regularly as part of their meaning-making was an important part of the dissemination of the project, as it was hoped that this would be used to inform the support of future students, and so anonymity was important here.

While the choice was made not to offer the option for identification in order to protect students and to provide a method in which students felt most comfortable and safe to take part, I wanted to give as much choice as possible to students in how they *participated* in the research. The method was therefore designed to allow students the freedom to tell their stories in the way that they wanted to, and it was hoped that this would capture the individual nature of meaning-making as well as making taking part in the research more enjoyable for the students.

About the research and choices offered

A benefit of this method is that students could be given a choice about how they could interpret the instructions for the photographs. This choice was given due to the challenge of how to explain the focus of the research in a way that would be inclusive of a range of meaning-making, that wouldn't privilege some forms over others, and that would capture what students do on a daily basis. The photo instructions first explained the research context and aim, then highlighted the difficulty of finding the right words to include a range of beliefs and practices. Students were then given different suggestions about how 'everyday beliefs and practices' could be understood and invited to use their own understanding of these terms when taking the photographs.

The photograph instructions also offered students the choice to include selfies and add filters to their photographs. Selfies offer the opportunity for participants to show their everyday behaviours themselves, illustrating 'not only "see this, here, now," but also "see me showing you me."' (Frosh, 2015, p. 1610) so this option would give students additional agency, an opportunity to include themselves in sharing their voice, 'this is me telling you my story'. The benefit of students knowing that their photographs will be anonymised is that they will be less likely to pose for the camera (Plummer, 2000) so the instructions informed students that they would be given a choice about whether they would like their photographs to be used in dissemination of the research and that even if permission to use their photographs was given, identifying features would not be shown. Participants were asked not to take photographs of others as the focus of their pictures and to send the photographs to me, the researcher, by email with a signed consent form.

Seventeen students from one institution took part in the study with (self-declared) religious identities such as: Christian, Muslim, Buddhist, Agnostic, 'own belief' and 'belief in a higher being', capturing the complexity and uniqueness of the students' meaning-making. Students were then invited for an interview to discuss the photographs that they had taken, and where students had sent their photographs prior to the interview they were printed on A4 card and given to the students for them to keep. Students were then asked to discuss the images in their order of preference and to describe any photographs that they would have liked to have taken but didn't, a question previously used by Williams (2010) when using photo-elicitation to explore lived religion.

Students were given the option to consent to their photographs being used for analysis only (with the content described in dissemination) or to give consent for their (anonymised) photographs to be included in both analysis and dissemination. Students were also given the option to give consent for anonymised audio-clips of the interview to be used in dissemination and this was literally a way of giving voice to students when sharing their data. Students could also give permission to be contacted about the research in future, and this was included to enable a future option for those participants who may wish to be visible a voice by hosting a one-off exhibition of their photographs that would allow participants to share their photographs without the risks of showing them in electronic form. Ethical clearance was gained from the research institution prior to the start of the research.

Capturing the diversity of meaning-making

In the interviews, students spoke about meaning coming from a range of sources such as their religion and spirituality, from being connected with others such as friends and family, and developing themselves such as through overcoming challenges. The method has been particularly useful here to capture students' everyday practices, with all but one of the students interviewed describing regular activities that support their meaning-making such as prayer, studying religious teachings, volunteering, mindfulness and spending time in nature. These were primarily private practices, with the majority of students only talking about these with their close friends (if at all), and with students findings ways to do these discreetly on campus such as praying 'on the go' and getting to campus early to spend 'ten minutes before a lecture [to] go out to the foresty patch and just walk there'. The students also spoke about how their meaning-making supports their student experience, including for many, as a way to manage stress and improve their well-being.

Taking part on their own terms

What was seen in the research is that students negotiated their own way through the research by creating and sharing their photographs on their own terms to tell their own stories in their own way. Students often chose to talk about their photographs in order of importance rather than the sequence in which they took them, and one student, Natalie, stretched the time that her contribution captured, reflecting that 'these kind of photographs have almost shown my journey through [the university]'.

Students created their photographs at their own level of disclosure with eleven of the seventeen students including photographs of themselves to varying degrees: Oliver for example included only one selfie while all seven of Natalie's photographs were selfies. Of particular note here was that only one of the students who took a photograph that illustrated a practice associated with their religion chose to use a selfie (a photograph of herself and her family giving 'donations to the monks'), the rest of these students chose instead to take pictures of private spaces and objects such as: 'my prayer wall in my dorm', 'the mat for when you pray' and 'an app that has the Bible' suggesting that these are private activities. Two students, Gamila and Ana, self-censored their pictures in what Allen refers to as anonymisation through photocomposition (Allen, 2015). Gamila cropped her head from a selfie that illustrated that she is the only student on her course to wear a scarf: 'This is a picture of me showing my scarf because I am the only one who is wearing a scarf.' Ana censored both 'a picture of a yoga class' by taking the photograph at a distance from behind, and a picture of herself showing only her arm when giving blood to illustrate 'doing something so simple but still helping other people' (Figure 8.1).

Kate used filters in her photographs and although in two of these they helped to anonymise faces, they also illustrated what she was trying to convey. Filters were used, for example to change the faces on her photographs of herself with her mum and her boyfriend, 'two of my most supportive people in my life' and hearts added to the photograph of her flatmates who are 'very meaningful' to her. Penny was also creative in her composition in order to convey that she uses music 'in all aspects' of her life: 'so

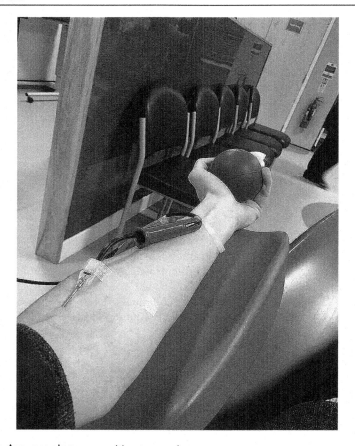

Figure 8.1 Ana uses photocomposition to remain anonymous.

I have made my headphones into a heart because music is the first way that I ever started to express myself ... I just put it in a heart shape because at university I feel like emotional intelligence is really really important' (Figure 8.2).

The students shared different amounts of photographs and on different mediums: fourteen of the students sent their photographs electronically prior to the interview, ranging from Taariq (who sent two photographs) to Kate and Oliver (who sent seventeen). Penny chose instead to bring the nine photographs that she had taken printed on paper rather than send them electronically, and Willow chose to withhold the photographs altogether, showing them to me on her phone in the interview but not sending them electronically.

While ten of the students chose to give permission for their images and audio clips to be used and to be contacted in future, the remaining seven students were selective about which permissions they gave. Maya and Kate, for example, gave

Figure 8.2 Penny illustrates the importance of music.

permission only for audio clips to be used, and Willow only for further contact. Asking whether there were any photographs that students would have liked to have taken but didn't in the interview was particularly useful to elicit conversations about meaning found from being with other people, with eight students here describing photographs of family and friends, and led to Taariq showing me a further nine photographs on his phone. During the interview students also commented that they had found taking part interesting and enjoyable, and that they liked the freedom that the method gave: 'you just let me talk about my thing'.

Concluding reflections

This method *has* captured the individual nature of the students' meaning-making on campus, contributing to an understanding of the diversity of meaning-making within higher education. A particular strength here is that it has captured what the students *do* as part of their meaning-making including when, where and why, and how this fits in with their life as a student, providing an insight that can be used to inform policy and practice to support students.

The strength of this diary-like photo-elicitation method is that it allowed for flexibility and choice in student participation, and as a result students have shared this sensitive and often private aspect of their everyday lives, one that they may not share with their peers. A visual rather than written diary allows participants greater control over privacy in its creation, and this was illustrated here in that some students chose to self-censor their photographs, and others used objects and private spaces to illustrate their religious practices.

There is inevitably a compromise when designing research, and what has been lost in the choice not to offer identification in this study (the potential to offer voice to students and to show their photographs as distinct from my descriptions and analysis of them), has been gained in that it created a safe space in which students could participate on their own terms and in their own way. Students took the choices offered (such as including selfies that they perhaps may not have included if they were to be shared beyond the interview), and made their own choices in the disclosure of their photographs (such as withholding them on their phone, or choosing to share more once in the interview).

It is therefore recommended that visual diary-like methods are considered when researching sensitive topics in higher education, and that in cases where identifiable photographs are created by participants a situated approach to ethics is taken in addition to consideration of current recommendations within visual research ethics. There is also potential here to encourage further inclusion by giving complete ownership of a photo diary to participants: inviting students to take photographs on their phone that would only be discussed in an interview rather than given to the researcher. While a private diary is not without limitations (Harvey, 2011), what would be gained is that it would enable the inclusion of students who might not otherwise take part, and a greater insight into private, not often shared topics.

Acknowledgements

This chapter is based upon my PhD research, which was funded by the Vice Chancellor's PhD Scholarship, Nottingham Trent University.

References

Advance HE. (2018) Religion and belief: Supporting inclusion of staff and students in higher education and colleges. Retrieved from www.ecu.ac.uk/publications/religion-and-belief (accessed 23 August 2019).

Allen, L. (2015) Losing face? Photo-anonymisation and visual research integrity. *Visual Studies*, 30, 3: 295–308.

Ammerman, N. (2014) 2013 Paul Hanly Furfey Lecture: Finding religion in everyday life. *Sociology of Religion*, 75, 2: 189–207.

Aune, K., Guest, M., Law, J. (2019) *Chaplains on campus: Understanding chaplaincy in UK universities.* Coventry/Durham/Canterbury: Coventry University, Durham University and Canterbury Christ Church University.

Bartlett, R. (2012) Modifying the diary interview method to research the lives of people with dementia. *Qualitative Health Research*, 22, 12: 1717–1726.

Beckers, R., van der Voordt, T. & Dewulf, G. (2016) Why do they study there? Diary research into students' learning space choices in higher education. *Higher Education Research and Development*, 35, 1: 142–157.

Chen, H.-Y., Yarnal, C., Hustad, J. T. P. & Sims, D. (2016) Take a selfie of life: A qualitative exploration of college students' self-reflections on free time use and personal values. *Journal of College and Character*, 17, 2: 101–115.

Clark, A. (2012) Visual ethics in a contemporary landscape. In S. Pink (ed.), *Advances in visual methodology*. London: Sage, pp.17–36.

Clark, A., Prosser, J. & Wiles, R. (2010) Ethical issues in image based research. *Arts and Health*, 2, 1: 81–93.

Day, A. (2010) 'Believing in belonging': An exploration of young people's social contexts and constructions of belief. In S. Collins-Mayo & P. Dandelion (eds), *Religion and youth*. Farnham: Ashgate, pp. 97–103.

Filep, C.V., Turner, S., Eidse, N., Thompson-Fawcett, M. & Fitzsimons, S. (2017) Advancing rigour in solicited diary research. *Qualitative Research*, 18, 4: 451–470.

Frosh, P. (2015) The gestural image: The selfie, photography theory, and kinesthetic sociability. *International Journal of Communication*, 9: 1607–1628.

Guest, M. (2017) From Jevons to Collini (via Douglas Davies): Reflections on higher education and religious identity. In M. Guest & M. Middlemiss Lé Mon (eds), *Death, life and laughter: Essays on religion in honour of Douglas Davies*. Abingdon: Routledge, pp. 201–220.

Guest, M., Aune, K., Sharma, S. & Warner, R. (2013) *Christianity and the university experience: Understanding student faith*. London: Bloomsbury.

Harvey, L. (2011) Intimate reflections: Private diaries in qualitative research. *Qualitative Research*, 11, 6: 664–682.

Hyers, L. (2018) *Diary methods: Understanding qualitative research*. Oxford: Oxford University Press.

Hyers, L., Swim, J. & Mallett, R. (2006) The personal is political: using daily diaries to examine everyday prejudice-related experiences. In S. N. Hesse-Biber & P. Leavy (eds), *Emergent methods in social research*. Thousand Oaks, CA: Sage, pp. 313–336.

Martinez-Vargas, C., Walker, M. & Mkwananzi, F. (2019) Access to higher education in South Africa: Expanding capabilities in and through an undergraduate photovoice project. *Educational Action Research*, May: 1–16.

McGuire, M. (2008) *Lived religion: Faith and practice in everyday life*. Oxford: Oxford University Press.

Nolas, S-M. (2018) Photo/stories from the field: Anonymous portraits and other practices in the ethics of representation. Blog post, 18 July. Retrieved from www.childhoodp ublics.org/anonymous-portraits-and-other-practices-in-the-ethics-of-representation (accessed 23 August 2019).

NUS (2012) No place for hate: Hate crimes and incidents in further and higher education: religion or belief. Retrieved from www.nusconnect.org.uk/resources/no-place-for-ha te-religion-and-belief-report-may-2012 (accessed 21 August 2019).

Papademas, D. & the IVSA (2009) IVSA code of research ethics and guidelines. *Visual Studies*, 24, 3: 250–257.

Plummer, K. (2000) *Documents of life 2: An invitation to a critical humanism*. London: Sage.

Punch, M. (1994) Politics and ethics in qualitative research. In N. K. Denzin & Y. S. Lincoln (eds), *Handbook of qualitative research*. Thousand Oaks, CA: Sage, pp. 83–97.

Rose, G. (2016) *Visual methodologies: An introduction to researching with visual materials*, 4th edition. London: Sage.

Scott, J., Green, P. & Cashmore, A. (2012) Bioscience students' first year perspectives through video diaries: Home, family and student transitions. *Bioscience Education*, 20, 1: 53–67.

Stevenson, J. (2013) Discourses of inclusion and exclusion: religious students in UK higher education. *Widening Participation and Lifelong Learning*, 14, 3: 27–43.

Stevenson, J. (2017) Exploring the lifeworld of international doctoral students: The place of religion and religious organisations. In L. T. Tran & C. Gomes (eds), *International student connectedness and identity, Cultural studies and transdisciplinarity in education, vol 6*. Singapore: Springer, pp. 61–74.

Taylor, Y. (2016) *Making space for queer-identifying religious youth*. Basingstoke: Palgrave Macmillan.

Wiles, R., Coffey, A., Robinson J. & Heath, S. (2012) Anonymisation and visual images: issues of respect, 'voice' and protection. *International Journal of Social Research Methodology*, 15, 1: 41–53.

Williams, R. (2010) Space for God: Lived religion at work, home, and play. *Sociology of Religion*, 71, 3: 257–279.

Woodhead, L. (2012) Religion in Britain has changed, our categories haven't. Retrieved from http://faithdebates.org.uk/debates/2012-debates/religion-and-public-life/main-trends-in-religion-and-values-in-britain (accessed 26 July 2019).

Part III

The importance of diaries for researching hidden issues

Chapter 9

Accessing silenced voices?

Diary method as a source of data for understanding higher education experiences of students from socially excluded groups

Nidhi S. Sabharwal, Roma Smart Joseph, Anil Chindha Bankar and Avinash Vasantrao Talmale

Introduction

An unprecedented expansion of the higher education (HE) sector in recent decades has led India to reach a stage of massification (Varghese, 2015). With a gross enrolment ratio (GER) of 25.8% and around 36.6 million students (MHRD, 2018), India has the second-largest HE system in the world. The expansion has been accompanied by diversification of the sector in terms of institutions, sources of financing, nature of programmes of study offered, and students' social background. From homogenous campuses dominated by students from privileged population groups, HE campuses are now increasingly being accessed by diverse student groups who are non-elite social group learners. In 2014, close to 63% of the student population in HE belonged to the socially excluded groups (NSSO, 2014) such as the scheduled tribes (STs: indigenous groups), scheduled castes (SCs: former untouchables in the caste hierarchy) and other backward classes (OBCs: other lower castes). Affirmative action policies followed in admissions in the form of reservation of seats, and various support schemes have contributed to upholding the Constitutional commitment to social justice (GOI, 1950).

In order to translate opportunity of access to academic success, and truly ensure social justice, warrants an enquiry into the nature of HE experiences of students from the socially excluded groups (SEGs) and to study how higher education institutions (HEIs) in India are taking into account the socio-educational requirements of diverse learners on their campuses. Such an investigation is necessary, as insights from the literature inform us of vulnerabilities associated with social belonging of students from the SEGs, which indicate disadvantaged life processes experienced in their journeys to HE. The socially excluded groups tend to suffer from a high incidence of poverty, malnutrition, illiteracy, poor health outcomes (Thorat & Newman, 2010), and inequitable conditions of study (Sabharwal et al., 2014), compared to the rest of the population (non-SC/ST/OBCs). In addition, these groups face exclusion and discrimination in access to opportunities associated with the institution of caste and ethnic backgrounds (Thorat & Newman, 2010).

Existing studies show exclusionary social experiences of students from the SEGs continue to shape their HE access, retention and success (Rao, 2013; Ovichegan, 2013; Sabharwal et al., 2014; Thornton et al., 2011; Henry & Ferry, 2017). These studies have drawn attention to social challenges confronting students from the SEGs, prevailing practices of prejudice (negative beliefs based on social group membership), and, discriminatory behaviours (differential treatment based upon social group membership) against these students on HE campuses. To examine forms of prejudice and exclusionary processes influencing HE experiences of students from the SEGs, some studies have made concerted efforts by either employing qualitative research methods such as interviews (Rao, 2013), or combined qualitative methods with quantitative instruments, such as student surveys (Sabharwal et al., 2014). However, diaries as a research method have been under-utilised in India (except by one study: Thornton et al., 2011), despite their potential to be a powerful medium of expression of sharing confidential insights, especially by those who are targets of everyday practices of social prejudices and discrimination (Swim et al., 2003).

The authors of this chapter included solicited diaries in a multi-institutional mixed method study that combined reflections from the diary data with other data sources (student survey and focus group discussions) to understand the interactional nature of HE experiences of students from the SEGs in academic and social spheres, and to study the existing institutional mechanisms to support student diversity (Sabharwal & Malish, 2016). We included solicited diaries largely to explore the research objective to uncover the nature and forms of academic and social challenges faced by students from the SEGs in HEIs which were geographically dispersed across India. Importantly, diaries were used to overcome difficulties in reaching out to students from the SEGs who were hesitant to be visibly identified, when they were approached to take part and interact in the focus group discussions (FGDs). These students were reluctant to reveal their identity in public, and participate in the FGDs. Their hesitation reflected a fear and a threat of discrimination. Fifty students from the scheduled castes, scheduled tribes, and women completed diaries to share their thoughts and emotions related to their everyday experiences of interactions in academic and social spheres, including with the administration.

Insights from this mixed method study showed a poor quality of educational experience of students from the SEGs, in the form of lower levels of integration in academic sphere and marginalisation in social spheres, with administration in HEIs not succeeding in effectively supporting students from the SEGs on their campuses (Sabharwal 2020). Undoubtedly, the diary method helped us in accessing spaces that we may have not been able to reach: silenced voices of students from the SEGs studying in HEIs in geographically dispersed locations across India.

The next section of this chapter reviews the literature on the versatile use of the diary method in HE research, internationally and in India. We then outline the methodology of the mixed methods study within which the diary method nests, its design and the process of data collection. After this, methodological reasons for using solicited diaries and the approach to data analysis are discussed, including challenges faced in the implementation process of the diary method. The chapter concludes by underlining the need for developing research capacities to fully explore the potential that the diary method offers for studying SEGs in higher education.

The use of diary method for studying HE experiences of students from SEGs

The diary method, as suggested by the literature review elaborated in this section, is flexible in terms of studying diverse topics and in the collection of both quantitative as well as qualitative data. It offers multiple advantages for researchers of all philosophies and all fields, by way of facilitating regular documentation of the human experience and its potential to capture time-sensitive and context-specific phenomena (Hyers, 2018). In research on HE, published academic articles indicate the use of the diary method to study experiences of students from the disadvantaged social groups, which is the key concern of this chapter.

The diary method has been used to reveal the chronic nature of everyday sexism, racism and prejudice, its frequency and its socio-psychological implications for women and African American college students' experiences (Swim et al., 2001; Swim et al., 2003; Hyers, 2007; Hyers et al., 2006; Hyers, 2010). Studies employing diaries have emphasised the benefit of diary method in reducing the issues with memory loss associated with retrospective recollection of accounts of experiences. The daily diary methodology (Swim et al., 2003) with a mixed design (an open-ended prompt and a structured format) and a grounded-theory coding procedure helped in capturing characteristics of perpetrators, frequency and nature of everyday experiences of racism faced by African American students attending a predominantly White/European US public university.

Furthermore, diary method has been useful to study women's agency and empowerment. Using an open-ended diary format, Hyers (2007) utilised a feminist approach in the diary method to explore how women students actively confronted oppression in their daily lives. Coding of the incidents reported in diaries and the response strategy which was discussed during focus groups involved an inductive, data-driven, grounded theory procedure. The diary-keeping period was followed by students meeting in small focus groups to discuss ways to confront the prejudicial experiences they had documented the week before.

More recently, Falconer and Taylor (2017) used the diary method combined with other methods to study intersectional HE experiences of students who identified both as queer and religious. This study included solicited diaries in a mixed method research design, along with individual face-to-face interviews and a mind-mapping exercise. The diarists were provided with open-ended instructions which related to interview themes, and had the freedom to tell their story in their way and record their reflections on their everyday life. The analysis involved triangulation of insights from the interviews with diary entries, providing thick descriptions which helped in developing the researchers' understanding of academic experiences of young, queer religious students.

The studies discussed so far have been carried out in the HE institutions located in the Global North. To the best of our knowledge, diary method has rarely been used in research on HE experiences of students from the socially excluded groups in India, except in one study (Thornton et al., 2011). This study was carried out jointly in India and the UK to explore issues of diversity and discrimination as experienced by minority, under-represented and disadvantaged students. Using a socio-constructivist perspective for data analysis, the study used diary entries in triangulation with insights from interviews and focus group discussions to show separation and subtle divisions in academic and social spheres of HE campuses based on caste, race, nationality, region, and language (Thornton et al., 2010).

In terms of its methodology, this study set out solely to employ 90 solicited diaries from students and staff as the source of data. However, due to difficulties faced in recruitment of diary participants, the study had to include additional methods. The difficulty in soliciting diaries was mainly related to the approach to recruitment of volunteers. The implementation of the diary method was successful in those institutions 'where there was a personal relationship or approach' (Thornton et al., 2011, p. 23), while accessing contacts and displaying adverts on Web-based Management Learning Environment (available in HE institutions in the UK), posters and invitations displayed on notice boards, and, leaflets left on tables, libraries and resource centres were unproductive (see also Chapter 5, this volume). The study supplemented diaries with additional methods such as interviews and group discussions in order to gain the necessary sample in institutes where the study was not able to recruit diarists.

To summarise, these studies show the versatile nature of the diary method reflected through multiple diary formats which can be used solely or in a mixed method research design, allowing for the possibilities of the use of deductive and inductive approaches in combination for data analysis, along with triangulation of findings from other forms of research instruments. For example, even when diary format has been open-ended, elements of a deductive approach have been used with application of themes emerging from other sources of information for analysis of diary entries (Falconer & Taylor, 2017). Importantly, studies have highlighted the usefulness of the diary method to uncover the nature and frequency of everyday experiences of students with casteism or racism that may be so familiar that they can easily be normalised. Despite its advantages, the use of the diary method to study experiences of students and faculty members from the disadvantaged social groups, globally and in India has been minimal.

Deploying learnings from previous studies, and with awareness of difficulties in implementing the diary method as indicated in the Thornton et al. (2010) study, we used solicited diaries as one of the research tools to understand social and academic HE experiences of students from the SEGs. The methodological information on this mixed methods study, within which the diary method was nested, is briefly discussed in the next section. This is followed by a detailed presentation of the methodological underpinnings, including the approach to analysis of data from the diary method.

The study: solicited diaries nested in a mixed method design

Diaries were incorporated as one of the qualitative tools in this mixed methods research, which used a multi-institutional case study design to gain a holistic understanding of the HE experiences of students and faculty members from the socially excluded groups in India. The case-study approach involved a careful selection of twelve HE institutions varying in their structure, size, and admission policies, located in six Indian States, which were situated across different geographical zones (Sabharwal & Malish, 2016).

A pragmatic triangulation mixed methods research design was used, in which the qualitative and quantitative data were collected to utilise the strengths of both methods (Creswell & Clark, 2007). Following this principle of 'methodological openness' (Hyers 2018), along with a range of other quantitative and qualitative insights through diverse sources, students' daily lived campus experiences were incorporated through diaries into case studies of HE institutions. While the quantitative data was collected to measure the extent of student diversity, patterns and differences between the experiences of diverse groups of students, qualitative data was used to understand processual aspects of classroom and out-of-classroom experiences, drivers of exclusion and discrimination, and to unpack causality.

Qualitative methods included solicited diaries and focus group discussions (FGDs) with students, and in-depth interviews with teachers, administrators and decision-makers in selected institutes. Second-year students at the under-graduate (UG) level and at the post-graduate (PG) level from the disciplines selected for the study (which included social sciences, humanities and STEM subjects) were selected for the FGDs and solicited diaries. Students studying in their second year (of undergraduate or postgraduate courses) were chosen, as this is the year when students are best placed to critically evaluate their college experience (Schaller, 2005; Zaitseva et al., 2013).

Solicited diary participants

50 diaries were completed by second-year students (including SCs and STs), comprising 33 male students and 17 female students across these social groups. In addition to being from the SEGs, students were also from low-income families, first-generation HE learners, from rural areas and who had studied in regional language as their medium of instruction. As informed by the literature (Ross et al., 2012), most of these background variables have links with academic transition, performance, and persistence. Furthermore, students from the SC social groups were members of more than one disadvantaged group and encountered a stigmatised ethnic identity (Thorat, 1979), which compounded the effects of the multiple barriers they faced. Diary entries depicted the campus life-world of these students, including their everyday campus experiences, their reflections on curricular transactions and teaching practices, and their social interactions with their higher-caste peers.

Semi-structured diary format with open-ended prompts

Existing studies (Hyers, 2007; Falconer & Taylor, 2017) inform us that semi-structured diary formats which ask for open-ended answers to prompts have the potential to allow reflections and recording of contextual information and provide introspective data. The diarists in our study too were provided with open-ended prompts which they could follow to record their campus experiences. In order to triangulate findings from multiple data sources, the prompts in the diaries were related to the topics being discussed in FGDs, and in the quantitative student survey questionnaire. For example, the topics in the FGDs with students included their classroom and out-of-classroom experiences, teaching methods and engagement with their peers, teachers, and administration. The diary prompts ranged from students' experiences of their journey from home to college, on their feelings on time spent in the classroom and on campus with friends in college, nature of engagement in the co-curricular activities, instances of feeling excluded, attitudes of their teachers and the administration.

These instructions were pasted on notebooks. The notebooks were handed over to the participants to record their experiences over a two-week period during the time that quantitative and other qualitative research instruments were being administered in the selected institutions. Importantly, instructions were translated into regional languages applicable to the Indian states where the HE institutions were located. Figure 9.1 provides shows an example of the diary, as well as the instruction page, translated in Marathi (an Indian regional language).

Students filled out their diaries in the language that they were most comfortable with to reflect their emotions and feelings. However, it should be noted that, in practice, translating diary entries from regional languages was time-consuming and resource-intensive, with some of the expressions of feelings and emotions lost in translation. The data collection involved a process which included seeking institutional clearances and consent from the participants, collection of students' demographic information, and gaining students' trust in order to sustain their motivation for sharing their feelings through diary entries. The next section discusses reasons for choosing the diary method, challenges encountered in the data collection process and the approach to data analysis.

Why choose diary method?

There were multiple methodological reasons for including diaries in this mixed method study. One of the main reasons was that, irrespective of institutions being studied, many students from the SC social group (former untouchables) were afraid to reveal their identity and engage in group discussions, while women were hesitant to speak in such open forums. Their reluctance was expressed when students were requested to take part in focus group discussions. At times, students were even

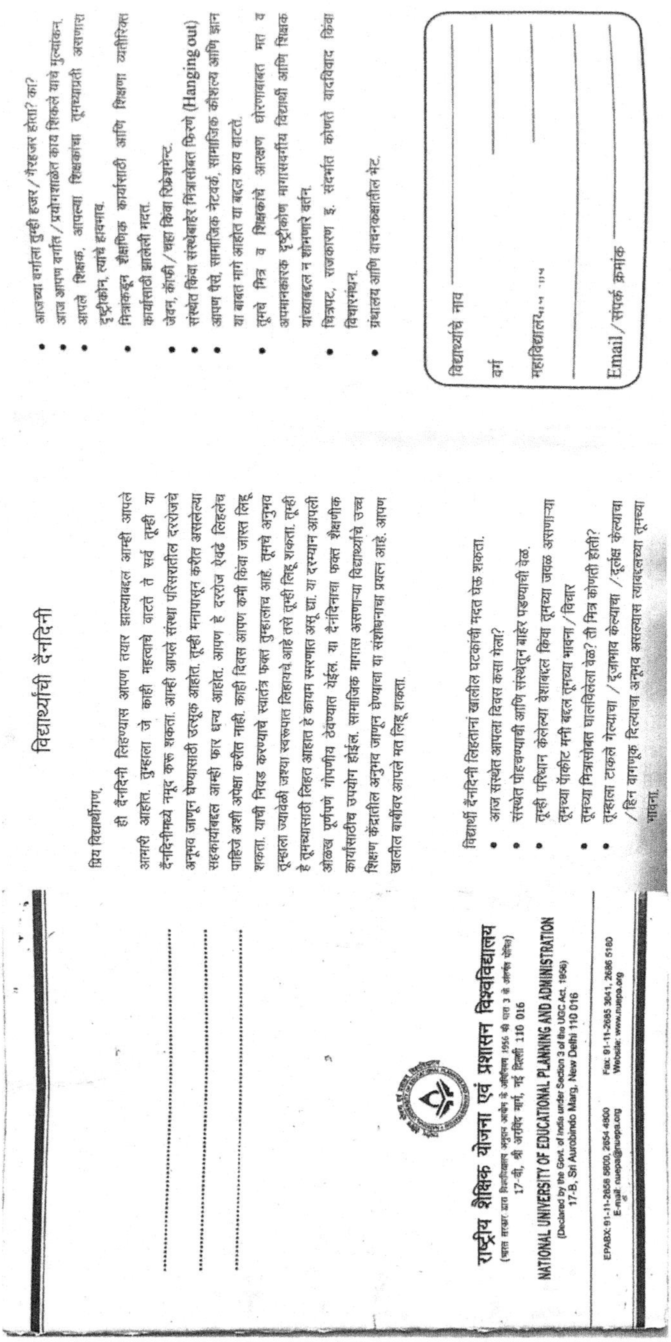

विद्यार्थ्यांची दैनंदिनी

प्रिय विद्यार्थीमित्रा,

ही दैनंदिनी लिहिण्यास आपण तयार झाल्याबद्दल आम्ही आपले आभारी आहोत. तुम्हाला जे काही महत्त्वाचे वाटते ते सर्व तुम्ही या दैनंदिनीमध्ये नमूद करू शकता. आम्ही आपले पारिसरातील दररोजचे अनुभव जाणून घेण्यासाठी उत्सुक आहोत. तुम्ही मनापासून करीत असलेल्या सहकार्याबद्दल आम्ही फार धन्य आहोत. आपण हे दररोज रेखुडे लिहिलेल पाहिजे अशी अपेक्षा करीत नाही. काही दिवस आपण कमी किंवा जास्त लिहू शकता. याची निश्चित काळण्याचे स्वातंत्र्य फक्त तुम्हालाच आहे. तुम्ही अनुभव घेतलेल्या जगाबद्दल जास्त स्पष्टपणे लिहिल्याने आहे तसे तुम्ही लिहू शकता. तुम्ही हे तुमच्यासाठी लिहित आहात हे कायम स्मरणात असू द्या. या दररोजच्या आपली ओळख पूर्णपणे गोपनीय ठेवण्यात येईल. या दैनंदिनाचा फक्त शैक्षणिक कार्यालयीन उपयोग होईल. सामाजिक मागास असलेल्या विद्यार्थ्यांचे उच्च शिक्षण केंद्रातील अनुभव जाणून घेण्याचा या संशोधनाचा प्रयत्न आहे. आपण खालील बाबींवर आपले मत लिहू शकता.

विद्यार्थी दैनंदिनी लिहिताना खालील घटकांची मदत घेऊ शकता.

• आज संस्थेत आपला दिवस कसा गेला?
• संस्थेत पोहचल्यावर आणि संस्थेतून बाहेर पडल्यानंतर वेळ.
• तुम्ही परिसरात केलेल्या वेगावरला किंवा तुमच्या जवळ असणाऱ्या तुमच्या पॉकेट मनी बदल तुमच्या भावना / विचार
• तुमच्या मित्रांसोबत घालविलेला वेळ? ते मित्र कोणते होती?
• तुम्हाला टाकलेले गेलेल्या / दुर्लाभ केल्याला / दुर्लक्ष केल्याच्या / हिन वागणूक दिल्याचा अनुभव असल्यास त्याच्याबद्दल तुमच्या भावना.

आजच्या वर्गात तुम्ही हजर / गैरहजर होता? का?
आज आपण वर्गात / प्रयोगशाळेत काय शिकले याचे मुल्यांकन.
आपले शिक्षक, आपल्या शिक्षकांचा तुमच्याप्रती असणारा दृष्टिकोन, त्याचे हावभाव.
मित्रांकडून शैक्षणिक कार्यासाठी आणि शिक्षण व्यतिरिक्त कार्यांसाठी झालेली मदत.
जेवण, कॉफी / चहा किंवा रिफ्रेशमेन्ट.
संस्थेत किंवा संस्थेबाहेर मित्रांसोबत फिरणे (Hanging out) आपला घेर, सामाजिक नेटवर्क, सामाजिक कोशल्य आणि ज्ञान या बाबत मागे आहोत वा बदल काय वाटते.
तुमचे मित्र व शिक्षकांचे आरक्षण धोरणाबाबत मत व अनुसूचित दृष्टिकोन मागासवर्गीय विद्यार्थी आणि शिक्षक यांच्याबद्दल न शोभणारी वागणूक.
विद्यापीठ, राजकारण इ. संदर्भात कोणते वादविवाद किंवा विचारमंथन.
ग्रंथालय आणि वाचनकक्षातील भेट.

विद्यार्थ्याचे नाव _____

वर्ग _____

महाविद्यालय/संस्था नाव _____

Email / संपर्क क्रमांक _____

राष्ट्रीय शैक्षिक योजना एवं प्रशासन विश्वविद्यालय
(भारत सरकार द्वारा विश्वविद्यालय अनुदान आयोग के अधिनियम 1956 की धारा 3 के अंतर्गत घोषित)
17-बी, श्री अरविन्द मार्ग, नई दिल्ली 110 016

NATIONAL UNIVERSITY OF EDUCATIONAL PLANNING AND ADMINISTRATION
(Declared by the Govt. of India under Section 3 of the UGC Act, 1956)
17-B, Sri Aurobindo Marg, New Delhi 110 016

EPABX: 91-11-2656 5800, 2654 4800   Fax: 91-11-2656 3641, 2686 5180
E-mail nuepa@nuepa.org   Website: www.nuepa.org

Figure 9.1 The diary and the instructions page (shown in Marathi).

hesitant to be seen to be visibly associated with the research team, because it was widely known in the college that we were there to research HE experiences of students from the socially excluded groups.

These responses reflected a fear of discrimination and of being reprimanded by those in authority. The reluctance of students to be 'visibly' engaging in group discussions led to a modification in the research design after the pilot, to include diaries as a choice of research instrument in the mixed methods study. Diaries helped our study in overcoming difficulties related to reaching out to respondents to participate in the research. These difficulties related to recruitment of respondents have also been acknowledged by other diary research on diversity, discrimination and exclusion (Thornton et al., 2011; Hyers, 2018).

Importantly, our research was informed by a theoretical understanding that, depending on the social-group dynamics and the social structures existing in respective Indian states, there would be students from other socially disadvantaged groups, such as from the indigenous groups and de-notified groups (previously notified as criminal tribes and who experience stigma of criminality; see Japhet et al., 2015), in the student body who may feel hesitant to reveal their identities. Equipped with this conceptual understanding and sensitivity towards multiple disadvantages and varying social structures, the research teams located across six states had the flexibility to select students from diverse population groups as diarists.

The diarists also consisted of students who had participated in FGDs, but remained silent. They chose to opt instead to use diary as a medium to voice their thoughts, emotions, and campus experiences. The diary method in a sense helped in giving participants a choice (Filep et al., 2017) and meeting the ethical considerations practiced while conducting FGDs of not pressurising participants to speak (Mason, 2002). The method provided an alternative to include participants in the study who were hesitant to interact in FGDs. For example, when students participated in the FGDs, some students interacted actively, while others did not. In that case, after group discussions, the research team individually reached out to silent students, and provided them with an alternative to complete diaries instead.

As diarists, these students reflected on their campus experiences in a detailed manner. Consistent with past research on discrimination and sexual harassment (Swim et al., 2003; Hyers, 2007), the diary method in our study offered privacy to students and a 'safe space' to record their experiences of caste-based discrimination, instances of sexual harassment and hurtful derogatory behaviours, along with other aspects of their campus life.

Another methodological reason for using the diary method was that it offered flexibility to those students who were physically unavailable to participate in FGDs. Group discussions were mostly held during college hours, especially after their regular classes. There were many students from the disadvantaged social groups and women who were leaving their campuses as soon as their classes finished. Many of the students cited part-time work, household chores, and safety concerns as reasons for leaving college earlier than the rest. For example, due to unsafe campuses as well as uncertainties related to the mode of commuting, women were not staying back after mid-afternoon hours. These students opted to write diaries. In other words, the diary method gave control to students to express themselves according to their convenience and in settings where they were most comfortable. Many students completed their diaries in the comfort of their home.

Importantly the choice of this method was informed by the existing literature on the potential of the diary method to reveal detailed information on everyday experiences of prejudice on campuses (Swim et al., 2003; Hyers, 2007), offer flexibility to reflect according to their convenience related to time and space (Filep et al., 2017; Chapter 2, this volume), and its power to raise consciousness within the diarist of these events (Milligan, 2001). Finally, the methodology was being informed by our social justice research objectives. The research objectives of this study were primarily focused on gaining insights on ways in which students' interactions with caste, class, ethnicity, and gender constructs shape their identities and influence HE experiences on college campuses. Through using the diary method, the aim was to find ways to generate best contextual findings and expressions of emotions (which other research tools may not have been able to capture in the mixed method study) that could inform institutional practices on ways of advancing social inclusion on its campuses.

Challenges faced in the process of diary data collection and data analysis

Participants' concerns during the data collection process

Even though we had clearly explained the purpose of the research, and had stated before the start of the data collection that diary entries would be anonymised, and had ensured the confidentiality of the data collected, students remained anxious. For example, when we distributed diaries to students, they felt apprehensive to share their views and experiences through the diaries as they were afraid of recording their personal experiences 'in writing'. Fear of backlash from higher authorities by the participants has also been highlighted in other research studies employing the diary method (Filep et al., 2017).

Some students, especially women students, were also fearful of documenting their private self-reflections and had anxieties concerning the security of diaries. The anxiety of women students was rooted in the cultural context, where neither in college nor at home could they escape from the patriarchal gaze and enjoy privacy (Sabharwal & Sonalkar, 2015). Additionally, at the beginning of data collection, despite instructions and prompts being included in diaries – students were not sure of the level of description that they needed to write as diary entries. While the literature has pointed out variations in participants' capacity to self-reflect (Hyers, 2018), in our study we do not believe it was so; we will elaborate on this in subsequent section.

To overcome difficulties related to the anxiety of participants, gain trust and increase their comfort levels, research team members included faculty members as researchers who shared participants' social group membership. In order to ensure participants' comfort and maintain quality of diary entries, studies on uncovering everyday prejudice have also included in-group research team members (Hyers, 2007). Furthermore, individual briefings on diary study instructions before the commencement of the study, regular contact by research team members through individual meetings with students during the data collection process to encourage participants to write, and being consistently available to answer their queries, helped in building confidence of students to continue and elaborate on their entries.

Retention of participants

Retention is a recognised issue in diary research (Hyers, 2018). Given this was the first time that we were all engaging with this method (not having been taught the method during our doctoral level studies or in research methodology courses), hence often we followed our intuition while implementing the method. This was especially the case when it was realised that this method involved regular individual meetings and follow-ups with diarists in order to retain their interests (see also Chapter 5, this volume). As advised by Hyers (2018), perhaps we should have elaborated the instructions to the participants more clearly and more explicitly to remind them of the purpose of the research, even though we had shared with them prior to start of data collection. Moreover, we now know that these instructions should have included the summary of the project, research questions and social justice objective of the research on the cover of their diary note-books to remind the participants the focus of the research.

However, almost all of the participants remained with the study and completed diaries with varying levels of reflections on their campus experiences. We believe the incentive for a sustained participation of students in the study mainly arose from students' internal motivation and developing a shared understanding of the aim of this research. The student-centric and social justice objective of this policy research was of their immediate concern, as it was addressing social inequities and unequal power relationships on college campuses. As noted by Hyers (2018), often when the focus of the research is on a social issue, the motivation of the participants to participate is rooted primarily in being included as diarists who can, as such, make their concerns heard.

Quantity and quality of diary data

The quantity and quality of entries were influenced by the sensitivity of research team members, their in-depth knowledge of the theoretical grounding of the research, and the relationship of trust established with participants to ensure their comfort (as noted before). Even though care was accorded in research design and data collection process, there were variations in the level of the description provided in diary entries. Diary entries ranged from a few entries of less than one page, with meagre information in the form of bullet point sentences as responses to the prompts, to 'thick description' reflecting rich contextual information on students' involvement in the teaching-learning process, which filled up the notebook. The description also included emotions of students' campus experiences shaped by their social background.

In the data collection phase, one of the challenges was that students had paucity of time to thoughtfully self-reflect on their experiences – this resulted in some students taking diaries and keeping them till the date of submission with no diary entries at all. Students who did not write any entries were generally those who were engaged in part-time work after college hours. Difficulty to spare time to write entries has also been noted in research on street vendors in Vietnam (Filep et al., 2017). Hence those whose experiences we wished to capture in this study were the very students who were unable to participate fully. But even so, through the mixed method diary design, we were able to study challenges facing students from the marginalised groups in HE in India.

Analysis process

The process of data analysis included transcription and translation of diary entries in English and Hindi from regional languages, as well as entries being typed as they were hand-written. This is an additional time resource requirement associated with this method. Names, institutional references, and subjects being studied were anonymised, while gender and social background were the characteristics retained for analysis.

The content in the diaries was read through and analysed for contextual insights and expressions of emotions concerning experiences (classroom, out-of-classroom, teacher-student interaction, peer-peer interaction, access to student support services) emerging from the quantitative data and other sources of qualitative data. Insights emerging from the diary data were integrated with patterns and themes emerging across multiple sources: questionnaires and FGDs. Words and sentences within diary entries as representation of emotions and feelings were selected and merged to provide meaning to the patterns emerging from the student survey and triangulated with the collective nature of experiences discussed during the FGDs. While qualitative methods such as FGDs facilitated interactions which helped in exploration of groups' opinions and greater clarity on the collectiveness of experiences related to students' stigmatised identity, student diaries provided an opportunity to explore their personal experiences.

For example, in relation to patterns and differences in experiences across student groups, quantitative analysis showed that students from the socially excluded groups were more likely to report that their teachers could not identify students by their names. The diary method helped 'harness the power of immediate personal witness' (Hyers, 2018, p. 27). The diary entries of the SC students reflected on the behaviour of their teachers and its negative impact. For example, a male SC student wrote 'teachers keep addressing them as, "*aesuno, haan kya hai tumhara naam*" ("*Hey ... yes you ... whatever is your name ... listen!*"), which was reported as heartbreaking and gave them a feeling of being inferior or worthless.

Diary entries also helped us to gain insights into the nature of experiences of students from the socially excluded groups. For example, related to classroom pedagogy, while the majority of the students in the survey reported that they were not encouraged to ask questions and participate in classroom discussion, it was only through student diaries and FGDs that we were able to understand in more detail that teachers generally adhered to lecture method in the classrooms and that questions were rarely used to elicit students' reflection and understanding. Another unique insight of the diary method for our study was that the in-depth reflections and expressions recorded by students from the SEGs negated negative stereotypes and beliefs held by teachers (faculty members) of their cognitive abilities. The dominant belief framed SEG students in deficit terms, which highlighted their academic deficiencies and considered their presence in HEI classrooms as a result of 'reservation' (i.e. the quota system) and not 'merit' (Sabharwal 2020).

Concluding observations

This chapter presented the method of using solicited diaries in the mixed methods research study to gain deeper insights into HE experiences of students from SEGs in India. We attempted to shine a light on this highly under-utilised (but useful) method in researching marginalised groups in India through a discussion on why we chose this method, including its design, the approach to data analysis and challenges encountered in the implementation process. It is the aim of this chapter to provide a reference point for others using this method to study experiences of not only students from SEG groups, but also of faculty members and administrative staff from these groups. While there were challenges related to variations in the quantity and quality of the information received through solicited diaries, through this method, we were able to understand emotions and feelings, attach meaning to patterns emerging on campus experiences, and come closer to gaining insights into challenges facing students from the socially excluded groups. Most importantly, diaries in our study offered a safe space to students from the SEGs to record their unspoken reflections on their everyday encounters with their social identity more freely.

In conclusion, in order to maximise the potential of diaries, we think a more systematic approach, clearer instructions and an improved data management process would have been appropriate. In the diary format, more clarity in instructions would have further improved the quality of diary entries. Perhaps following the diary method with face-to-face interviews (as in the diary-interview method proposed by Zimmerman & Wieder, 1977) would have increased insights gained through the diary study. The importance of piloting cannot be over-emphasised. Finally, including the diary method along with traditional qualitative methods in the teaching of research methodologies would be helpful in generating awareness on its potential, as well as contribute to developing the capacity of future researchers to efficiently manage and analyse data collected through the diary method.

Acknowledgements

The authors express their gratitude to Professor N. V. Varghese, Dr C. M. Malish, CPRHE/NIEPA, and members of the regional research teams from Bihar, Delhi, Karnataka, Kerala, Maharashtra & Uttar Pradesh.

References

Creswell, J. W. & Clark, V.L. (2007) *Designing and conducting mixed methods research.* Thousand Oaks, CA: Sage.

Falconer, E. & Taylor, Y. (2017) Negotiating queer and religious identities in higher education: Queering 'progression' in the 'university experience'. *British Journal of Sociology of education,* 38, 6: 782–797.

Filep, C.V., Turner, S., Eidse, N. & Thompson-Fawcett, M. (2017) Advancing rigour in solicited diary research. *Qualitative Research,* 18, 4: 451–470.

GOI (1950) Constitution of India. Retrieved from http://legislative.gov.in/con stitution-of-india.

Henry, O. & Ferry, M. (2017) When cracking the JEE is not enough. *South Asia Multidisciplinary Academic Journal,* 5, 1–28.

Hyers, L. L. (2007) Resisting prejudice every day: Exploring women's assertive responses to anti-black racism, anti-semitism, heterosexism, and sexism. *Sex Roles,* 56, 1–2: 1–12.

Hyers, L. L. (2018) *Diary methods.* Oxford: Oxford University Press.

Hyers, L. L. (2010) Alternatives to silence in face-to-face encounters with everyday heterosexism: Activism on the interpersonal front. *Journal of Homosexuality,* 57, 4: 539–565.

Hyers, L. L., Swim, J. K. & Mallett, R. K. (2006) The personal is political: Using daily diaries to examine every day prejudice-related experiences. In S. Nagy Hesse-Biber & P. Leavy (eds), *Emergent methods in social research.* London: Sage, pp. 313–329.

Japhet, S., Balgurumurthy, G., Diwakar, D. & Sabharwal, N. S. (2015) *Criminal stigma and livelihood: Socio-economic study of de-notified tribes in Karnataka.* Working paper, IX, 1. New Delhi: IIDS.

MHRD (2018) *All India survey of higher education: 2017–2018.* New Delhi: Government of India.

Milligan, C. (2001) *Geographies of care: Space, place and the voluntary sector.* Aldershot: Ashgate.

Mason, J. (2002) *Qualitative researching.* London: Sage.

NSSO (2014) *India: Social consumption – education survey 2014, 71st round.* New Delhi: Ministry of Statistics and Programme Implementation, Government of India.

Ovichegan, S. (2013) Social exclusion, social inclusion and passing: The experience of Dalit students at one elite Indian university, *International Journal of Inclusive Education* 18, 4: 359–378.

Rao, S. S. (2013) Structural exclusion in everyday institutional life: Labelling of stigmatised groups in an IIT. In G. Nambissan & S. Rao (eds), *Sociology of education in India: Changing contours and emerging concerns.* Delhi: Oxford University Press, pp. 199–223.

Ross, T., Kena, G., Rathbun, A., KewalRamani, A., Zhang, J., Kristapovich, P. & Manning, E. (2012) *Higher education: Gaps in access and persistence study. Statistical Analysis Report.* Washington, DC: National Center for Education Statistics.

Sabharwal, N. S. (2020) Managing student diversity in Indian higher education institutions: achieving academic integration and social inclusion. In N. V. Varghese & G. Malik (eds), *Governance and management of higher education in India: India higher education report.* New Delhi: Sage: 315–344.

Sabharwal, N. S. & Malish, C. M. (2016) *Diversity and discrimination in higher education: A study of institutions in selected states of India.* CPRHE Research Report. New Delhi: Centre for Policy Research in Higher Education, National University for Educational Planning and Administration.

Sabharwal, N. S. & Sonalkar, W. (2015) Dalit women in India: At the crossroads of gender, caste, and class. *Global Justice: Theory Practice Rhetoric,* 8, 1: 44–73.

Sabharwal, N. S., Thorat, S. K., Balasubramanyam, T. & Diwakar, D. (2014) *Diversity, academic performance, and discrimination: A case study of a higher educational institution.* IIDS Working Paper. New Delhi: Indian Institute of Dalit Studies.

Schaller, M. A. (2005) Wandering and wondering: Traversing the uneven terrain of the second college year. *About Campus,* 10, 3: 17–24.

Swim, J. K., Hyers, L. L., Cohen, L. L. & Ferguson, M. J. (2001) Everyday sexism: Evidence for its incidence, nature, and psychological impact from three daily diary studies. *Journal of Social Issues,* 57, 1: 31–53.

Swim, J. K., Hyers, L. L., Cohen, L. L., Fitzgerald, D. C. & Bylsma, W. H. (2003) African American college students' experiences with everyday racism: Characteristics of and responses to these incidents. *Journal of Black Psychology,* 29, 1: 38–67.

Thorat, S. K. (1979) Passage to adulthood: Perceptions from below. In S. Kakar (ed.), *Identity and adulthood.* Delhi: Oxford University Press, pp. 65–81.

Thorat, S. & Newman, K. S. (2010) Introduction: Economic discrimination, concept, consequences, and remedies. In S. Thorat & K. S. Newman (eds), *Blocked by caste: Economic discrimination in modern India.* Delhi: Oxford University Press, pp. 1–34.

Thornton, M., Bricheno, P., Iyer, P., Reid, I., Wankhede, G. & Green, R. (2010) Diversity and social integration on higher education campuses in India and the UK: Student and staff perspectives. *Research in Post-Compulsory Education,* 15, 2: 159–176.

Thornton, M., Bricheno, P., Iyer, P., Reid, I., Wankhede, G. & Green, R. (2011) Getting diverse students and staff to talk about equality and social integration issues on higher education campuses in India and the UK. *Research in Education,* 85, 1: 17–29.

Varghese, N. V. (2015) *Challenges of Massification of Higher Education in India, CPRHE Research Papers* 1. New Delhi: Centre for Policy Research in Higher Education, National Institute of Educational Planning and Administration.

Zaitseva, E., Milsom, C. & Stewart, M. (2013) Connecting the dots: Using concept maps for interpreting student satisfaction. *Quality in Higher Education,* 19, 2: 225–247.

Zimmerman, D. H. & Wieder, D. L. (1977) The diary: Diary-interview method. *Urban Life,* 5, 4: 479–498.

Chapter 10

Using photo diaries as an inclusive method to explore information experiences in higher education

Ben Watson and Jennifer Leigh

Introduction

In this chapter we describe the use of a multi-method solicited diary approach that we call diary-photograph: diary-interview. It was used with an aim of comparing the information experiences of students with and without print disabilities in higher education (HE). We asked participants to create a log of their learning activities over the course of a 'typical week', and supplement the written log with photographs that highlighted particular issues when accessing information. The students then had the opportunity to discuss their entries in detail with researchers in an interview. They reflected on their entries and explained the context and feelings behind the events that impacted either positively or negatively on their learning experiences.

We use this study to highlight the ways in which diary methods, and in particular this variation of a diary method, can challenge the researcher in HE and provide unexpected insight. For example, what was perceived as straightforward accessibility of print materials through information services actually impinged on larger issues of identity and belonging.

In addition to critically appraising the methodology, we share some of our findings, as they highlight some criticism often directed at diary methods. The first issue is variation in quality and quantity of entries. The nature of participant responses can leave the method open to standard criticisms levelled at qualitative research methods. However, diaries, particularly when the structure and format is left open as here, can result in a huge variety of types and richness of data depending on the level of engagement, involvement and situation of the individual respondent. This can be a strength, as the data may reach beyond that gathered using a more structured or rigid technique. Our study showed how using an open diary-photograph: diary-interview method led to the data encompassing a range of areas of HE that were not originally anticipated.

Connected to this, the second issue might be a lack of control from the perspective of the researcher. They are in control of neither content nor nature of the data, and it could easily go beyond what would be manageable and relevant. We choose to see this as a creative opportunity (Brown & Leigh, 2019), bringing in possibilities of genuine discovery, and creation of knowledge. However, there is a tension between keeping the brief absolutely clear to all participants at the beginning of the study to minimise the risk, and allowing it to be open to new connections.

A third issue is the selectivity of participant responses, which is in turn connected to the final issue of inequity of the form. Diary research may be a form that encourages engaged students to provide more information than respondents who are not so confidant or whose personal circumstances do not elicit the same level of emotional involvement in the study. In this chapter, we will discuss, using examples from our data, how some of these issues seemed to us to be positive benefits, all the while aware of Alaszewski's (2006, p. 80) constant dilemma of diaries 'attaining relevant data without restricting the diarists' writing flow unnecessarily'.

Information, print and accessibility in HE

The nature of modern university education requires the smooth flow of large amounts of information. Technological and cultural barriers may mean that students (or staff) with a print disability are not always enabled to access information as fluidly as their non-disabled counterparts. Print disability is defined by the Copyright Licensing Agency (CLA) as 'a visual, cognitive or physical disability [that] hinders the ability to read print' (CLA, 2016).

A person with a print disability may have a number of different impairments. They might have a visual impairment, so they cannot access text visually or at the same size as those without a disability. They may have dyslexia, or a similar specific learning disability. They may have a physical disability that prevents them from being able to handle a physical copy of a print publication. Any type of print disability may have negative implications for academic outcomes, as it would affect the ability they would have to access and process information. A typical barrier to accessing information is when a source is not available in a format that is accessible to their requirements. For example, this might be a visually impaired person being unable to access module reading because the resource does not work with their screen reading software, or a person with a hearing impairment finding multimedia content difficult due to a lack of captions or transcripts. Beyene (2018, p. 126) highlights the potential impact this could have:

> Users with print disability who rely on screen reader technologies could effectively be excluded from digital services if the search interfaces are not easily navigable, or if resources such as ebooks cannot be 'read' by screen readers.

There has been a welcome shift towards a more mainstream and inclusive approach to supporting students with disabilities in HE. The adoption of the social model of disability seeks to embed inclusive design in an effort to deliver accessible by design services at the point of need without any retrospective adaptation. The traditional medical (individual) model of disability would posit that it is the 'functional limitations' of disabled people that are the reason for exclusion rather than institutional oversight:

> Firstly, it locates the 'problem' of disability within the individual and secondly it sees the causes of this problem as stemming from the functional limitations or psychological losses which are assumed to arise from disability. These two points are underpinned by what might be called 'the personal tragedy theory of disability' which suggests that disability is some terrible chance event which occurs at random to unfortunate individuals.
>
> (Oliver, 1990, n.p.)

The social model of disability demands a fundamental overhaul of thinking around how the preeminent culture has developed:

> The genesis, development and articulation of the social model of disability by disabled people themselves is a rejection of all of these fundamentals. It does not deny the problem of disability but locates it squarely within society. It is not individual limitations, of whatever kind, which are the cause of the problem but society's failure to provide appropriate services and adequately ensure the needs of disabled people are fully taken into account in its social organisation. Further, the consequences of this failure does [*sic*] not simply and randomly fall on individuals but systematically upon disabled people as a group who experience this failure as discrimination institutionalised throughout society
>
> (Oliver, 1990, n.p.)

This is reinforced by the Disabled Students Sector Leadership Group (DSSLG, 2017, p. 12) which calls for the implementation of an inclusive, and technologically advanced practice to support students with disabilities:

> HE providers could embrace and adopt this approach as it supports and guides the ways in which pedagogy; curricula and assessment are designed and delivered to engage students in learning that is meaningful, relevant and accessible to all. It embraces a view of the individual and individual difference as the source of diversity that can enrich the lives and learning of others.

It is imperative that a university looking to change their practice and ensure it is inclusive seeks feedback from people with disabilities to understand the barriers from the user perspective (DSSLG, 2017). This helps to identify and address the patterns of difficulties experienced by all students (Newman et al., 2018). Solicited narrative diary research is a good option for the 'methodological and theoretical flexibility' (Mackrill, 2008, p. 12) it offers and the facility to capture the everyday lives of participants' experiences, practices, habits, and actions in order to gain an authentic insight into 'their inner world' (Milligan & Bartlett, 2019,

p. 1450) in a more holistic way than the 'snapshot views' of social practice (Mackrill, 2008, p. 9).

At Kent, the university has sought to embed inclusive approaches to the delivery of information and the use of assistive technologies for all; and take a holistic approach to the mainstreaming of adjustments as an approach to learning, teaching, research and support as a key strategy to benefit from the new opportunities to improve access for everyone. The aim is for the general information services to be as accessible as possible.[1] Beyene (2018, p. 122) notes that the 'advent of digital technology and the production of information in electronic formats, coupled with the introduction of accessibility guidelines, have created a favorable ground for pursuing the ideals of all-inclusive information services'. In order to achieve this, it is important to know where the barriers are for students with print disabilities, so that work can be put in place to eliminate them. We as authors undertook this diary-photograph: diary-interview study to help understand the different ways that students access information in order to shed light on:

- barriers that print disabled students experience (with a view to removing those barriers); and
- how positive or negative information experiences make people feel about their place within the institution.

The diary method provides a very effective means of 'shadowing' the student to reveal differentiated or inequitable experiences to inform strategies to improve educational opportunities. A particular benefit of the diary-photograph: diary interview format was the richness and feeling of the responses it enabled us to document, and the potential to 'access data that subjects otherwise conceal' (Milligan et al., 2005, p. 1892). This is reiterated by Harvery who recommends diary method 'particularly in research that seeks to track changes and differences' (Harvery, 2011, p. 66).

We were very aware that while the definition of print disability is encompassing, the nature of a profound physical impairment is not the same as dyslexia or a visual or hearing impairment. While there are many things an HE institution can put into place in order to increase accessibility, there will always be individuals with specific requirements or needs that have not been anticipated. By acting to increase accessibility in ways that we know affect many students we would be able to indicate to the university where it was possible to free up specialist time to support those with additional requirements. Where possible we did not want to assume and negate the experiences of our students, and instead, we wanted to capture their voices and learn from them.

Our diary-photograph: diary-interview study

Our phenomenological study incorporated twelve students, six with a print disability and six without. After gaining institutional ethical approval we asked for volunteers through our Careers and Employability Service who run a scheme that incentivises and rewards students for their active engagement in co-curricular activities with experiences of work. We found these were more than sufficient incentive and reward to attract a cohort of research participants. The students were chosen carefully in order to provide a varied sample spanning a range of year groups, disciplines and types of print disability.

We asked each student to keep a diary of their day-to-day experiences of accessing information at the university (both educationally and socially) for one week. We asked them to highlight positive and negative experiences, and reflect on the way the success or failure of the interaction made them feel. We specified that we were interested in barriers to information, and where the students felt a specific experience was particularly impactful, we asked them to take a photograph. With every image, the students gave us context with a textual annotation describing the barrier, how it hindered their research or study progress and how it made them feel. The students emailed their diaries and images to us at the end of the week.

Following the submission of the diaries, we set up interviews with each student, where we could meet them, and review and use their diary as 'a basis for further interviewing and communication between researcher and participants' (Crilly et al., 2006, p. 210). We wanted to make sure that we understood the diary entries, and had opportunity to clarify details relating to the reflective textual and photo elicitation elements. We wanted to make sure that we could understand as much as possible about the context of information interactions and associated factors the students experienced when comparing similar print disabled and non-print-disabled experiences.

We used a form of comparative analysis between the responses from print-disabled students and their non-print-disabled peers as a 'basic logical approach of observation and interpretation' (Teichler, 2014, p. 394) to understand the experience of information access at Kent, and to begin to understand the potential causes of any difference in experiences. In analysis, any differences in experiences were categorised in order to seek to establish a 'borderline' (Teichler, 2014, p. 394) between the experiences of these two groups and understand the reasons for difference. In order to do this, we used contextual information about the participants as it was essential for ensuring the relatability of findings between those who identified as print disabled and those who did not. For example, these contextual differences included the subject of study, nature of print disability and academic stage. These influenced the relevance of subsequent qualitative comparative analysis and the identification of relatable trends and themes.

Although we had not specified a format for the diaries, we were surprised that every student took a similar approach, writing a reflective diary and captioning images - either integrated into the main narrative diary or included as an appendix. The reflexivity precipitated by the diary method (Mackrill, 2008) was particularly useful for distinguishing between perceptions of similar information experiences and digging deeper in to how these experiences made the participants feel.

For example, a visually impaired student included the following entry in her diary (Figure 10.1). She was highlighting the steps outside the university library where the poor contrast directly affected her experience of accessing information as it inhibited her use of the service, and elicited the following commentary at the interview stage:

Figure 10.1 Lack of contrast on the library steps (participant photo).

> But these stairs outside can just completely put a stop on my day and they made me really nervous, and the threat of falling down because they're all the same– same facing brick, there's no distinction between the stairs.
>
> I think it's something like the fact that I do get on with things so independently, it's the fact that such a small thing can so regularly just jar me back into this having to stop and go, 'Oh I'm disabled, I'm gonna have to go over here and do this.'

We shared this feedback immediately with key stakeholders, who were moved and convinced by the sheer detail and emotional impact of the student's words to resolve this issue. The architects and our Estates department worked with the student to identify and test a range of solutions.

In a second example, a postgraduate mature student without a print disability recorded the following signage indicating the location of lecture theatres as problematic (Figure 10.2). The student expanded on her difficulty in interpreting the sign in the interview:

Figure 10.2 Image taken by participant indicating confusing use of acronyms to signpost lecture theatre location.

INTERVIEWER: What happened there? [referring to photo of Darwin lecture theatre sign]

PARTICIPANT 6: So, well I think that was also me just being a bit ridiculous, because … So, this is at the back of the ground floor, and in front are, like, wooden benches. And the people, I didn't know anyone that was going to be in this talk, but there was a group of maybe five or six people waiting outside to go in. But, not directly outside the lecture hall, they were waiting just in the middle milling around. So, I just, I don't use Darwin that much, I came in and the last time I'd been in Darwin I'd had to go upstairs, that's going back a bit. So, I didn't know the layout, I went upstairs, realised I had no idea where I was or where the hall was. And I came downstairs, again, and looking around, like, is it, could it possibly be on the ground floor? Is it here? And then I saw the sign and there was clearly an arrow and I just missed it. It was probably because there was this group of people that I didn't know that were stood in the middle, and I didn't want to stare at them. And it's different in every building, it's coded. And a lot of the time, I have my timetable on my phone also, it will say the lecture hall I'm in, but not the building. And the, so I have to google Kent and then this weird string of numbers and then find out what building it's in. Yeah. [laughs]

She felt uncertain, and as if it was her mistake, which impacted on her confidence and raised her stress levels as she had an unsettled entry into the lecture theatre.

Diary-photograph: diary-interview in practice

Our primary aim in the study was to capture a range of student experiences in text and visual means to categorise a variety of barriers to information access that all students might face, and through careful analysis begin to identify how far issues might relate to the nature of a participant's disability. In this discussion, we explore how by incorporating creative and participatory research (Brown & Leigh, 2019) into what could have been a more conventional evaluation or assessment of accessibility, we felt we were able to access a deeper understanding of students' experiences, and some of the implications of the diary-photograph: diary-interview method. Through using a combination of photo diaries and interviews we got beyond descriptions of simple processes and barriers and were able to tap into how the information experience made people feel as students and about their place within the institution. As one of the print disabled students commented in the follow up interview: 'I guess that's kind of the big thing about accessibility: you just want to feel the same as everyone else.' This reinforced our desire and mission to build in accessibility, so that all students (and staff) had those barriers minimised where possible.

Variation in quality and quantity of entries

The facility offered by the diary method to enable the 'absent' researcher to be 'present' (Gibson, 2005, p. 36) was particularly valuable to us. It provided the opportunity to see and attend to detail critical to understanding lived experiences of students (with and without disabilities) and to begin to understand differences in the broader student journey through HE:

> We need to know a lot about how people with atypical functions get around and get along ... This kind of information is no different from that routinely elicited from nondisabled people in designing facilities. But it requires the representation of people with a wide array of impairments, and it requires respectful attention to the minutiae of their daily lives
>
> (Wasserman et al., 2016, n.p.)

The essence of Wasserman's comment is echoed by Gill and Liamputtong (2009, p. 1452) who identify that the diary form 'can also be useful where a researcher is interested in uncovering routine, everyday processes and events that may be viewed by the participant as trivial and hence easily forgotten' (see also Chapter 12, this volume). The 'relatively unobtrusive' (Milligan and Bartlett, 2019, p. 1450) nature of this approach proved to be very beneficial. The range of responses subverted our initial expectations of what students would report.

Based on the National Student Survey, we assumed that the topics covered by our students would relate mainly to technical issues, such as the library catalogue or electronic resources, or to access to physical resources such as finding library books. However, the experiences students shared included far more nuanced preferences for print or electronic resources, building access, signage, teaching spaces, university communication and processes, the student union, the importance of wellbeing for studying, and the natural environment of the campus.

In fact, the 'freedom of expression' (Mackrill 2008, p. 13) engendered by the diary method meant that the data we received was wide-ranging, even to the point where we thought students had misunderstood the brief and began to question our strategy in relation to mitigating 'data overload, selectivity and manageability' (Cohen et al., 2013, p. 529). Mackrill (2008, p. 13) similarly highlights this as a challenge of the diary method but also considers it equally a strength:

> The diarist may choose to record data about topics other than the one the researcher set out to study. Thus, the diarist may reveal connections between topics that the researcher had not foreseen. Similarly, the diarist may present data about a topic in ways that do not immediately make sense to the researcher, but which, upon further investigation, prove to be useful. In diary studies this is more likely to occur than in an interview study, as in a diary study there is no interviewer to get the subject back on the researcher's track. This can lead to surprising data, as the tracks the diarist goes off on may be highly relevant. This challenges the researcher to be extra open to the diary data and search for possible relevancies that do not immediately catch the eye.

However, in every case when we explored the diaries with participants in interviews, even apparently irrelevant issues (like the campus shop stocking culturally appropriate items or access to food and drink while studying) directly impacted their access to information. In one case, the student described how not being able to afford to eat or get a hot drink on campus meant that they did not get to the library and physical copies of the text at all.

The range of data presented a definite challenge to how we would process the findings. The range of barriers to information was broad. Topics covered included: library borrowing, library search systems, University events, teaching and teaching spaces, student support, wellbeing, study space, time management, forms, access to PCs and printing, software issues, storage, physical access on campus, e-resources, food and drink, web access, lecture recording and University communication methods.

The data was textual and visual. It was sometimes emotive and difficult to categorise as it was so rich, capturing the surrounding data (Mackrill, 2008). It revealed many facets of students' informational experiences. Even identifying a means to code and categorise each participant's range of responses and information was challenging. Before using NVivo to manage and analyse the data, we used 'old school' Post-it notes on a wall attempting to make sense (Figure 10.3):

Figure 10.3 Our initial efforts to use Post-it notes to begin the process of filtering.

Although time-consuming to analyse, generating lots of data to process is a strength of this type of study. Our data was a good vehicle for providing 'unique insights into the life-worlds inhabited by individuals; their experiences, actions, behaviors, and emotions and how these are played out across time and space' (Milligan & Bartlett, 2019, p. 1447), such was the diversity of topics identified and the detail with which they were described. Indeed, the range of topics covered by our participants served to highlight how unique each student's experience is (regardless of print disability) and made it particularly noteworthy and meaningful where commonalities and trends were identified.

Lack of researcher control

A related criticism levelled at such diary methods is the lack of control the researcher has concerning the structure of the data that is going to be returned. Mackrill (2008, p. 14) notes that 'solicited diary methods require the researcher to relinquish control of part of the research process'; however, again, this represented one of the key advantages of the format for us, namely 'participant independence' (Gibson et al., 2013, p. 396), which supported the researcher's ability to act as a passive observer of real lived experiences from a diverse range of areas of student life that we would otherwise be unable to enter.

Each one of our participants was provided with a basic framework detailing the parameters of our research, and clearly outlining what kinds of experience we would like them to capture, for how long, and advising of ethical steps to ensure their wellbeing and privacy. We did not offer a prescribed format or template – preferring an unstructured approach to enable participants to create responses they felt would best reflect their personal experiences.

Although this lack of structure posed a potential risk in that we could not control what we got back (see also Chapter 11, this volume), we found the participants brought their individual understanding to the brief, and, as a result, provided us with a very rich source of qualitative data and an insight into their lives across a range of stages, subjects and social experiences. These were relatable enough to be effectively dissected at the interview stage with careful questioning based on each diary entry and supporting image. Even the images and text which did not immediately seem to relate to information accessibility, had clear connections once placed in its context in the interview.

The unstructured approach had the advantage of being less likely to be directly influenced by the researcher, enabling participants to document authentic and immediate experiences. Indeed, Cohen et al. (2013, p. 530) note that photo elicitation can be a good method to provide alternative focus, avoiding 'awkward silences' and 'intimidating eye contact' between researcher and researched and therefore may provide a good record of the genuine 'lived' experiences. This was particularly beneficial as an approach for participants with autistic spectrum conditions who stated that they felt more comfortable with the freedom of the diary format to document their thoughts in their own time and space. This corresponds with the findings of Filep et al. (2015, p. 461) who observed that 'if participants are comfortable with the method, diaries can provide space in which…[participants] feel free to reflect or reminisce'. This not only allows elaboration on the complexity of thoughts and emotions at any moment, but also challenges temporal and relational sequences of how we process the world.

However, to be successful, it is vital that participants are clear about the basic parameters of the study and the relevance of experiences they should be aiming to record to avoid the risk that the entries of each participant will not be relatable (notwithstanding similar subject focus, stage etc.) which would ultimately limit the verisimilitude of the comparative analysis stage.

Selectivity of participant responses

The 'difference' or 'selectivity' in what is recorded is interesting in itself as a form of data and 'these choices reveal aspects of the self as much as diary content' and can be probed further within an interview (Mackrill, 2008, p. 14). This was evident as we attempted to distinguish experiences of students with and without disabilities. Indeed, as our analyses of the data progressed, we noticed alternate perspectives and areas of differentiation that we had not initially anticipated. For example, international students had concerns about lack of availability of culturally diverse food in the student shop, while most students expressed concerns over costs of refreshments on campus. Visually impaired students highlighted physical access alongside the digital and informational, while commuting students included photographs of public transport to indicate the challenges faced by commuting students when university communications are unclear around the cancellation of classes (Figure 10.4).

In relation to the selectivity of photo elicitation, Cohen et al. (2013, p. 529) highlight the potential pitfalls of the camera being selective and fleeting and failing to therefore deliver a 'singular objective reality':

> Whilst cameras report what they see and what really happens (rather than the selective observation of the human observer), nevertheless images are

Figure 10.4 Photograph of inside of bus taken by a student to indicate inconvenience to commuting students when classes are cancelled.

selective, in that the image maker has already decided what to include or not to include, what to focus on and what not to focus on, where to point the camera and where not to point the camera. Images also create their own representational and symbolic forms and they are time-bound – they catch a particular moment (or several).

In a study such as ours there were many variables to be aware of. How can we be certain that the barriers experienced are genuinely related to the nature of a person's print disability and how can this be disaggregated from other factors such as general academic performance, motivation and engagement? These may also have a bearing on how students perceive (and feel about) barriers to information access. For example, some students may be more resourceful and able to find solutions to problems and may therefore not experience them as negatively. The relatability of the qualitative experiences of each student will also be dependent on factors such as subject of study and their academic stage.

Inequity of the format for all participants

There is criticism of the potentially inequitable nature of keeping a diary as something that is hostile to people with differing abilities and that the form 'favor[s] more literate and better-educated participants' which can be 'exclusionary to those with poor literacy skills or those with cognitive or physical limitations that hinder their ability to perform the task of diary keeping' (Milligan & Bartlett, 2019, p. 1457). This was a particular concern for us given our focus on print disability, and because we were asking visually impaired students to document their experiences visually. This is feasible using talking camera type applications such as Seeing AI which the researchers provided to all participants in the form of a briefing summary that gave ideas for record keeping (to gently suggest an approach without seeking to overly prescribe one). However, this was not borne out in our findings – our perception based on the student feedback we received was that any differences in quality of diary entry were more a product of the student's lack of time or general organisation.

The photo elicitation part of the diary was, in fact, quite a leveller in terms of capturing 'knowledge that is not reducible to language' (Bagnoli, 2009, p. 547) and proved a helpful methodology to apply to understanding the potential differentiation of user experiences in modern university education. Gibson et al. (2013, p. 386) note this by stating 'photographs…provide a visual illumination of the unthought or unstated that, when combined with other methods, reveals how identities are produced and reproduced in the everyday'.

Bagnoli (2009, p. 547) argues that 'the inclusion of non-linguistic dimensions in research … may allow us to access and represent different levels of experience' – offering new and unforeseen insights that traditional methods may not be able to elicit:

> The use of interviews relies on language as the privileged medium for the creation and communication of knowledge. However, our daily experience is

made of a multiplicity of dimensions, which include the visual and the sensory, and which are worthy of investigation but cannot always be easily expressed in words, since not all knowledge is reducible to language.

(Bagnoli, 2009, p. 547)

While we are aware of the issues and considerations that using the diary-photograph: diary-interview method entailed with regard to variation in quality of data; lack of researcher control; selectivity of participant responses and potential inequity of the method; we feel strongly that its benefits added much value to our research.

Conclusion

The study exceeded our expectations in relation to the range of information access issues it helped us to identify, and this is due to the methodology that we employed. The relatively unstructured approach of diary-photograph: diary-interview elicited a wide range of responses by offering all participants the freedom to creatively document their information access processes for the week of the study. By not limiting our participants to a particular format or by being too controlling about a structure, we were able to find out how they perceived 'information access' as a much wider topic than just the technological or physical aspects of library searches and software we were expecting. To the contrary, the students shared barriers to information that shadowed larger aspects of inclusion for students with disabilities or from different cultural backgrounds. We also gained insights into how information barriers made them feel which enabled us to begin to formulate a sense of the collective impact of even apparently small barriers to a broader sense of wellbeing. This is important for understanding factors around digital inclusion which requires a thorough examination of issues related to access, skills, participation, and usage in context (Beyene, 2018, p. 136).

We feel that there is much here of relevance to the sector, particularly in light of the rollout of the Public Sector Bodies (Websites and Mobile Applications) Accessibility Regulations (2018) (PSBAR), which require all public sector bodies to meet the requirements of Web Content Accessibility Guidelines (WCAG) by September 2020 (W3C, 2018). We feel that to meet these requirements it is paramount that universities have an understanding of usability as well as technical accessibility criteria (meeting WCAG standard). One way to meaningfully achieve this is through dialogue with users to understand how they feel about the services at a deeper, emotional level. The diary-photograph: diary-interview method is highly suited to this type of work.

Among the students' own words, we found much inspiration to inform our future work at the University, well in excess of what we had originally hoped to gain from the study. We end with a participant's words on how best to support students with disabilities:

I am always telling non-disabled people that the best way to approach a disabled person is with the question 'How can I help?' Because from that I know that you want to help, you don't know how to help, you trust me that I can explain, and you don't have any preconceptions which can destroy the helping process.

Acknowledgements

Huge thanks to Angela Groth-Seary for all her help, inspiration and support.

Note

1 The University of Kent was awarded the Times Higher Education Award for Outstanding Support for Students for the OPERA (Opportunity, Productivity, Engagement, Reducing barriers, Achievement) project, which is aimed at ensuring information services are accessible to all.

References

Adams, M. & Brown, S. (2006). *Towards inclusive learning in higher education: Developing curricula for disabled students*. London: Routledge.

Alaszewski, A. (2006). *Using diaries for social research*. London: Sage.

Bagnoli, A. (2009) Beyond the standard interview: The use of graphic elicitation and arts-based methods. *Qualitative Research*, 9, 5: 547–570.

Beyene, W. M. (2018) Digital inclusion in library context: A perspective from users with print disability. *Journal of Web Librarianship*, 12, 2: 121–140.

Brown, N. & Leigh, J. (2019) Creativity and playfulness in higher education research. In M. Tight & J. Huisman (eds), *Theory and method in higher education research*, Vol 4. Bingley: Emerald, pp. 49–66.

CLA (2016) User guidelines: Higher education licence. Retrieved from www.cla.co.uk/sites/default/files/HE-User-Guidelines.pdf (accessed 20 March 2019).

Cohen, L., Manion, L. & Morrison, K. (2013) *Research methods in education*. London: Taylor & Francis.

Crilly, N., Blackwell, A. & Clarkson, P. (2006) Graphic elicitation: Using research diagrams as interview stimuli. *Qualitative Research*, 6, 3: 341–366.

DSSLG (2017) Inclusive teaching and learning in higher education as a route to excellence. Retrieved from www.gov.uk/government/uploads/system/uploads/attachment_data/file/587221/Inclusive_Teaching_and_Learning_in_Higher_Education_as_a_route_to-exc ellence.pdf (accessed 28 April 2019).

Filep, C. V., Thompson-Fawcett, M, Fitzsimmons, S. & Turner S. (2015) Reaching revelatory places: The role of solicited diaries in extending research on emotional geographies into the unfamiliar. *Area*, 47, 4: 459–465.

Gibson, B. (2005) Co-producing video diaries: The presence of the 'absent' researcher. *International Journal of Qualitative Methods*, 4, 4, 34–43. https://doi.org/10.1177/160940690500400403.

Gibson, B., Mistry, B., Smith, B., Yoshida, K., Abbott, D., Lindsay, S. & Hamdani, Y. (2013) The integrated use of audio diaries, photography, and interviews in research with disabled young men. *International Journal of Qualitative Methods*, 12, 1: 382–402.

Harvey, L. (2011) Intimate reflections: Private diaries in qualitative research. *Qualitative Research*, 11, 6: 664–682.

Latham, A. (2003) Research, performance, and doing human geography: Some reflections on the diary-photograph, diary-interview method. *Environment and Planning A*, 35, 11: 1993–2017.

Mackrill, T. (2008) Solicited diary studies of psychotherapy in qualitative research – pros and cons. *European Journal of Psychotherapy and Counselling*, 10, 1: 5–18.

Meth, P. (2003) Entries and omissions: Using solicited diaries in geographical research. *Area*, 35, 2: 195–205.

Milligan, C. & Bartlett, R. (2019) Solicited diary methods. In P. Liamputtong (eds), *Handbook of research methods in health social sciences*. Singapore: Springer.

Milligan, C., Bingley, A. & Gatrell, A. (2005) Digging deep: Using diary techniques to explore the place of health and well-being amongst older people. *Social Science and Medicine*, 61: 1882–1892.

Newman, I., Healey, C., Osborne, A. & Newman, V. (2018) Diversity for everybody, achievement for all, patterns not labels. *The Journal of Inclusive Practice in Further and Higher Education*, 10, 1.

Oliver, M. (1990) *The individual and social models of disability*. Paper presented at Joint Workshop of the Living Options Group and the Research Unit of the Royal College of Physicians on People with Established Locomotor Disabilities in Hospitals, 23 July. Retrieved from https://disability-studies.leeds.ac.uk/wp-content/uploads/sites/40/library/Oliver-in-soc-dis.pdf (accessed 8 April 2019).

Teichler, T. (2014) Opportunities and problems of comparative higher education research: The daily life of research. *Higher Education*, 67.

Wasserman, D., Asch, A., Blustein, J. & Putnam, D. (2006) Disability: Definitions, models, experience. In E. N. Zalta (ed.), *The Stanford encyclopaedia of philosophy* (summer edition). Retrieved from https://plato.stanford.edu/archives/sum2016/entries/disability (accessed 7 April 2019).

W3C (2018) Understanding WCAG 2.1. Retrieved from www.w3.org/WAI/WCAG21/Understanding (accessed 12 April 2019).

Chapter 11

Closer to the feeling?

Exploring diary methods for higher education research on affective phenomena

James Burford

Introduction: diary methods and higher education research on affective phenomena

In recent years, there has been increasing interest in affect, emotion, and felt experience in the field of higher education (HE) research. Scholars have investigated the desires that draw people to universities (Mitchell, 2019), the affective forces shaping policy imaginaries (Hey & Leathwood, 2009), and the wave of feelings that ebb and flow across any given campus on any given day (Kelly, 2015). While this body of research is sometimes described as an affective 'turn', as Hey and Leathwood (2009) remind us, scholarly interest in emotion in HE can be traced across a long line of feminist and critical studies (e.g. hooks, 1994; Lee & Williams, 1999). Whether or not this is a 'turn' or a spurt of activity within an ongoing flow, HE researchers have recognised that accounts of knowledge production, teaching and learning require theorisation of emotion because 'accounts of the university ... which dwell solely on the rational are analytically impoverished' (Beard, Clegg & Smith, 2007, p. 263).

The growth of interest in emotion has also occurred across HE sub-fields, including doctoral education, which is the thematic focus of this chapter. Researchers have increasingly challenged prevailing discourses which configure emotions as ideally absent, phases to be overcome, or personal issues which suggest that a student may not be a good fit for doctoral study (Aitchison & Mowbray, 2013). Rather than viewing doctoral education as properly rational and passionless, researchers have argued instead that emotions are integral to both knowledge production, and the production of doctoral subjects (e.g. Herman, 2008; Aitchison & Mowbray, 2013; Cotterall, 2013). Increasingly, doctoral education scholars have examined doctoral identity development, looking at whether specific milestones in the doctoral experience might be knotted up with certain feelings. Another stream of thinking has linked felt experience to relations of power (Aitchison & Mowbray, 2013), arguing that emotions are not only individual psychological states but are also socially and culturally produced. Writing is a particular doctoral practice that has been recognised as ripe for affective inquiry (Badenhorst & Guerin, 2016; Bosanquet & Cahir, 2015; Burford, 2017; Cameron, Nairn & Higgins, 2009), with accounts emerging about the complex felt experiences of doctoral women (Aitchison & Mowbray, 2013), and disciplinary accounts of the affective dimensions of writing in the sciences (Aitchison, Catterall, Ross & Burgin, 2012), for example. Others have closely examined supervision dynamics (Cotterall, 2013; Lee & Williams, 1999), and post-doctoral careers (Guerin, 2019) as zones that are laden with affective intensity.

Given growing interest in doctoral emotions as an object of inquiry, this chapter aims to illuminate how HE researchers might design empirical projects to investigate affective phenomena. I begin by explaining the concepts emotion and affect and how they are understood within HE and doctoral research. I also track some existing methods that doctoral education researchers have used to investigate affective phenomena and outline some of their limitations. Following this, I survey how other researchers have used diaries to research emotions and affective phenomena, including how researchers have designed diary instruments. The second half of this chapter takes these debates forward by reflecting on my own research project, 'Uneasy Feelings' (Burford, 2016a). I offer detailed description of the diary instrument I used in an empirical study on the affective-political subjectivities of doctoral students in Aotearoa New Zealand, reflecting on the strengths and weaknesses of my research design. Ultimately, across this chapter I make a case for diary research being a valuable tool for HE researchers investigating affective phenomena. I argue that diary-interview method enabled rich understandings of the context in which emotions were felt, the duration of affective patterns, and the ways in which felt experiences were interwoven with the political context of the contemporary university. The use of solicited diaries also allows emotionally intense data to be collected in a manner that is less intrusive for research participants. Undertaking diary research enabled the collection of nuanced and detailed data that was temporally 'closer to the feeling' than other qualitative research methods might be.

Doctoral education research on emotion, affect and felt experience

Before proceeding to examine how other doctoral education researchers have explored 'emotion', 'feeling' and 'affect', it is important to clarify some of the dis/ connections between these terms. As I remarked at the outset of this chapter, doctoral education researchers have had an interest in emotion and 'the irrational' for quite some time (e.g. Lee & Williams, 1999). However, as a part of the wider affective turn in the social sciences, scholars of doctoral education have become more interested in these keywords. Many doctoral education researchers proceed with an understanding that affect and emotion describe related pathways to understanding felt experience. Among doctoral education researchers, 'affect' tends to be used to describe embodied states which are asignifying, a sort of pre-cognitive sensation (Kennedy & Gray, 2016). In contrast, 'emotions' are often understood to be products of cognitive recognition and representation, cultural constructs which draw on affective states (ibid.), for example 'envy' or 'joy'. Many researchers mediate between these two positions, as Aitchison and Mowbray (2013, p. 861) argue: 'We see emotions as more than just biology or behaviour but as intertwined psychology and biology within a social context.' In my own contributions to these conversations (e.g. Burford, 2015b, 2017), I have tended to use generic terms like feeling and felt experience, because they enable 'the ambiguity between feelings as embodied sensations and feelings as psychic or cognitive experiences' (Cvetkovich, 2012, p. 4) to be retained. Across the doctoral education literature researchers have drawn on a range of conceptual resources to approach felt experience, including Wetherell's (2012) affective practice (e.g. Burford, 2015b; Kennedy & Gray, 2016), Hochschild's (1983) work on emotional labour (e.g. Aitchison & Mowbray, 2013; Herman, 2008), activity theory (e.g. Cotterall, 2013) and threshold concepts (e.g. Bosanquet & Cahir, 2015).

So far, I have identified that competing theories of emotion operate within doctoral education scholarship, and that scholars have focused their inquiries on the felt experience of various doctoral practices. In the remainder of this chapter I focus on *how* HE researchers might capture emotional phenomena in their research projects. Before outlining the possibilities of diary research as a possible method for approaching felt experience, I want to consider some other methods that HE scholars have commonly used. While it is clear that many approaches may be considered, and also that scholars also employ mixed methods designs to explore doctoral emotions (e.g. Doloriet, Sambrook & Stewart, 2012), I will limit my focus here to two of the most common methods: questionnaires and interviews.

Questionnaires are very popular research tools for researching felt experience in HE in general (e.g. Trigwell, 2012; Zhang & Zhu, 2008) and doctoral education in particular (e.g. Doloriet, Sambrook & Stewart, 2012; Kennedy & Gray, 2016). Questionnaires are popular because they are easily administered and have temporal adaptability across both momentary and habitual emotional reactions (Pekrun & Stephens, 2010). Additionally, results are easily quantifiable and enable comparability across contexts. Despite their advantages, questionnaires are often less helpful when it comes to tracking the chronological sequencing of affective practices. They are also often less useful when seeking to understand how emotions are patterned in relation to interactions, relationships and thoughts experienced by a participant, as this information often exceeds their level of detail.

Interviews are also frequently used methods for doctoral education researchers of felt experience (e.g. Wall, 2008). Unlike questionnaires, interviews tend to enable participants to offer richer detail about emotional episodes (e.g. Chubb, Watermeyer & Wakeling, 2017; Pekrun and Stephens, 2010). Indeed, many doctoral education scholars design interview schedules within a narrative inquiry framework to generate stories of felt experience (e.g. Cotterall, 2013; Guerin, 2019). The depth of data collected in interviews can be helpful for tracing how personal histories, and social relations interact with affective patterns. However, the one-off nature of many interview designs prevents researchers from gathering longitudinal personal insights. In order to address this limitation, some doctoral education researchers have used multiple interviews over extended periods, as can be seen in

Cotterall's (2013) study which interviewed participants over a two-year period. Another challenge with interviews is that they are less attuned to capture ordinary experiences that may lose significance over time. Within interviews there can be a tendency for participants to re-construct a linear and coherent story which emphasise a single dominant emotion (Cottingham & Erickson, 2019). Often minor, shifting or incoherent felt experiences can be forgotten or seem too insignificant to report, leaving interview methods less suited to capturing ordinary affective routines.

Because of the retrospective nature of both interviews and questionnaires, they share a tendency to reduce complexity, contradiction and incoherence when it comes to capturing affective phenomena. While recognising there is no single way to undertake rigorous affective research in HE, and that research methods must always respond to the aims of a particular study, I am interested in highlighting research methods that are able to attend to the 'patterning' and 'flow' of ordinary felt experience over time (Wetherell, 2012). In contrast, event-based methods (such as diaries) are valuable when it comes to capturing emotion because they enable researchers to get more information about the 'specific emotion-provoking event and context, and meaning of that event' (Briner & Kiefer, 2005, p. 308). In the next section I survey diary research which takes emotion as an object of inquiry, including HE research studies of emotion which use diary methods.

Diary research on emotions and affective phenomena in HE and beyond

Social scientists have identified diary research as an innovative method with significant potential to address some methodological challenges that arise when researching emotions (Filep et al., 2018). Diary research has already been identified for its capacity to offer deep reflection, and longitudinal understandings, while minimising imposition on participants (Eidse & Turner, 2014). Scholars have argued that, by allowing participants time and privacy to reflect (rather than the immediate question and answer format of interviews, for example), diaries allow for nuanced, detailed understandings of everyday experience (ibid.). In contrast to retrospective methods such as interviews and questionnaires, diaries arguably facilitate more attentive recording of the mixed experiences of ordinary life. Another argument in favour of diary methods is that they facilitate a more participant led approach, offering participants more control over the research process; a feature which is especially valuable for sensitive topics (ibid.).

In addition to these more general strengths of diary research, there are some specific reasons why researchers of felt experience might take up diaries. Researchers who address topics that are seen to be emotionally complex – such as the experience of breastfeeding (Williamson, Leeming, Lyttle & Johnson, 2011), the emotional experience of living with HIV/AIDS (Myers, 2010; Thomas, 2007) and everyday sexism (Swim et al., 2001) – have argued that diaries can help to elicit more emotional and relationally complex responses than other ethnographic methods. Researchers who have taken emotion as an object of inquiry have drawn on a variety of diary forms including audio diaries (Cottingham & Erickson, 2019), written diaries (Spowart & Nairn, 2014; Travers, 2011) and photo diaries (Myers, 2010). In this section I identify previous studies which have drawn on diary methods to capture affective phenomena, paying close attention to their research design. While I cannot present an exhaustive list of all possible studies, I hope that the snapshot I offer illuminates the diversity of possible diary approaches for researching emotion.

A group of studies take up diary research to measure the frequency of phenomena, and affective responses to phenomena, over a specific time period. For example, Swim et al. (2003) used a daily diary format combining qualitative and quantitative elements in a study exploring the everyday racism experienced by African American students on campus. Arguing that diary methods correct some limitations of past research (e.g. retrospective questionnaires), Smith et al. (2003, p. 41) set out to capture 'more mundane or patterned experiences with everyday racism'. First, the 51 participants in this study completed pre-diary baseline measures, rating (on a scale ranging from 1 = very unrepresentative to 7 = very representative) the extent to which 24 emotions were representative during typical interactions with white Americans. Participants were then given a notebook with daily diary forms inside and were asked to complete these over a period of two weeks. Participants in this study responded to a detailed instrument which included open-ended descriptions of race-related incidents, questions about the characteristics of the incident (e.g. overt or nonverbal), the location and perpetrator of the incident, and their levels of certainty with regard to whether the incident reflected prejudice. A final section asked participants to assess their emotional responses to the incidents, rating the extent to which the same 24 emotions used in the pre-diary measures were representative of their emotions during the incident. Smith and colleagues argue that a daily diary method enabled participants to:

> report everyday experiences as soon after they occur as possible, better capturing some of the more subtle, sometimes ambiguous, and often forgotten experiences of racism that may be quickly brushed off as a function of everyday living and survival.
>
> (Smith et al., 2003, p. 41)

HE researchers have taken up similar approaches to measure the frequency of affective phenomena. For example, Ouweneel, Le Blanc, Schaufeli and van Wijhe (2012) invited 59 participants to fill out a booklet in their study on positive emotions, work-related hope, and work engagement among employees at a Dutch university. Participants were asked to fill in the questionnaire-like diary instrument for five consecutive working days before and after work, and were given reminders either via text or email to do so. Like the study by Smith and colleagues, baseline emotions were assessed to enable comparison to pre-diary levels.

Health researchers Cottingham and Erickson (2019, p. 1) have also taken up diaries as 'a method for capturing the sequential and varied experience of emotions as they emerge from everyday life'. Using audio diaries with 48 nurses in their research on the emotional experiences and emotional management of nursing in US hospitals, Cottingham and Erickson justified their methodological choice by stating that research tools to study emotion 'must attend to the intimate connection between emotion, self and interactions with others' (ibid., p. 3). The authors also argue that diary methods can have advantages over other qualitative methods (e.g. interviews) because rather than reconstructing coherent stories, diaries enable individuals to record experiences of multiple or contradictory emotions. Nurses participating in this study were given a digital voice recorder and were asked to make a recording during and/or after each of six consecutive shifts. Participants were instructed to reflect on their feelings after a shift, to describe how they felt during and after a shift, and who/what influenced their feelings.

Cottingham and Erickson (2019) argue that diary methods enabled them to capture emotional candour, arguably promoting more personal disclosure of private feelings than may be possible with other methods. In particular, the authors argue that diaries were more likely to capture negative emotions (which could be taboo for care workers to express in a research interview, for example). In addition to capturing candid emotions, Cottingham and Erickson (ibid.) also argue that diaries can be a tool for documenting the self as an unfinished project (e.g. identities which are multiple and fragmentary) and to identify processes of emotional reflexivity. In conducting their analyses of audio diary data, the authors undertook both qualitative analysis and waveform visualisations of audio recordings to allow greater representation of the 'texture' of spoken words (ibid.).

Another popular form of diary for capturing emotional data is a free-form written diary. Travers (2011) undertook reflective diary research with thirty Business and Management students in the final year of undergraduate study at a UK university. Her study focused on the lived experiences of stress and associated coping strategies. Students completed the diary as a part of their assessment in an optional module on 'Advanced Interpersonal Skills' where students had chosen to focus on stress management as a development goal. Students received coaching on diary keeping, and then Travers asked students to write regularly, and not only when significant events took place. Travers also sent participants periodic reminders and gave opportunities to ask questions, obtain advice and receive feedback on their diaries (ibid.). In terms of the analysis of the data, content analysis was undertaken to understand sources of stress and reactions to it. Travers found that using diaries enabled her to see 'which stressors may lead to which outcomes, reactions, and emotions, which is not always possible with questionnaires and other qualitative data gathering such as "one-shot" interviews' (ibid., p. 210).

The study that is closest in design to my own (introduced below) was a diary-interview project conducted by Spowart and Nairn (2014). The authors used a diary-interview approach with 8 mothers who snowboard. The study involved three primary components: an initial interview (to obtain basic demographic information and introduce the diary), a period of independent data collection, and finally a follow-up in-depth interview. Following an initial interview, participants were given lined notebooks within which they would handwrite their diaries. Participants were asked to complete 10 diary entries during the course of the snow season (approximately 4 months in duration). Two weeks after the initial interview, a check-in phone call was made to participants to provide support and help keep up motivation. In terms of their methodological reasoning, Spowart and Nairn advocate for the strengths of diary approaches to capture affective phenomena because 'first, they [diaries] are written closer to the time of the event, and second, they are written in the privacy of the participants' own homes (usually) without the researcher being physically present' (ibid., p. 328). Working within a post-structuralist framework, the authors describe emotions as relational in nature. For Spowart and Nairn, 'the process of this relational work produces the subjectivities of mother, snowboarder and research participant, and the diary-interview method offers the possibility of glimpsing this process in action' (ibid., p. 328).

Clearly, there are a diverse array of possibilities for HE researchers who are interested in researching emotion to think alongside. Each of these studies has demonstrated that diary methods have the potential to offer unique insights into the emotional worlds of participants, and that diaries can offer features that other common methods (e.g. interviews and questionnaires) cannot. In the next sections, I critically reflect on the opportunities and challenges of diary research via a consideration of my own research project, 'Uneasy Feelings' (Burford, 2016a).

Using diary method to investigate felt experience: the 'Uneasy Feelings' study

In this section I evaluate my own use of diary methods in a doctoral project focused on capturing data about felt experience. The 'Uneasy Feelings' project sought to explore the felt experience of doctoral education in Aotearoa New Zealand. The aims of my study were, firstly, to develop understandings about how the felt experience of doctoral education may be shaped by political transformations to HE, and secondly, to use conceptual resources of queer and feminist scholars to 'read' these affective-political contexts. My study was underpinned by a body of literature which has examined the affective experience of academic work amid growing neoliberalism (Hey & Leathwood, 2009; Kelly, 2015), and my goal was to extend these considerations to explore whether doctoral students were similarly impacted by wide-scale political transformations to the HE sector.

Recognising that affective phenomena are complex and multifaceted, and wishing to experiment with multiple methods, I opted for a multi-pronged research design. The entire study involved three dimensions: (1) cultural analysis of an online photo blog (Burford, 2015a); (2) autoethnographic self-reflection and the production of poetic inquiry (Burford, 2014) and ethnographic fiction (Burford, 2016b); and (3) a qualitative study conducted with 10 doctoral researchers in faculties of Arts and Education at a research-intensive university in Aotearoa New Zealand. In this chapter I focus solely on the third dimension, the qualitative study. Data were generated for the qualitative study in 2013 via two connected phases of data collection: (a) diary-interview method, involving an initial interview, independent diary-keeping, and a final semi-structured interview which ranged in duration from 45 minutes to over two hours; and (b) a three-day residential writing retreat, which involved solo and group-based research activities, producing verbal and visual data (see Burford, 2018). In this chapter I focus narrowly on the diary-interview component of the empirical study, where candidates were invited to record details about their felt experience of doctoral education and ordinary research practices, and then took part in a final semi-structured interview. However, as I outline my study it is important to remember that this diary-interview method sat alongside a wider suite of methods.

I recruited ten doctoral students in faculties of Arts and Education to my empirical study, and nine participated in the diary-interview component of the research. Participants varied in terms of their progress through the doctorate, with some nearing confirmation of candidature and others close to submission and examination. Participants ranged in age from their 20s through to their 50s. Five were women, four were men, and one participant was non-binary. Five participants were Pākehā/NZ European domestic students, four were international students and one participant chose not to specify their background.

Mirroring the process used by Spowart and Nairn (2014), there were three components to the diary-interview method used in this study. The first began with an orientation meeting with each participant via video conference. At this meeting I introduced myself to participants, described the research project, explained the diary data collection purpose and process, and discussed ethical considerations. Participants who consented to complete a diary were then given detailed verbal and written instructions (via email) and asked to document their routine feelings as they undertook their doctoral research and writing. An unstructured diary design was adopted, similar to that outlined by Spowart and Nairn (2014, p. 331), in order to keep the diaries 'open', and 'easy to complete, allowing space for the participants to write their thoughts and opinions without being constrained too much by instructions'. In my invitation to participants I suggested that diaries could be 'either be a virtual writing journal (using a private blog, or saved in a word document) or a pen and paper diary, or any mixture of these' (personal communication). I suggested participants produce a minimum of four entries within a month, but more entries were encouraged to enable greater tracking of affective patterns across time. In the instructions I explained that the purpose of the diary was to better understand the activities and felt experience of students' day-to-day doctoral lives. While Travers (2011) oriented her participants mostly toward reflection, I asked for both reflection and description:

> Often it can be tempting to record only the experiences that feel important and extraordinary – and please do feel encouraged to record intense events. However, don't forget to also record what is ordinary and run-of-the-mill.

The next phase involved a period of mostly independent diary writing. I sent 'check-in emails' in order to allay anxieties and to maintain an ongoing relationship with participants (see also Chapter 5, this volume). These were sent at least once, and then I made a judgement if I would send further check-in emails depending on the individual response of the participant. Some participants did send through draft entries, and two participants requested some short prompts during the period. Participants were invited to submit their writing diary at least two weeks prior to one-on-one interviews. Of the nine diaries that were returned, all were saved as word documents, some of which had images and examples of written work embedded. The range in terms of the number of entries was substantial, with two participants completing one entry, three completing four, two completing five entries, one completing 12 entries and one completing 14 entries. The range in terms of the number of words produced per participant spanned 597 words to 7637 words. Most participants completed their diaries over a period of one month, but two participants continued up until two and a half months. The combined tally of diary data amounted to almost 25,000 words.

Finally, I scheduled semi-structured interviews to enable additional contextualising information. The interviews were flexible, and often began with a simple question, 'How has your writing been going?'. In all cases the interview was scheduled after the diary was submitted, in order to allow areas of interest to be explored. I also used the interview to clarify aspects of the diary data that I did not understand. Enacting both of these steps offered critical benefits.

A reflexive account of methodological decision-making

It is my view that diary methods have considerable strengths for HE researchers of felt experience. As previous studies have noted, a key benefit of solicited diaries is that they allow data to be collected over a longer duration than other common methods. The longitudinal nature of diaries is important because it enables researchers to identify affective flows and patterns over time. Solicited diaries also enable data to be generated 'closer to the feeling'. This is of particular value to researchers of emotion given the fleeting nature of much affective experience. This feature was especially helpful for my project, because it facilitated the recording of affective phenomena that may be disregarded as unimportant or easily forgotten (e.g. routine boredom or numbness, small pleasures). In addition to this, solicited diaries are written at a time and place that is convenient for the participant, making them appropriate for capturing intimate felt experiences which may be challenging for others to observe (Chapter 9, this volume). Diaries are not only useful for research projects where the presence of the researcher may be intrusive, but on a more practical level the fact that recordings can occur without the need for the researcher to 'be there' also makes longitudinal research more feasible for researchers undertaking small projects, like my own. Diary research also involves more choice about the direction of data collection on the part of participants. Unlike interviews, where often interviewers lead the questioning, with diaries participants can determine what is meaningful to them, giving them greater agency over the direction of inquiry.

While many researchers view the interview component of the diary-interview as a means of triangulation in order to 'interrogate' diary data for its consistency and 'truthfulness', I did not. This is because the theoretical framework I work within is critical of the notion of objective and rational subjects (Harvey, 2011). It is my view that neither diaries nor interviews can be viewed as windows onto the truth. Firstly, this is because solicited diaries are not 'natural' documents. As Elliot (1997, p. 9) reminds us, 'from the outset, they are written with a particular reader and their agenda in mind'. And, as Harvey (2011) notes, diaries cannot tap into 'reality' because participants are always self-editing and performing versions of themselves. But more fundamentally, I do not believe diaries or interviews can access 'the truth', as all forms of telling are made up of competing discourses. As I was working within a post-structuralist paradigm (see Spowart & Nairn, 2014), it was my understanding that 'identity is a performative struggle, always destabilized and deferred' (Smith & Sparkes, 2006, p. 175). Thus, any formation of affective subject positions of doctoral students that I could glimpse via diary data was necessarily partial and constrained. While diary-interview method allowed data to be captured 'closer to the feeling' this does not mean that it is necessarily 'closer to the truth'.

Like all methods, diary-interviews have limitations. One key limitation of diaries is the time and effort required to complete them. It is important to think carefully about using time intensive methods, and whether participants are likely to have the motivation to complete them. In my study, some diaries were marked by limited depth, a factor which, in some cases, grew over time. Another challenge that I encountered in carrying out my study was that participants sometimes struggled to believe that seemingly ordinary activities may be of interest. Some participants required regular reassurance that detailed descriptions of feelings and activities were indeed valuable. It could be that some of the up-front training used in Travers (2011) study could have been useful, or perhaps more time could have been spent at the initial orientation interview emphasising the value of description for the purposes of the study.

While across this chapter I have made the case for diary research for studies of felt experience, in offering retrospective accounts of methodological decision-making, such as this, there is often a temptation for researchers to narrate research as a much more tidy, logical and linear process than the one that researchers themselves experience! This tug toward tidiness is prompting some uneasy feelings right now as I conclude these reflections. As readers will notice from my sketch of my own study, mine was a complex and multifaceted project, where I pursued an interest in methodological juxtaposition: what would happen if different 'ways in' to research were presented alongside each other? What possibilities for knowing the felt experience of doctoral education might emerge as a result? In line with my wider queer knowledge project, I imagined this as a queer orientation to methodology. I was inspired by Halberstam's (1998) vision of queer as a 'scavenger methodology' which mixes and matches methods, and resists calls to disciplinary coherence. When accounting for one's methodological decision making it is commonplace to describe a careful process of reading and deliberation; I will confess that I did not read a wide body of research on diary methods for capturing emotional data before designing my own. I had read Spowart and Nairn's (2014) paper closely and was persuaded that diary-interview method could be a valuable tool for generating thick and nuanced accounts of personal experience. As my project focused on exploring doctoral students' felt experiences, and I required an approach that could capture sequential and fluid affective practices, diary-interview method seemed to be a particularly appropriate method. I also felt that, given my qualitative study also required me to build rapport with participants over time in order to gather and share time together at the writing retreat, that a process of diary-keeping would also enhance this. If I was given the opportunity to re-design my study, I would opt for a more regular entries (e.g. daily) over a shorter duration. The images and photographs that participants sent me throughout their studies were also immensely valuable, so I would also encourage this more in orientation interviews.

Concluding thoughts

This chapter has introduced diary methods, positioning them as valuable methods for HE researchers who seek to examine affective phenomena. After surveying existing diary studies which examine felt experience, I introduced my own study which drew upon diary-interview method to investigate the affective-politics of doctoral education in Aotearoa New Zealand. In so doing, I have extended existing diary research which has taken affective phenomena as an object of inquiry (e.g. Spowart & Nairn, 2014), including previous HE studies (Ouweneel et al., 2012). Across this chapter I have revealed that solicited diaries brought with them a number of strengths and complexities. The space and time that diaries gave doctoral students to tell their own stories of doctoral life allowed me to gain nuanced understandings of their everyday felt experiences. Solicited diaries enabled data to be generated closer to an affective event, in a less-intrusive manner, and in a way that was efficient for me as a researcher. Importantly, the longitudinal nature of diaries also enabled me to access accounts of affective flows and patterns over time. In concluding this chapter, I hope that future HE researchers might benefit from my experience as they consider using diary research designs to research affective phenomena. Whether HE researchers find themselves in agreement or opposition with my methodological choices, I hope that by writing this chapter I might prompt further dialogue. There remain many questions left to consider about the potentials of diary methods for researching emotion and I look forward to the ongoing discussion.

Acknowledgements

I would like to thank the participants in the 'Uneasy Feelings' study for their generous participation. Thanks are also owed to the editors of this collection for helpful feedback on an earlier draft of this chapter.

References

Aitchison, C. & Mowbray, S. (2013) Doctoral women: Managing emotions, managing doctoral studies. *Teaching in Higher Education*, 18, 8: 859–870.

Aitchison, C., Catterall, J., Ross, P. & Burgin, S. (2012) 'Tough love and tears': Doctoral writing in the sciences. *Higher Education Research and Development*, 31, 4: 435–447.

Badenhorst, C. & Guerin C. (2016) Post/graduate research literacies and writing pedagogies. In C. Badenhorst & C. Guerin (eds), *Research literacies and writing pedagogies for masters and doctoral writers*. London: Brill, pp. 3–28.

Beard, C., Clegg, S. & Smith, K. (2007) Acknowledging the affective in higher education. *British Educational Research Journal*, 33, 2: 235–252.

Bosanquet, A. & Cahir, J. (2015) 'What feelings didn't I experience!': Affect and identity in PhD writing. In C. Badenhorst & C. Guerin (eds), *Research literacies and writing pedagogies for masters and doctoral writers*. London: Brill, pp. 132–148.

Briner, R. B. & Kiefer, T. (2005) Psychological research into the experience of emotion at work: Definitely older, but are we any wider? In N. M. Ashkanasay, C. Hartel & J. W. Zerbe (eds), *Research on emotion in organizations: The effects of affect in organizational settings*. Oxford: Elsevier, pp. 289–315.

Burford, J. (2014) A meditation on the poetics of doctoral writing, *Higher Education Research and Development*, 33, 6: 1232–1235.

Burford, J. (2015a) Dear obese PhD applicants: Twitter, tumblr and the contested affective politics of fat doctoral embodiment. *M/C Journal*, 18, 3. Retrieved from http://journal.media-culture.org.au/index.php/mcjournal/article/view/969.

Burford, J. (2015b) Queer(y)ing the affective politics of doctoral education: Toward complex visions of agency and affect. *Higher Education Research and Development*, 34, 4: 776–787.

Burford, J. (2016a) Uneasy feelings: Queer(y)ing the affective-politics of doctoral education. Doctoral thesis, Auckland University.

Burford, J. (2016b) Doctoral induction day: An ethnographic fiction on doctoral emotions. In J. Smith, J. Rattray, T. Peseta & D. Loads (eds), *Identity-work in the contemporary university: Exploring an uneasy profession*. Rotterdam: Sense Publishers, pp. 117–128.

Burford, J. (2017) Conceptualising doctoral writing as an affective-political practice. *International Journal of Doctoral Studies*, 12: 17–32.

Burford, J. (2018) The trouble with doctoral aspiration now. *International Journal of Qualitative Studies in Education*, 31, 6: 487–503.

Cameron, J., Nairn, K. & Higgins, J. (2009) Demystifying academic writing: Reflections on emotions, know-how and academic identity. *Journal of Geography in Higher Education*, 33, 2: 269–284.

Chubb, J., Watermeyer, R. & Wakeling, P. (2017) Fear and loathing in the academy? The role of emotion in response to an impact agenda in the UK and Australia. *Higher Education Research and Development*, 36, 3: 555–568.

Cotterall, S. (2013) More than just a brain: Emotions and the doctoral experience. *Higher Education Research and Development* 32, 2: 174–187.

Cottingham, M. D. & Erickson, R. J. (2019) Capturing emotion with audio diaries. *Qualitative Research*, 20, 5: 549–564.

Cvetkovich, A. (2012) *Depression: A public feeling*. Durham, NC: Duke University Press.

Doloriet, C., Sambrook, S. & Stewart, J. (2012) Power and emotion in doctoral supervision: Implications for HRD. *European Journal of Training and Development*, 36, 7: 732–750.

Eidse, N. & Turner, S. (2014) Doing resistance their own way: Counter-narratives of street vending in Hanoi, Vietnam through solicited journaling. *Area*, 46, 3: 242–248.

Elliott, H. (1997) The use of diaries in sociological research on health experience. *Sociological Research Online*, 2, 2: 38–48.

Filep, C., Turner, S., Eidse, N., Thompson-Fawcett, M. & Fitzsimons, S. (2018) Advancing rigour in solicited diary research. *Qualitative Research*, 18, 4: 451–470.

Guerin, C. (2019) Stories of moving on: HASS PhD graduates' motivations and career trajectories inside and beyond academia. *Arts and Humanities in Higher Education*, 19, 3: 304–324.

Halberstam, J. (1998) *Female masculinity*. Durham, NC: Duke University Press.

Harvey, L. (2011) Intimate reflections: Private diaries in qualitative research. *Qualitative Research*, 11, 6: 664–682.

Hey, V. & Leathwood, C. (2009) Passionate attachments: Higher education, passionate attachments, knowledge, emotion and social justice. *Higher Education Policy*, 22, 1: 101–118.

Herman, C. (2008) Negotiating the emotions of change: Research, restructuring and the doctoral student. *South African Journal of Higher Education*, 22, 1: 100–115.

Hochschild, A. (1983) *The managed heart: Commercialization of human feeling*. Berkeley: University of California Press.

hooks, b. (1994). *Teaching to transgress: Education as the practice of freedom*. New York: Routledge.

Kelly, F. (2015) A day in the life (and death) of a public university. *Higher Education Research and Development*, 34, 6, 1153–1163.

Kennedy, E. & Gray, M. (2016) 'You're facing that machine but there's a human being behind it': Students' affective experiences on an online doctoral programme. *Pedagogy, Culture and Society*, 24, 3: 417–429.

Lee, A. & Williams, C. (1999) 'Forged in fire': Narratives of trauma in PhD supervision pedagogy. *Southern Review*, 32, 1: 6–26.

Mitchell, C. (2019) The dreams and promises of the university: Narratives of first-generation students in doctoral education. Doctoral thesis, University of Auckland, New Zealand.

Myers, J. (2010) Moving methods: Constructing emotionally poignant geographies of HIV in Auckland, New Zealand. *Area*, 42, 3: 328–338.

Ouweneel, E., Le Blanc, P. M., Schaufeli, W. & van Wijhe, C. I. (2012) Good morning, good day: A diary study on positive emotions, hope, and work engagement. *Human Relations*, 65, 9: 1129–1154.

Pekrun R. & Stephens E. J. (2010) Achievement emotions in higher education. In J. Smart (ed.), *Higher education: Handbook of theory and research*, vol 25. Springer: Dordrecht, pp. 238–255.

Smith, B. & Sparkes A. C. (2006) Narrative inquiry in psychology: exploring the tensions within. *Qualitative Research in Psychology* 3, 3: 169–192.

Spowart, L. & Nairn, K. (2014) (Re)performing emotions in diary-interviews. *Qualitative Research*, 14, 3: 327–340.

Swim, J., Hyers, L., Cohen, L. & Ferguson, M. (2001) Everyday sexism: Evidence for its incidence, nature and psychological impact from three daily diary studies. *Journal of Social Issues*, 57, 1: 31–53.

Swim, J. K., Hyers, L. L., Cohen, L. L., Fitzgerald, D. C. & Bylsma, W. H. (2003) African American college students' experiences with everyday racism: Characteristics of and responses to these incidents. *Journal of Black Psychology*, 29, 1: 38–67.

Thomas, F. (2007) Eliciting emotions in HIV/AIDS research: A diary-based approach. *Area*, 39, 1: 74–82.

Travers, C. (2011) Unveiling a reflective diary methodology for exploring the lived experiences of stress and coping. *Journal of Vocational Behavior*, 79, 1: 205–216.

Trigwell, K. (2012) Relations between teachers' emotions in teaching and their approaches to teaching in higher education. *Instructional Science*, 40: 607–621.

Wall, S. (2008) Of heads and hearts: Women in doctoral education at a Canadian university. *Women's Studies International Forum*, 31, 3: 219–228.

Wetherell, M. (2012) *Affect and emotion: A new social science understanding*. Los Angeles, CA: Sage.

Williamson, I., Leeming, D., Lyttle S. & Johnson, S. (2011) 'It should be the most natural thing in the world': Exploring first-time mothers' breastfeeding difficulties in the UK using audio-diaries and interviews. *Maternal and Child Nutrition*, 8, 4: 434–447.

Zhang, Q. & Zhu, W. (2008) Exploring emotion in teaching: Emotional labor, burnout, and satisfaction in Chinese higher education. *Communication Education*, 57, 1: 105–122.

Chapter 12

The diary method and its power to record the routine and forgettable in the language lives of international students

Olivia Groves

Introduction

Diaries are valuable research tools due to their facilitation of rich and detailed information (Swim et al., 2003) that may be inaccessible by other research methods (Cucu-Oancea, 2013; Debreli, 2011). The diary method may also contribute to the integrity of a project through collecting data which is more accurate than that obtained via other methods such as interviews and questionnaires (Cucu-Oancea, 2013).

Despite these benefits, diaries have been relatively neglected as a social science research method (Milligan, Bingley & Gatrell, 2005). They have not become part of mainstream qualitative research methods which include questionnaires, interviews and focus groups (Reid, Hunter & Sutton, 2011). Higher education research, particularly, has been slow to adopt this method. The author, however, comes from the field of second language education, and in this discipline, diary studies written from the perspective of the language learner are well documented (Lally, 2000) and were an inspiration for the project described here that spanned the fields of applied linguistics and higher education.

Low rates of application of the diary method in higher education may be reflective of the methodological issues identified as being problematic in its use. The most significant of these is the burden of effort and time required by participants to keep a diary and the associated respondent fatigue and attrition that this may cause (Furness & Garrud, 2010; Tanaka, 2009). However, there are ways in which these weaknesses can be minimised or overcome, and the full benefits of the diary method obtained.

This chapter draws on a research project which investigated the situated (immersive, informal and authentic), English language learning of international students studying at an Australian university. It discusses the benefits and challenges of using solicited diaries as a data collection tool to gather information about participants' English language interactions. The chapter will outline the benefits that the method provided to the project, specifically, the power of the diary to collect data about the micro-level, every day and forgettable activities of the students. It will also discuss the challenges faced in using the method, including respondent fatigue and the fullness and quality of data. The discussion will conclude by offering suggestions as to how the method can be successfully used in future higher education research.

The following sections outline the benefits and challenges of the diary method for higher education studies, and approaches to maximising the potential of the approach.

The usefulness of the diary method in capturing micro-level data

One of the major advantages of using diaries in social research, and the appeal of the diary method for this study, is that diaries provide a way of uncovering routine or everyday processes and events that may be viewed as trivial and therefore easily forgotten by participants (Falconer & Taylor, 2017; Milligan et al., 2005). Higher education diary studies highlight the benefits of the method for accessing the ambiguous (Swim et al., 2003); easily forgotten (Swim et al., 2003); insignificant (Travers, 2011); less salient (Swim et al., 2003); micro-level (Dietrich, Kracke & Nurmi, 2011); mundane (Falconer & Taylor, 2017; Swim et al., 2003); patterned (Swim et al., 2003); routine (Falconer & Taylor, 2017); regular (Beckers, van der Voordt & Dewulf, 2016); and subtle (Swim et al., 2003). For example, through diaries, Beckers, van der Voordt and Dewulf (2016) captured the learning activities that university students worked on during a week, where they occurred and why that location was chosen. Chen et al. (2016) tracked all the daily activities of university students including information about the duration, location, company kept, emotions felt, and stress experienced over seven 24-hour periods. Such data would not be accessible via other methods, for example interview or questionnaire. Thus, one of the main reasons for using diaries is epistemological and relates to facilitating access to issues that are not normally accessible through other instruments (Cucu-Oancea, 2013; Debreli, 2011).

Diaries are able to capture everyday activities because they require participants to record these events close to when they unfold rather than through recall at a later time (Cucu-Oancea, 2013; Hyers et al., 2012; Milligan et al., 2005; Nonis, Philours & Hudson, 2006). Indeed, Travers's (2011) use of daily reflective diaries allowed university student stress to be recorded 'as it happened', capturing participants' immediate and spontaneous assessments of stressful events. Similarly, Swim et al. (2003) used daily diaries to capture immediate emotional and behavioural responses to racism on an American campus. Its use in capturing data this way has the advantage of increasing the accuracy and fidelity of data by counteracting or even eliminating memory errors (Cucu-Oancea, 2013). Solicited diaries are less subject to the vagaries of memory, retrospective censorship or reframing of data given by participants than other methodological techniques (Bartlett & Milligan, 2015; Heng, 2017; Scott, Green & Cashmore, 2012; Swim et al., 2003). Travers (2011) found that the diary method allowed university student participants to make more accurate judgements about their stressors. Bartlett (2012) claims that what people write in their diaries is likely to be accurate accounts of what they did and how they felt at that time. Thus, diary techniques are useful where accuracy about an individual's experiences, actions and practices are important to determine (Bartlett & Milligan, 2015).

Lastly, higher education studies which have utilised the diary method emphasise the richness, detail and intricacy of data that the method allows access to (Heng, 2017; Martinez-Vargas, Walker & Mkwananzi, 2019; Scott et al., 2012; Swim et al., 2003; Travers, 2011). The unique findings from such studies highlight the potential of the diary method to gain access to rich information on the activities of various participants across higher education.

The challenges in capturing micro-level data

Capturing detailed, micro-level data requires a commitment of time and effort by participants (Furness & Garrud, 2010; Tanaka, 2009). Depending on the study, participants might be required to write at length; write in a second or other language; interrupt their activities to make records; attend to the diary hourly, daily or weekly; carry the diary with them; or invest emotionally as they record personal or sensitive information. The burden of such activities may deter participants from joining the research and, for those who do participate, lead to fatigue and demotivation, with consequences for the quality of data (Furness & Garrud, 2010), or even attrition from the study (Bucarelli & Purdon, 2015; Scott et al., 2012). Significant attrition was experienced in Reid et al.'s (2011) study with participant numbers dropping from 93 to 48 once participants realised the time commitment required of the diary study. Similarly, in Swim et al.'s (2003) project, out of 70 college students agreeing to participate, 19 did not arrive at the orientation meeting or return their diaries. Thus, recruitment and retention of participants is a challenge in implementing a diary study (see also Chapter 5, this volume).

The quantity and quality of diary data are also at risk due to variable participant commitment to the project and lack of the researcher's control over a diarist's writing frequency (Travers, 2011). In Dietrich et al.'s (2011) weekly diary study, the 46 adolescent participants completed between 2 and 21 assessments with the mean number of weekly assessments completed being 8 – far from the 21 assessments anticipated by the researchers. This highlights a problem with the diary method of full and continuing participation. Similarly, Furness and Garrud (2010) found that there were clear differences in the number and intricacy of diary entries both within and between diaries. Swim et al. (2003) suggest that participants might underreport incidents in their diaries due to the labour intensiveness of the diary keeping. However, for other participants, the novelty of both the diary itself and the events being recorded might result in entries which are numerous and detailed (Furness & Garrud, 2010).

The recording of irrelevant data can also be a problem for data collection using the diary method (Debreli, 2011). In Debreli's (2011, p. 4) study it was concluded that the 'the recording of irrelevant information by the participants could not be avoided' and that although instructions were given, they 'seemed not to work'. This may be because the interpretation of instructions can be subjective (Furness & Garrud, 2010). Debreli (2011, p. 64) suggests that the problem of irrelevant data is 'a natural process of diary data collection'. However, the literature does reveal many techniques that can be used to reduce problems such as this and these are explored in the following section.

Approaches to maximising the potential of the diary method

Diary researchers highlight the need to keep diaries simple, short and user friendly, so as not to overburden and fatigue participants (Hyers et al., 2012; Reid et al., 2011). A pre-dated checklist was implemented to this effect in Hyers et al.'s (2012) study.

Increased researcher contact and support throughout the period of diary keeping might ameliorate participation which is less than full (Milligan et al., 2005). To this end, Bucarelli and Purdon (2015) provided the researcher's contact information to participants and were encouraged to call if there were any questions or concerns. Swim et al. (2003) employed research assistants who were assigned a 'caseload' of approximately ten participants with whom they had regular contact in case they had any questions, concerns, or problems with the study. In Travers's (2011) study, university student diarists were sent periodic reminders and given regular chances to ask questions, obtain advice and receive feedback on their diaries.

Some diary studies required that participants turn in their diaries periodically through the study to increase the likelihood that they would complete the diaries correctly (Reid et al., 2011; Swim et al., 2003). Remuneration can also be combined with this strategy to support full participation (Bucarelli & Purdon, 2015; Swim et al., 2003). In Swim et al.'s (2003) study, participants turned in their forms four times during the study and were paid $5 each time they did so. Careful consideration of how to guide participants through the diary-keeping process, whether through simple prompts, coaching, sample diaries, remuneration or other means may improve the success of a diary study (Filep et al., 2018).

The timing of journal entries should also be given much thought (Tanaka, 2009). Diaries can be used to collect data over varying lengths of time, from as short as a week (Nonis et al., 2006) to months (Scott et al., 2012). The length of the study should balance the need to obtain a comprehensive picture of the issue but not at the expense of participation (Reid et al., 2011). Chen et al. (2016) required participants to make a diary entry every 30 min for seven consecutive 24-hour periods. Other higher education studies required participants to make a diary entry three times a day (Bucarelli & Purdon, 2015), once per day (Swim et al., 2003), or once a week (Scott et al., 2012) depending on the data being captured. Across many studies, however, a regular habit of recording entries ensures that events are recorded before they fade from short-term memory and are forgotten (Milligan et al., 2005). Thus the importance of completing diary entries regularly and soon as possible after the episode should be emphasised to participants (Bucarelli & Purdon, 2015; Swim et al., 2003).

The next section provides an overview of the study and examines the value of the diary method for researching the international student experience.

The study

Background

There is an assumption that when international students arrive in an English-speaking country that they are 'immersed' in the language and automatically improve their English language skills (Benzie, 2010). Yet, general language proficiency is cited as a significant ongoing problem for international students (Murray, 2010; Oliver, Vanderford & Grote, 2012). A factor in this may be the reported difficulties faced by international students in accessing host communities (Yates & Wahid, 2013) and the resulting isolation and social exclusion (Guilfoyle & Harryba, 2011; Khawaja & Stallman, 2011; Paltridge & Schapper, 2012), conditions not conducive to situated English language learning. In order to support the English language development of international students and improve the outcomes of their study abroad, it is necessary to understand exactly how students participate in the local English-speaking community. Previous studies (e.g, Guilfoyle & Harryba, 2011; Khawaja & Stallman, 2011; Yates & Wahid, 2013) used interview and focus group methods to understand students' interactions with local members of the community. However, these methods, applied at a distance from and after the events, are susceptible to issues of memory loss and distortion (Bartlett, 2012).

The purpose of this chapter is to examine how the dairy method was used to capture detailed, reliable and previously inaccessible data about international students' language learning, as well as the challenges that emerged in its application in order to inform future studies. The following section briefly outlines the current study.

Study overview

This chapter draws on a qualitative research project which explored the participation in situated English language learning of international students studying at an Australian university. The project sought to describe the nature of the students' off-campus interactions and discover the factors which influence their participation and take up of opportunities for language development. The participants in the study were ten Saudi Arabian international students studying at a regional Australian university. Initially the project sought to investigate the female experience and due to its success, twelve months later, it was expanded to examine the male experience and to compare gender difference.

Methodology

The project adopted a diary-interview methodology (Cucu-Oancea, 2013) where data were constructed through detailed diary records of interactions generated daily by participants; a series of interview conversations in relation to these diaries; and semi-structured interviews.

Before commencing the diary study, a semi-structured interview was conducted with participants to collect data towards the research questions, provide an opportunity for participants to ask questions about the project, and negotiate their involvement in it.

In diaries, participants were asked to document every English language interaction that they had off-campus. Details of the interactions such as where it occurred, with whom, for how long, for what purpose and any other comments about the interactions were logged. Table 12.1 below is the header provided to participants under which they recorded their interactions. A semi-structured diary design was chosen to provide participants with guidance and support in their writing. This was important for two reasons. Firstly, it was crucial for the analysis to have specific details about the interactions which were consistent across all participants. Secondly, as English as a second language speakers and culturally different from the researcher, the participants may not have been familiar with the task of logging activities in a diary. Participants were asked to keep their diary for six weeks.

Every two weeks, the researcher met with the participants to discuss their diary entries. These meetings were to clarify what was recorded, and to explore further interesting and significant interactions. These meetings were audio recorded and the researcher kept a reflective journal in which aspects of the context of the interviews and meetings were recorded.

Three analyses were conducted on the data: a reflexive analysis of the cross-cultural interviews, analysis of register of the learner diaries, and a thematic analysis of the interview data.

Why the diary method?

Seeking a more accurate understanding of international student interactions than had previously been acquired, the author considered having participants wear recording devices to capture their English conversations. It was considered to be a way to gain highly accurate data but was disregarded for being unnecessarily intrusive and laborious to analyse. However, the author did not need to know the entire contents of each conversation but simply the contexts of them. A method of learner diaries was suggested by Halliday as useful for data collection to this end:

Table 12.1 Diary entry prompts

Date and time of interaction	Who did you interact with? What is your relationship with them?	Where or how did you interact with them?	How long did the interaction last?	Why did you interact? What was the purpose?	Was the interaction planned or unplanned? Who started the interaction?	General comments. How did you feel about the interaction?

To gain some impression of 'language in the life of an individual', it is hardly necessary, or possible, to keep detailed records of who says what, to whom, when and why. But it is not too difficult to take note of information about register, with entries for field, mode and tenor in the language diary.

(Halliday, 2009, p. 78)

Therefore, inspired by Halliday, data about the interactions were recorded and an analysis of register was done on that data, rather than on transcripts of conversations. Register is a variety of language use for a particular purpose and in a particular context comprising of the field (the nature of the activity), tenor (role relationships) and mode (the symbolic organisation of text) (Halliday, 2009). In this study, participants were asked to keep a diary record of all interactions that they had in English beyond the university campus. The actual 'diary' was a small folder which contained a set of printed instructions and a number of tables, blank except for the header shown in Table 12.1. Participants were encouraged to fill in the tables each night while the day's events were still fresh.

The following analysis examines in detail how the researcher's plans for the application of the diary method 'played out' with this group of participants in this study.

Successes and challenges of the diary method

The analysis presented here examines the diary method's success in capturing routine and forgettable, micro-level data toward the research questions, as well as the challenges which were encountered in acquiring this data.

Capturing the routine and forgettable

The first analysis of the diaries consisted of a simple counting of the recorded interactions of each participant. This count, an analysis similar to that used by Swim et al. (2003), enabled an understanding of the frequency of occurrences for individuals in a specific time period. Table 12.2 shows how many times each participant interacted in English off campus during the six-week period.

In this study, the diary method facilitated an accurate understanding of how often each participant spoke English off campus, a finding on which other analysis built. Arguably, it is not possible to gather this information through an interview or questionnaire administered long after conversations have ended. In this way, the diary method made possible the capturing of the everyday, routine and forgettable in the language lives of international students.

The interactions recorded in the diary entries were then analysed for the *field, tenor* and *mode* according to their components summarised in Table 12.3.

The analysis of the register of the conversations recorded in the diaries revealed the nature of English-speaking activity of each of the participants as well as the quality of connection that they experienced within those interactions (Groves,

Table 12.2 Number of interactions by participant (all names are pseudonyms)

Participant	Interactions
Habibah	25
Aamina	18*
Jahira	6*
Medina	15*
Raabia	3
Rushdi	12
Haydar	26
Riyad	35
Ahmed	28
Hafiz	16

* Number of interactions during a three-week (Jahira), four-week (Medina), or five-week period (Aamina).

Table 12.3 Analysis categories

Field	Tenor	Mode	Length	Comments
Purpose: pragmatic or casual conversation Language activity Subject matter	Status relations: taking on and attributing relevant social roles Affective involvement: the degree to which we 'matter' to those with whom we are interacting Contact: level of familiarity Orientation to affiliation: extent to which we seek to identify with the values and beliefs of those we interact with	Spoken or written Face-to-face, email or phone Language of interactants		How was this interaction significant? Participation: action and connection?

Source: adapted from Eggins and Slade (1997); Halliday (2009); Mohan (1987)

2015; Groves, Verenikina & Chen, 2016). The findings from this analysis offers a more detailed understanding of participation than what existing studies have provided. Previously, international students' experience of participation has been described generally as withdrawing, separating, being excluded, or involving themselves in an enclave of co-culturals (Edgeworth & Eiseman, 2007; Paltridge & Schapper, 2012). Similarly, acculturation research labels community involvement in a general way – through the four acculturation strategies: assimilation, integration, separation and marginalisation (Sam & Berry, 2010). A new perspective and more detailed understandings on the phenomenon of international student participation in local communities was afforded by the method used in this study, that is, the solicited diary.

These benefits could not have been possible without the time and effort given to the research by the participants. With a diary study, that contribution can often be considerable. The following section discusses the burden of the diary study on the participants and how this impacted the quantity and quality of data.

The burden of diarising and implications for the research

In designing the study, the researcher took much time to consider how to successfully fulfil the research aims without overburdening the participants. A time frame of six weeks was chosen as being long enough to capture the required data and achievable for participants to maintain the required motivation to participate. Eight of the ten participants maintained their diaries into the sixth week. Aamina finished hers at in the fifth week and Jahira only kept the diary for 13 days after the initial interview (see Table 12.4). Three weeks after commencing the diary study, Jahira attended a meeting with the researcher and had filled in the diary for some of that period. At the second meeting, however, Jahira had not completed any more of the diary. The researcher took this as an indication that Jahira did not wish to participate any longer and did not schedule a third meeting with her.

Interview conversations were used by the researcher to maintain motivation and encouragement for the participants to complete their diaries as fully and regularly as possible. Most of the participants attended two or three of these meetings during the diary keeping phase. One participant, Medina, did not fill out her diary in between the first and second interview conversations (i.e. weeks three and four) of the study as she had been away on holiday. In an attempt to move beyond the lapse in record keeping, the meeting provided the researcher with an opportunity to encourage Medina to continue keeping her diary, which she did, for the next two weeks. The interview conversations were successful at avoiding attrition and motivating this participant to re-engage with the project and contribute further data to it.

Table 12.4 Diary completion

Participant	Days kept	Interview conversations attended
Jahira	13	2
Aamina	34	2
Habibah	39	3
Raabia	38	3
Medina	41	3
Ahmed	40	3
Hafiz	39	2
Rushdi	44	2
Riyad	37	3
Haydar	40	3

Respondent fatigue and commitment to keeping a diary was a challenge for the project which resulted in less data for three of the female participants (Aamina, Medina and Jahira) than was hoped for by the researcher. The possible reasons for this are twofold. Firstly, due to their traditional roles and responsibilities, Saudi women are kept very busy with the domain of the home in addition to their studies (Groves, 2015) and probably have less time to attend to their diaries. Secondly, the data collection with the male participants took place 12 months after that of the females and the researcher was able to achieve a better response and participation rate in the second round as a result of learning from the first. Specifically, the researcher learnt to be more confident and direct in asking the participants to maintain their diaries accurately and fully and imparting the importance of that for the research.

A second issue for this study was related to the data recorded in the diaries. Analysis of the diaries began with cleaning of the data and exclusion of irrelevant records. Most of the diaries had good levels (71–87%) of relevant entries. However, Haydar, Raabia and Jahira's diaries contained high levels of irrelevant entries, that is, entries that were not of interest to the study (44%, 87% and 50%, respectively). These were excluded from analysis (see Table 12.5). Table 12.6 provides some examples of irrelevant diary entries.

The main problem with the diary entries was the inclusion of on-campus interactions. Although the researcher thought that she had made the directions for diary completion clear, looking back at the printed instructions included with the diaries and the participant information sheet, this was not so. There was actually no written instruction to include only off-campus events, only instructions given verbally by the researcher. Fortunately, in this study, the inclusion of extra, irrelevant entries had little impact on the data as they could be excluded however, participants should be given clearly written printed instructions about what to include in their diaries to complement verbal instructions. Clearly written instructions to participants might

Table 12.5 Diary entry relevance

Participant	Entries	Relevant entries	Percentage relevant
Jahira	12	6	50%
Aamina	22	18	82%
Habibah	29	25	86%
Raabia	23	3	13%
Medina	21	15	71%
Ahmed	32	28	87%
Hafiz	21	16	76%
Rushdi	17	12	71%
Riyad	42	32	76%
Haydar	46	26	56%

Table 12.6 Examples of irrelevant diary entries

Participant	Date and time	Who?	Where?	How long?	Why?	Planned or unplanned?	Comments?
Raabia	Wed 13/5	my supervisor	Via email	2 min writing in English	ask about assignment	planned	I am still using the computer spell checking, so no improvement
Jahira	Wed.	my research supervisor	the uni	5 min	about collecting data	planned – I start	she was satisfied
Haydar	25/3	my group in my subject	the library	2 hours	preparing for our group assignment	planned	we use simple English in these meetings so it's easy to show our ideas

reduce the likelihood that irrelevant records are recorded in diaries, the burden of diary completion on participants and any unnecessary time spent by researchers in the analysis phase.

The following section draws on the analysis to recommend a series of approaches and techniques which might guide future researchers in the use of the diary method and enable the potential of the method to be maximised.

Maximising the potential of the diary method

This section proposes a series of recommendations for researchers seeking to use the diary method in higher education research in light of reflection on the challenges and successes experienced in this project and the published experiences of others in the field.

Firstly, researchers should keep diaries simple, short and user-friendly. Pre-printed tables with guiding headers (Table 12.1) provided to participants in the current study were successful in allowing participants to record their data efficiently. Pilot testing of diaries prior to implementation can allow them to be checked for usability (Beckers, van der Voordt & Dewulf, 2016).

Also, it is recommended to attach written instructions to diaries for participants to refer to during the study to complement verbal instructions. Clearly written instructions regarding the substance, form, language, and timing of entries expected will aid diary completion (Harvey, 2011; Tanaka, 2009). An emphasis should be made to participants on the importance of recording entries as soon as possible while they are fresh in their minds. Instructions in participants' first languages might further support clear communication.

Researcher contact and support during the diary study should be maximised. In the current project, the researcher had face-to-face contact with participants up to three times during the diary study, however, it is possible that SMS or emails could have been sent weekly to support and motivate participants and improve their participation. Requiring participants to submit their diaries regularly might facilitate full participation and diary completion. In this project it motivated the participants to complete the diary more fully and supported the quality of data collected. Additionally, remuneration might be offered where appropriate to motivate participants to participate fully in completing the study. Offering a reward or compensation to the Saudi students in this study may have motivated them to complete the diary more fully and for longer.

Conclusion

In this study into the English language learning of international students, the diary method made possible the capturing of detailed, micro-level data not obtainable through other qualitative methods such as interviews and questionnaires. The minutia of everyday and routine interactions was not likely to be stored in the memories of participants and recalled at a later date but could be recorded as they occurred in diaries. Thus, solicited diaries provided this project with timely and dependable data about participants' language lives. Furthermore, the level of detail and richness of data obtained afforded more specific understandings and new perspectives about international student participation in local communities than had previously been gained.

However, respondent fatigue and incomplete participation were issues for this project's implementation of a diary study. To overcome these challenges, careful consideration must be given to the form of the diary and timing of diary entries, as well as providing participants with clear instructions as to what is required of them, and frequent contact with the research team throughout the data collection phase.

With these aspects well attended to, higher education researchers might fully capitalise on the diary method's power to capture rich, micro-level, subtle, and reliable data about the lives of a range of higher education participants. In the future, the diary method might be usefully applied in, for example, analyses of processes of learning; student transitions to higher education; socialisation of students and academics to new communities; administrative processes; and academic work practises. The issue of respondent fatigue within diary studies has only just begun to be explored in higher education literature (see also Chapters 1 and 5, this volume) and is also an area for future research.

This chapter contributes to methodological understandings in its exploration of the power of the diary method to capture routine, forgettable, and micro-level data. Specifically, it has shown how new perspectives and understandings can be created with rich, detailed data which is largely inaccessible through more popular research methods. The chapter also contributes specifically to higher education research methods in its consideration of how the minutiae of higher education activities might be captured and better understood through the diary method.

References

Bartlett, R. (2012) Modifying the diary interview method to research the lives of people with dementia, *Qualitative Health Research*, 22, 12: 1717–1726.

Bartlett, R. & Milligan, C. (2015) *What is diary method?* London: Bloomsbury Academic.

Beckers, R., van der Voordt, T. & Dewulf, G. (2016) Why do they study there? Diary research into students' learning space choices in higher education, *Higher Education Research & Development*, 35, 1: 142–157.

Benzie, H. (2010) Graduating as a 'native speaker': international students and English language proficiency in higher education. *Higher Education Research & Development*, 29, 4: 447–459.

Bucarelli, B. & Purdon, C. (2015) A diary study of the phenomenology and persistence of compulsions, *Journal of Behavior Therapy and Experimental Psychiatry*, 49: 209–215.

Chen, H., Yarnal, C., Hustard, J. & Sims, D. (2016) Take a selfie of life: A qualitative exploration of college students' self-reflection on free time use and personal values. *Journal of College and Character*, 17, 2: 101–115.

Cucu-Oancea, O. (2013) Using diaries – a real challenge for the social scientist. *Procedia Social and Behavioural Sciences*, 92: 231–238.

Debreli, E. (2011). Use of diaries to investigate and track pre-service teachers' beliefs about teaching learning English as a foreign language throughout a pre-service training program. *Procedia Social and Behavioural Sciences*, 15, 60–65.

Dietrich, J., Kracke, B. & Nurmi, J. (2011) Parents' role in adolescents' decision on a college major: A weekly diary study, *Journal of Vocational Behavior* 79, 134–144.

Edgeworth, K. & J. Eiseman (2007) Going bush: international student perspectives on living and studying at an Australian rural university campus. *Journal of Research in Rural Education* 22, 9: 1–13.

Eggins, S. & Slade, D. (1997) *Analysing casual conversation*. London: Equinox.

Falconer, E. & Taylor, Y. (2017) Negotiating queer and religious identities in higher education: queering 'progression' in the 'university experience'. *British Journal of Sociology of Education*, 38, 6: 782–797.

Filep, C., Turner, S., Eidse, N., Thompson-Fawcett, M. & Fitzsimons, S. (2018) Advancing rigour in solicited diary research. *Qualitative Research*, 18, 4: 451–470.

Furness, P. & Garrud, P. (2010) Adaptation after facial surgery: Using the diary as a research tool. *Qualitative Health Research*, 20, 2: 262–272.

Groves, O. (2015) Language learning as participation. PhD thesis, University of Wollongong.

Groves, O., Verenikina, I. & Chen, H. (2016) Mapping participation in situated language learning. *Higher Education Research & Development*, 35, 2: 267–281.

Guilfoyle, A. & Harryba, S. (2011) Understanding Seychelles international students' social and cultural experiences during transition to an Australian university. *The International Journal of Learning*, 16, 11: 1–22.

Halliday, M. A. K. (2009) *The essential Halliday*. London: Continuum.

Harvey, L. (2011) Intimate reflections: Private diaries in qualitative research. *Qualitative Research*, 11, 6: 664–682.

Heng, T. (2017) Voice of Chinese international students in USA colleges: 'I want to tell them that …' *Studies in Higher Education*, 42, 5: 833–850.

Hyers, L., Syphan, J., Cochran, K. & Brown, T. (2012) Disparities in the professional development interactions of university faculty as a function of gender and ethnic under-representation, *Journal of Faculty Development*, 26, 1: 18–28.

Khawaja, N. & Stallman, H. (2011) Understanding the coping strategies of international students: A qualitative approach. *Australian Journal of Guidance and Counselling*, 21, 2: 203–224.

Lally, C. (2000) Language teaching and learning diaries: French conversation from two different perspectives. *Foreign Language Annals*, 33, 2: 224–228.

Martinez-Vargas, C., Walker, M. & Mkwananzi, F. (2019) Access to higher education in South Africa: Expanding capabilities in and through an undergraduate photovoice project. *Educational Action Research*, 28, 3: 427–442.

Milligan, C., Bingley, A. and Gatrell, A. (2005) Digging deep: Using diaries techniques to explore the place of health and well-being amongst older people, vol. 2. *Social Science & Medicine*, 61: 1882–1892.

Mohan, B. (1987) The structure of situations and the analysis of text. In R. Steele & T. Threadgold (eds), *Language topics: Essays in honour of Michael Halliday*. Amsterdam: John Benjamins Publishing Company, pp. 507–522.

Murray, N. (2010) Conceptualising the English language needs of first year university students. *The International Journal of the First Year in Higher Education* 1, 1: 55–64.

Nonis, S., Philours, M. & Hudson, G. (2006) Where does the time go? A diary approach to business and marketing students' time use, *Journal of Marketing Education*, 28, 2: 121–134.

Oliver, R., Vanderford, S. & Grote, E. (2012) Evidence of English language proficiency and academic achievement of non-English-speaking background students. *Higher Education Research & Development*, 31, 4: 541–555.

Paltridge, T. & Schapper, J. (2012) Covering the gap: Social inclusion, international students and the role of local government. *Australian Universities Review*, 54, 2: 29–39.

Reid, L., Hunter, C. & Sutton, P. (2011) Rising to the challenge of environmental behaviour change: Developing a reflexive diary approach. *Geoforum*, 42: 720–730.

Sam, D. & Berry, J. (2010) Acculturation: When individuals and groups of different cultural background meet. *Perspectives on Psychological Science*, 5, 4: 472–481.

Scott, J., Green, P. & Cashmore, A. (2012) Bioscience students' first year perspectives through video diaries: Home, family and student transitions. *Bioscience Education*, 20, 1: 53–67.

Swim, J., Hyers, L., Cohen, L., Fitzgerald, D. & Bylsma, W. (2003) African American college students' experiences with everyday racism: Characteristics of and responses to these incidents. *Journal of Black Psychology*, 29, 1: 38–67.

Tanaka, T. (2009) Diary studies: their potential to explore learner perspectives on second language learning. *Doshisha Studies in English*, 85: 57–70.

Travers, C. (2011) Unveiling a reflective diary methodology for exploring the lived experiences of stress and coping. *Journal of Vocational Behavior*, 79: 204–216.

Yates, L. and Wahid, R. (2013) Challenges to Brand Australia: International students and the problem with speaking. *Higher Education Research & Development*, 32, 6: 1037–1050.

Afterword

Ensuring the continued success of diary research in higher education

Lauri L. Hyers and Jenna Walmer

> The diary no longer leads to the contingency of an absurd ending, but toward the transcendence of one or several future re-readings.
> – Philippe LeJeune (2000, p. 102)

Diary researchers harness the transcendent potential of the diary so revered by LeJeune (2020). They commission diarists to document personal moments in research diaries, then they curate those diary entries for future contemplation by a wider audience. The intricacies of this process of soliciting diaries for qualitative research studies are well described by the contributors to this volume. Seasoned diary researchers surely identify with the reflexive accounts in these chapters, and those new to diary research have much to gain from reviewing this volume before they embark on their own studies.

We would like to focus this Afterword on some important takeaways regarding diary research in higher education settings. First, we discuss why participants from the higher education community get involved in our studies and the implications of their involvement. Second, we identify two key strengths of diary research that speak to its suitability for higher education research. Finally, we discuss pedagogical strategies to ensure a robust future for diary research.

Participants' personal investment in diary studies

In the busyness of campus life at universities and colleges around the world, our students, faculty, and staff are becoming increasingly overburdened with demands on their time (Berg & Seeber, 2016; Thorogood, Faulkner & Warner, 2018). Unlike many qualitative and quantitative research studies, where extra credit or small payments might be sufficient incentives for a volunteer's time, diary studies are more daunting. Diarists take the study home with them, they must be vigilant for the phenomena of interest, and their participation can last days, weeks, and even months. Certainly, some volunteers who value the university setting as a place of involvement and self-development, may have their interest sparked at such a unique and novel undertaking. However, by necessity, diary studies must also rouse a potential volunteer's *personal* interest. As a result, diary volunteers are motivated to get involved because the topic is of immediate relevance to them.

Across all studies described in this volume, the researchers designed diary studies of phenomena that were directly relevant to the lives of their diarist recruits. Many focused on vivid experiences of *identity and marginalisation*: Mathebula and Vargas's diarists (Chapter 4) were students from low-income and rural backgrounds; Keenan's diarists (Chapter 6) were bisexual or trans-identifying students; Watson and Leigh's diarists (Chapter 10) were students with print disabilities; and Lawther's diarists (Chapter 8) represented varied faith traditions and spiritual orientations. Some were focused on *interpersonal challenges*, such as Groves' international students managing sometimes intimidating intercultural interactions (Chapter 12), and Mittelmeier, Rienties, Zhang and Jindal-Snape's doctoral students navigating social life in new university programs (Chapter 1). Others focused on critical *career and professional development matters*: Henderson (Chapter 2) focused on how academic professionals balanced family care demands with academic career responsibilities; Baker (Chapter 7) examined youth decision-making about their future higher educational plans; Burford (Chapter 11) explored the interplay of emotions and politics in doctoral thesis writing; and both Dangeni, Elliot and MacDiarmid (Chapter 3) and Cao (Chapter 5) examined the training and career development concerns of international Master's students. As Cao put it, when qualitative diary participants have a personal stake in the subject matter, it is 'a "win–win" for both researchers and participants in the research cooperation' (p. 74).

To further enhance participant investment, many researchers in this volume described elaborate community building with their participants, typical of participatory action research strategies (Fine & Torre, 2019). As Sabharwal, Joseph, Bankar and Talmale described (Chapter 9), the methodology is 'informed by our social justice research objectives' (p. 139). Many held welcome meetings and retreats. They kept in touch with their participants. Some even provided ongoing monitoring and feedback on their participants' diaries. They were making personal connections, sharing personal contact information, and even becoming friends. As Mathebula and Vargas (Chapter 4) described:

> It was important for our approach to be encouraging and supportive… Meaningful engagement on our part as facilitators meant not just listening to but also affirming students' stories and recognising them as having an important role to play… to begin to acknowledge themselves as members of a community of knowers and tellers and epistemic contributors.
>
> (p. 66)

This sense of community alters the research endeavour from a one-sided data grab to a shared activity of meaning making. Cao even described how her participants 'had a sense of responsibility to help me complete my research, because I was a friend, a listener, an adviser, and an emotional supporter during their very difficult time' (p. 82). Involvement in diary research at this level is a unique experience for participants that may never be forgotten. As one of Mathebula and Vargas's participants described, 'I felt part of something big and life changing' (p. 66).

With such engagement follows a requisite degree of loss when a diary study concludes (Hyers, 2018). Of course, university life is full of endings – classes wrap up, semesters conclude, groups disband, students graduate, faculty retire – however, when a diary study ends, the participant loses the (virtual or literal) diary relationship with the researcher who has become injected into some aspect of the participant's daily life. It is not unheard of for enthusiastic diary research participants to continue contacting the researcher to share musings and observations years after a study has ceased. For the research team, too, there may be a sense of loss. The close of a diary study may mean an end to regular contacts with participants and/or research team members with whom they have bonded. To ease this palpable sense of loss, a concluding research group meeting to express gratitude and engage in some collective reflexivity can help provide closure, along with personal outreach to individually thank each participant (e.g. Hyers, 2010; Hyers, 2007; Swim, Hyers, Cohen & Fergusen, 2001). A structured reconnection with participants can be organised in the form of a 'member check' (Doyle, 2007). Member checks are typically designed to provide the researcher feedback on the integrity of the coding and analysis (Thomas, 2017), but they can also provide another opportunity for a comforting follow up with participants (Harper & Cole, 2012; Hyers, 2018; Hyers & Hyers, 2008).

Once analysis is complete, the rich data or 'thick description' (Geertz, 2003) that makes qualitative diaries so interesting also presents ethical challenges when preparing presentations, reports, and publications in the higher educational context. While anonymising is a fairly straightforward process with regard to *written* diary studies, use of other media in visual, audio, or audio/visual, or mixed methods diary studies will present more difficulties when the goal is to keep the participants identity concealed. As Mittelmeier, Rienties, Zhang and Jindal-Snape described of their multifaceted project:

> We were taking an in-depth look at doctoral students' experiences within single departments, the participants were well known to one another and to other non-participants in the department (including their supervisors or other staff), which increased risks that participants may be identifiable in the dissemination of our findings. This was exacerbated in a mixed methods design, as triangulating multiple pieces of sensitive information about individuals could make it easier to 'guess' who the individual might be.
>
> (p. 22)

In the higher education context, diary participants are recruited from a special interest community that is nested within the university or college community. We can assure that their diary data is confidential in that 'information that is kept hidden from everyone except the primary researcher' (Saunders, Kitzinger & Kitzinger, 2015, p. 616); however, full anonymity may be harder to guarantee (Scott, 2005).

Lawther offers a number of important points regarding how these concerns become further amplified in photo diary studies – and there is very little precedent to guide decision-making. Mathebula and Vargas described how photo diaries are often used in activist and participatory designs addressing a community concern, contributing to a social justice action, or spurring a policy change. If final reports may involve a community presentation of diaries, traditional standards of participant anonymity can become irrelevant. Sometimes the participants themselves will attend the unveiling of the diary themes. In such cases, stories, photos, and other revealing aspects of their experience would likely be shared. If present, participants' own consent and control dictates testimonials, however if others in the community are characters in participant's textual diary entries or if others appear in photos or videos diaries, the researcher may have little ability to obtain their consent. Such issues will need to be addressed in initial consent forms and reviewed carefully and thoughtfully with the researcher's respective institutional ethics review board.

Extending these challenges further, a better distinction is needed between consent for participation and consent for revealing reportage. Lawther and Dangeni, Elliot and MacDiarmid describe the care they took to engage in ongoing reflexive ethical decision making with regard to consent and anonymity. Due to the richness of qualitative data obtained in a diary study, it may be advisable to adopt the narrative research approach to 'rolling consent', where consent is obtained as a regularly negotiated process, rather than as a one-time event only occurring at the beginning of the study (Smythe & Murray, 2000). Especially given the richness of participant involvement in diary studies, there may be a need to gain subsequent consent before a presentation or report is shared. Participants might feel one way about writing in their confidential diaries for the research project, and another way about having direct quotes or images displayed in a presentation, as part of social advocacy, or in an academic publication. As Lawther points out, once an article is published, there is little that can be retracted. Yet we need to give our participants as much freedom as possible to withdraw their diary data. In tight knit university communities, these issues need to be carefully communicated to all concerned parties.

The revelatory and creativity strengths of diary research are consistent with the mission of higher education

The contributors to this volume all share a high degree of enthusiasm for the diary method. Praise for the method abounds; however, we want to emphasise two aspects of the method that are well suited for the higher educational context. Echoed across the chapters are that the diary method has the *power to reveal* new phenomena and that it has strong *creative potential*. These two strengths make the diary method well-suited to the aims of higher education to foster learning, insight, and innovation.

Researchers in this volume unanimously valued the revelatory power of the diary method. Consistent with the goals of higher education for learning, self-growth, and mutual understanding, revelations that can emerge from diary research are subtle and multifaceted. There is the power of the diary method to reveal diarists' experiences *to others*. For example, soliciting diaries from international higher education students, Groves spoke of the 'power of the diary' to reveal 'micro-level, everyday and forgettable activities of the students' (p. 175). In addition, the diary method was valued for its power to reveal diarists' experiences *to themselves*. For example, Sabharwal, Joseph, Bankar and Talmale found in their diary study of socially marginalised students attending higher educational institutions that the diaries became a place for revealing 'confidential insights' that led to consciousness raising. The diary study also has the power to reveal a different research scope to *the researchers*. Keenan described how a photo diary study of bisexual and transgender undergraduate students led participants to 'break the frame of both the researcher and the participant', revealing new 'borders of relevance' for the researcher (p. 90).

Researchers also praised the creativity of diary method as a real asset in the higher educational context. As Cao and Henderson recommend in the Introduction, to support diversity in higher education, creative research approaches are needed. Dangeni, Elliot and MacDiarmid point out that, in the digital age, alternative modalities of self-expression can engender so much creativity. And it is not only the researchers who can be creative with varied diary modalities; participants can be, too, as Lawther noted. Creative modes of diary documentation allowed for barriers of understanding to fall in Watson and Leigh's study of disability and accessibility: 'We felt we were able to access a deeper understanding of students' experiences' (p. 152). Part of the creativity comes from not being limited to linguistic narrative, as Keenan emphasized: 'The many textures and aspects of the reality of Higher Education are done a disservice by research limiting itself to text and speech' (p. 91). Although it is still the norm in academic research for video/ audio diaries to be converted to script, handwritten diaries to be typeset, and photo/visual diaries to be replaced with captions, diary researchers are beginning to look beyond these potentially reductive practices.

We need to adopt pedagogical strategies to ensure a robust future for diary research

One of the qualitative diary method's earliest advocates, Allport (1942) encouraged researchers to use diaries as a regular part of our research programmes, in order to keep 'our acquaintance with concrete individuals...in their natural complexity' (p. 44). Those of us who have come to appreciate the diary as a research tool are actually a complex group ourselves. Some researchers have adopted diary methods as the main focus of their research programmes, exclusively selecting topics of inquiry that suit the diary modality and extensively employing the method. Some who identify as 'qualitative researchers' use the diary as a one of an array of narrative tools in their qualitative toolbox. There are also mixed methodologists who employ the diary occasionally in eclectic combinations of qualitative and quantitative approaches. Our own research lab is currently qualitative leaning (e.g. Hyers, in preparation; Walmer & Hyers, 2020) having evolved from more mixed methods roots (Hyers, Syphan, Cochran & Brown, 2012; Ritz, Lawson, Hyers, 2002; Swim, Hyers, Cohen & Fergusen, 2001; Swim, Hyers, Cohen, Fitzgerald & Bylsma, 2003). Looking across the higher education context, the overwhelming majority of diary researchers use the method for just one project. They quickly bone up on diary research design, find their way through the data collection, analyse their data, share their results, and move on. Fortunately, diary research is intuitive enough for beginners, yet it is also interesting enough for those who return to the method throughout their career.

Whether researchers are diary dabblers or diary devotees, each has some degree of pedagogical obligation to educate consumers of diary research. It is inevitable that diary researchers of any ilk will find themselves educating their research assistants and participants, the institutional review board, colleagues, students, grant funders, professional organisations and journal editors about the nature of the diary method. The more advocacy and effort we diary researchers engage in to inform others about qualitative diary research methods, the stronger the foundation we will build for practitioners and consumers of all diary studies.

As a complement (or for some, an antidote) to the positivistic standards of research in the higher educational context, there is a growing effort to increase the visibility of qualitative diary methods, as this volume represents. The effort is part of the 'Narrative Turn' that began in the latter part of last century to promote and reinvigorate a range of qualitative approaches such as narrative, phenomenological, feminist standpoint, multicultural, and social constructionist methodologies (Burr, 1995; Connelly & Clandinin, 1990; Denzin, 2010; Gergen & Gergen, 2018; Hyers, Swim & Mallet, 2006; Kreiswirth, 1992; Tomes, McBride, Martin & Hyers, 2020). Qualitative diary methods in particular can contribute to challenging and changing research methods and theoretical constructs across academic disciplines by destabilising constants and honouring the intersectionality of experience (Gergen & Gergen, 2018; Hyers, 2018). Diary methods also contribute to social justice, to understanding complexities of identities in context, and to improving human relations (Hyers, 2018). Yet, diary methods are rarely taught in higher education methods training. Several of the authors who have shared their forays into diary methods in this volume went into the process unaided by any prior training. Depending on the discipline, much social sciences university research education is quantitative and positivistic, yet even when qualitative and social constructionist methods courses are taught, they tend to favour single-measure data collection methods, such as interviewing, over diary designs. This is partly due to the pressures of time and productivity that favour quick data collection methods, and partly due to the mysteriousness and obscurity that surround diary methods. We would hope that all diary researchers in the higher education context will do their part to educate the academy about the value of conducting and consuming qualitative diary research. Such efforts should be viewed as part of the tasks of finishing a diary study.

One practical way to advance diary methods in the higher education context is through encouraging students of different levels and upcoming professionals to dive into diary research. The diary is often a comfortable and familiar form of expression to students, many of whom have kept diaries or journaled at some point in their schooling, so students are often curious about the use of diaries as a research method. At the undergraduate level, as part of a senior capstone seminar, our university has been offering a course focused on diary methods for several years. In this class, students study the method, read examples, and ultimately build toward designing and pilot testing a diary study of their own. Recently, we have built a diary study into the course, with students writing and thematically coding a diary during the semester (Hyers, in preparation). At the graduate level, diary methods can be an excellent choice for master's level students to explore a research question for an independent project. Diary methods encourage our graduate students to slow down and explore a topic, rather than jump right into positivistic frameworks of making predictions about the phenomena of interest, for which they may lack expertise. Seeing the scientific value of beginning research slowly, with diary documents, Allport (1942, p. 2) hailed this more organic perspective gained as 'the beginning of all knowledge, scientific and otherwise', 'the font and origin of our curiosity' and an 'essential first step'. For new scholars just beginning a research career, a diary study can help build their expertise through a medium that is more accessible and more relatable.

Because solicited diary research can be so time consuming, one method for teaching new scholars about the diary is to use archival diaries, which is a form of unsolicited diary research that has much potential in the higher education field (exploring, for example, the diaries of scholars), but which was not employed by researchers represented in this volume. In addition to millions of published diaries and memoirs, there are also archived solicited diaries which can be re-analysed by new scholars (e.g. www.massobs.org.uk) and diary archives in museums, libraries, and collections worldwide (e.g. www.thegreatdiaryproject.co.uk). Working with archival sources helps new researchers to explore diary data they might not be able to obtain easily themselves. For example, our research group recently included an undergraduate student who was interested in forensic criminal profiling, so we worked with her to catalogue and examine existing forensic diary material available online (Greulich & Hyers, 2020). She uncovered a variety of diary source materials that provided rich psychological details that a student at her stage would not have been able to acquire through solicited diary methods. An archival diary project we are currently working on in our research team concerns adolescent resilience in situations of genocide (Walmer & Hyers, 2020). Solicited diaries would not be possible for our research team for several practical reasons: we are working within the restricted time frame of a master's thesis program; we have resource limitations that prevent obtaining in-person solicited diaries; and there could be insurmountable dangers to solicited participants. Thus, archival diary research enabled us to explore our research question in a powerful way as we turned to two well-known diarists who wrote during the Holocaust: Anne Frank and Renia Spiegel. We felt there were several advantages to using their diaries, the first being that we could acquire them from the library with ease. In addition, these young women provided well-known, first-person accounts that were candid and detailed. Furthermore, substantial supplementary resources exist to help with triangulation as we explored their lives. Nonetheless, we still faced challenges that are typical of archival designs. For one, we do not have access to the original diaries, meaning we are relying on the transcription, translation, and editing of others (a notorious problem when choosing which version of Frank's diary to use). Most obviously, we could not ask the diarists any follow-up questions, and nor would we ask our specific research questions – namely, how their adolescence affected their resilience through the horrors of their time. It can be frustratingly instructive to visualise how, with greater resources, a solicited diary study would have provided more targeted answers to our research questions. Nonetheless, archival voices can be so compelling precisely because they were not writing directly to a researcher; as Anne Frank wrote, 'it seems to me that, later on, neither I nor anyone else will be interested in the musings of a thirteen-year-old schoolgirl' (Frank 2003: 200). Ms. Frank was not writing to us, but contrary to her remark, her archival musings are of the utmost interest to us and countless others.

It is also important that we engage in more research process reflexivity *within* the articles we publish and the presentations we deliver. This book supplies what scholarly journal articles often do not make room for – a place for diary researchers to tell the 'back story' of their research process. Ideally, the entire process of data analysis should be documented by the primary researchers using what is called an 'audit trail' (Rodgers & Cowles, 1993; Scharp & Sanders, 2019) or a 'research diary' (Li, 2018), in which the researcher notes all aspects of the process throughout the course of reading and familiarising, coding, and report writing. This practice heightens the researcher's awareness of the decisions made along the way, and thereby contributes to the integrity of the study. Auditing provides a nice framework to promote the qualitative research practice of 'reflexivity' (Braun & Clarke, 2019; Mruck & Mey, 2019; Palaganas, Sanchez, Molintas & Caricativo, 2017). A researcher who engages in reflexivity during the research process is attending to their values, expectations, emotions, and learning, as they explore and represent their participants experiences (Gilgun, 1994; Rubin & Babbie, 2012). Auditing, research diary keeping, and reflexivity can be practiced throughout a diary project from start to finish, though they are most indispensable to during coding, analysing, and synthesising of research conclusions. Researchers can then draw from this careful meta-processing to more accurately communicate, not just their results, but the steps and decisions along the way. Reflexivity, if shared with others, is itself a form of embedded pedagogy, so that readers of fine-tuned manuscripts and audiences of polished presentations have a better sense of how the researchers got there.

* * *

Long after participants have completed their final diary entries, the researcher's work of reading, re-reading, and retelling has only just begun. The greatest reward comes when the diary researcher completes a study that makes a meaningful contribution to all who have a stake in the project, from the research team and diary participants, to the academy of professional peers and students, to policy makers and community members. It is our hope that the chapters of this volume have inspired many readers to take up a new qualitative diary project. This is a method that one discovers in the richest sense by doing. Diary researchers and participants alike are guaranteed to learn more about the topic of study than they anticipated. Diary research is an extraordinary method, so all involved should expect extraordinary results.

References

Allport, G. W. (1942) *The use of personal documents in psychological science*. Bulletin 49. New York: Social Science Research Council.

Berg, M. & Seeber, B. K. (2016) *The slow professor: Challenging the culture of speed in the academy*. Toronto: University of Toronto Press.

Braun, V. & Clarke, V. (2019) Reflecting on reflexive thematic analysis. *Qualitative Research in Sport, Exercise, and Health*, 11, 4: 589–597.

Burr, V. (1995) *An introduction to social constructionism*. London: Routledge.

Connelly, F. M. & Clandinin, D. J. (1990) Stories of experience and narrative inquiry. *Educational Researcher*, 19, 5: 2–14.

Denzin, N. K. (2010) *The qualitative manifesto: A call to arms*. Walnut Creek, CA: Left Coast Press.

Doyle, S. (2007) Member checking with older women: A framework for negotiating meaning. *Health Care for Women International*, 28, 10: 888–908.

Fine, M. & Torre, M. E. (2019) Critical participatory action research: A feminist project for validity and solidarity. *Psychology of Women Quarterly*, 43, 4: 433–444.

Frank, A. (2003) *The diary of Anne Frank: The revised critical edition*. New York: Doubleday.

Geertz, C. (2003) Thick description: Toward an interpretive theory of culture. *Culture: Critical Concepts in Sociology*, 1, 173–196.

Gergen, K. J. & Gergen, M. (2018) The performative movement in social science. In P. Leavy (ed.), *Handbook of arts-based research*. New York: Guilford Press, pp. 54–67.

Gilgun, J. F. (1994) Hand into glove: Grounded theory and social work practice research. In E. Sherman & W. J. Reid (eds), *Qualitative research in social work*. New York: Columbia University Press, pp. 115–125.

Greulich, K. & Hyers, L. (2020) *Diaries and other personal documents from the lives of violent killers: A catalog of qualitative archival sources of rich forensic research materials*. Society for Qualitative Research in Psychology Conference, Boston, MA.

Harper, M. & Cole, P. (2012) Member checking: Can benefits be gained similar to group therapy. *The Qualitative Report*, 17, 2: 510–517.

Headland, T. N., Pike, K. L. & Harris, M. (eds). (1990) *Emics and etics: The insider/outsider debate*. Newbury Park, CA: Sage.

Hyers, L. L. (2007) Challenging everyday prejudice: The personal and social implications of women's assertive responses to interpersonal incidents of anti-Black racism, anti-Semitism, heterosexism, and sexism. *Sex Roles*, 56, 1–12.

Hyers, L. L. (2010) Choosing alternatives to silence in face-to-face encounters with everyday heterosexism. *Journal of Homosexuality*, 57, 539–565.

Hyers, L. L. (2018) *Diary methods: Understanding qualitative research.* Oxford: Oxford University Press.

Hyers, L. L. (In preparation) Teaching by doing: Diary keeping and diary coding in a capstone qualitative research methods course.

Hyers, L. L. & Hyers, C. (2008) Everyday discrimination experienced by conservative Christians at the secular university. *Analysis of Social Issues and Public Policy,* 8: 113–137.

Hyers, L. L., Swim, J. K. & Mallet, R.M. (2006) The personal is political: Using daily diaries to examine everyday prejudice-related experiences. In S. Hesse-Biber & P. Leavy (eds), *Emergent methods in social research.* New York: Sage.

Hyers, L. L., Syphan, J., Cochran, K. & Brown, T. (2012) Disparities in the professional development interactions of university faculty as a function of their gender and ethnic underrepresentation. *Journal of Faculty Development,* 26, 1: 18–28.

Kreiswirth, M. (1992) Trusting the tale: The narrativist turn in the human sciences. *New Literary History,* 23: 629–657.

LeJeune, P. (2000) *On diary.* Honolulu, HI: University of Hawai'i Press.

LeJeune, P. (2001) How do diaries end? *Biography,* 24: 99–112.

Li, S. (2018) The natural history of a doctoral research study: The role of a research diary and reflexivity. In H. T. Allan & A. Arber (eds), *Emotions and reflexivity in health & social care field research.* Cham, Switzerland: Palgrave Macmillan, pp. 13–37.

Mruck, K. & Mey, G. (2019) Grounded theory methodology and self-reflexivity in the qualitative research process. In A. Bryant & K. Charmaz (eds), *The Sage handbook of current developments in grounded theory.* London: Sage, pp. 470–496.

Palaganas, E. C., Sanchez, M. C., Molintas, V. P. & Caricativo, R. D. (2017) Reflexivity in qualitative research: A journey of learning. *Qualitative Report,* 22, 2: 426–438.

Ritz, S. R., Lawson, D. J. & Hyers, L. L. (2002) *Everyday ableism.* Augusta, GA: Society for Southeastern Social Psychologists.

Rodgers, B. L. & Cowles, K. (1993) The qualitative research audit trail: A complex collection of documentation. *Research in Nursing & Health,* 16: 219–226.

Rubin, A. & Babbie, E. R. (2012) *Essential research methods for social work.* Belmont, CA: Brooks/Cole.

Saunders, B., Kitzinger, J. & Kitzinger, C. (2015) Anonymising interview data: Challenges and compromise in practice. *Qualitative Research,* 15, 5: 616–632.

Scharp, K. M. & Sanders, M. L. (2019) What is a theme? Teaching thematic analysis in qualitative communication research methods. *Communication Teacher,* 33, 2: 117–121.

Scott, C. R. (2005) Anonymity in applied communication research: Tensions between IRBs, researchers, and human subjects. *Journal of Applied Communication Research,* 33, 3: 242–257.

Smythe, W. E. & Murray, M. J. (2000) Owning the story: Ethical considerations in narrative research. *Ethics & Behavior,* 10, 4: 311–336.

Swim, J. K., Hyers, L. L., Cohen, L. L. & Fergusen, M. J. (2001) Everyday sexism: Evidence for its incidence nature and psychological impact from three daily diary studies. *Journal of Social Issues,* 57, 31–54.

Swim, J. K., Hyers, L. L., Cohen, L. L., Fitzgerald, D. & Bylsma, W. (2003) African American college students' experiences with everyday racism: Characteristics of and responses to incidents. *Journal of Black Psychology,* 29, 38–67.

Thomas, D. R. (2017) Feedback from research participants: Are member checks useful in qualitative research? *Qualitative Research in Psychology,* 14, 1: 23–41.

Tomes, Y., McBride, E., Martin, A. & Hyers, L. L. (2020) *Introducing psychology undergraduates to qualitative methods.* St Petersburg, FL: National Institute for Teaching of Psychology.

Walmer, J. & Hyers, L. L. (2020) *Resilience in Frank and Spiegel's diaries.* Austin, TX: Association for Women in Psychology.

Thorogood, J., Faulkner, S. & Warner, L. (2018) Slow strategies for student (and staff) engagement. *Student Engagement in Higher Education Journal,* 2, 2: 105–123.

Index

Page numbers in **bold** denote figures, those in **italics** denote tables.